Lecture Notes in Artificial Intelligence   3847

Edited by J. G. Carbonell and J. Siekmann

Subseries of Lecture Notes in Computer Science

T0238096

Klaus P. Jantke   Aran Lunzer
Nicolas Spyratos   Yuzuru Tanaka (Eds.)

Federation over the Web

International Workshop
Dagstuhl Castle, Germany, May 1-6, 2005
Revised Selected Papers

 Springer

Series Editors

Jaime G. Carbonell, Carnegie Mellon University, Pittsburgh, PA, USA
Jörg Siekmann, University of Saarland, Saarbrücken, Germany

Volume Editors

Klaus P. Jantke
FIT Leipzig, Forschungsinstitut für InformationsTechnologien
Postfach 30 11 66, 04251 Leipzig, Germany
E-mail: jantke@meme.hokudai.ac.jp

Aran Lunzer
Yuzuru Tanaka
Hokkaido University, Meme Media Laboratory
North 13 West 8, Sapporo 060-8628, Japan
E-mail: {aran,tanaka}@meme.hokudai.ac.jp

Nicolas Spyratos
Université Paris-Sud, Laboratoire de Recherche en Informatique
LRI-Bât. 490, 91405 Orsay Cedex, France
E-mail: spyratos@lri.fr

Library of Congress Control Number: 2005938389

CR Subject Classification (1998): I.2, H.2.8, H.3, H.4, J.1

ISSN   0302-9743
ISBN-10   3-540-31018-5 Springer Berlin Heidelberg New York
ISBN-13   978-3-540-31018-1 Springer Berlin Heidelberg New York

Springer is a part of Springer Science+Business Media

springer.com

© Springer-Verlag Berlin Heidelberg 2006
Printed in Germany

Typesetting: Camera-ready by author, data conversion by Scientific Publishing Services, Chennai, India
Printed on acid-free paper   SPIN: 11605126   06/3142   5 4 3 2 1 0

Preface

The lives of people all around the world, especially in industrialized nations, continue to be changed by the presence and growth of the Internet. Its influence is felt at scales ranging from private lifestyles to national economies, boosting the pace at which modern information and communication technologies influence personal choices along with business processes and scientific endeavors.

In addition to its billions of HTML pages, the Web can now be seen as an open repository of computing resources. These resources provide access to computational services as well as data repositories, through a rapidly growing variety of Web applications and Web services.

However, people's usage of all these resources barely scratches the surface of the possibilities that such richness should offer. One simple reason is that, given the variety of information available and the rate at which it is being extended, it is difficult to keep up with the range of resources relevant to one's interests. Another reason is that resources are offered in a bewildering variety of formats and styles, so that many resources effectively stand in isolation.

This is reminiscent of the challenge of enterprise application integration, familiar to every large organization be it in commerce, academia or government. The challenge arises because of the accumulation of information and communication systems over decades, typically without the technical provision or political will to make them work together. Thus the exchange of data among those systems is difficult and expensive, and the potential synergetic effects of combining them are never realized.

Motivation for overcoming this challenge with respect to the Web is found in many domains. In academia there is a recognized need for interdisciplinary and international availability, distribution and exchange of intellectual resources, which include both static information (such as publications and other research results) and the tools that support research activities. Similar pressure derives from the development and deployment of pervasive computing, which extends the types of resources that are present on the Web to encompass embedded devices and mobile computing resources, communicating over wireless networks. In such domains, just as for enterprise application integration, the rich variety of resources and the boundless human creativity applied in developing new solutions conspire to increase the number of compatibility barriers.

To what extent can this challenge be addressed by standardization? While the development and broad adoption of standards are crucial to the advance of information and communication technologies, any attempt to find a general solution to resource incompatibility through global standardization is doomed to fail because of the diversity of resources and the pace at which they change. That said, given an appropriately narrowed target scope, it is reasonable for providers to agree on a shared middle ground that will increase the mutual compatibility of their resources. This is the key to the approach known as *mediation*. Mediation, at least as usually understood in the area of databases, requires cooperation among providers in specifying (a) a well-defined community of co-operating sources, and (b) a common schema (called the mediator schema) to which the sources address their queries and/or provide answers.

In contrast to mediation, the study of *federation* involves working to bridge the differences between resources without such a predefined common ground. The process of resource federation in general involves selecting the resources that are to be combined, discovering the relationships that will allow them to work together, establishing the necessary connections, then driving the assembly in a coordinated way to achieve certain desired goals. The science of federation requires new theoretical foundations and enabling technologies for analysis of syntactic and/or semantic interrelations among resources, matching of service requesters and providers, and reliable and secure establishment and coordination of their execution.

Federation over the Web has attracted the attention of researchers aiming to support interdisciplinary and cross-border reuse and interoperation of heterogeneous intellectual resources, for example in support of scientific research, simulation, and digital libraries. Federation over enterprise intranets, also based on Web technologies, is being pursued as a way to bring large numbers of legacy application systems into cooperation with each other.

Existing work on federation can be divided broadly into programmatic and interactive approaches. Programmatic approaches are based on standardization at the level of communication protocols and languages for discovering compatibilities between resources, including the run-time matching of requesters and providers; for the Web, such federation tends to be based on Web-service technologies. On the other hand, interactive federation places in the hands of the user all responsibility for judging which resources are suitable for connection, then establishing and coordinating such connections. A simple example of interactive federation on the Web is the use of visual operations to connect result elements of one Web application, found at predictable locations within its HTML results, to input fields within an HTML form of another application.

From 1 to 6 May 2005 we held a workshop at Dagstuhl Castle to discuss advances in this area, drawing together active researchers from several institutes in Japan and Europe. The workshop focused on theoretical foundations and enabling technologies for federation of resources offered over the Web or within pervasive computing environments. We invited the participants to present and discuss work falling under any of the following topics:

- Knowledge look-up and matching
- Knowledge search and clustering
- Knowledge ontology and mediation
- Interoperation of Web-based resources
- Knowledge extraction and Web wrappers
- Computational models for knowledge federation

Based on the 18 workshop presentations, we went through a process of consultation, reviewing and editing to arrive at the 12 papers in this book. As shown in the table of contents, these papers touch on most of the above topics.

Future research and development of Web-based federation stands to influence how humans use intellectual resources in local and global networks. In combination with the rise of ubiquitous computing, introducing new forms of mobile computing devices and smart objects, computer systems will increasingly form location-based, on-demand federations. By the meeting and cooperation of these systems, humans will be dynamically connected with other humans and with a greater variety of systems and services. One can envisage future workshops on resource federation including contributions from the humanities, including sociology and psychology.

Let the present volume set the stage for such exciting developments.

October 2005

Klaus P. Jantke
Aran Lunzer
Nicolas Spyratos
Yuzuru Tanaka

Table of Contents

Knowledge Evolution

Text Mining Using Markov Chains
of Variable Length

Björn Hoffmeister[1] and Thomas Zeugmann[2]

[1] RWTH Aachen, Lehrstuhl für Informatik VI, Ahornstr. 55, 52056 Aachen
hoffmeister@i6.informatik.rwth-aachen.de
[2] Division of Computer Science, Hokkaido University,
N-14, W-9, Sapporo 060-0814, Japan
thomas@ist.hokudai.ac.jp

Abstract. When dealing with knowledge federation over text documents one has to figure out whether or not documents are related by context. A new approach is proposed to solve this problem.

This leads to the design of a new search engine for literature research and related problems. The idea is that one has already some documents of interest. These documents are taken as input. Then all documents known to a classical search engine are ranked according to their relevance. For achieving this goal we use Markov chains of variable length.

The algorithms developed have been implemented and testing over the Reuters-21578 data set has been performed.

1 Introduction

When one is aiming at knowledge federation over the web, one is often looking for information around a specific topic. In a first step, one may find one or more papers dealing with the topic of interest. Then, the next task is to find related papers. Another situation to which our research may apply is to enable documents to communicate to one another when trying to form a knowledge federation over the web. Again, in such cases it may be very important to answer a question like "is document A on the same subject as document B?" If the answer is affirmative, then a federation is made, otherwise it is rejected.

For dealing with such problems, we propose an approach based on Markov Chains of variable length. We exemplify this approach by constructing a search engine taking as inputs papers and returning a list of semantically related papers.

Currently used search engines do not take documents as input. They rely on queries of one or a few words describing the desired information. Basically, there are two different search strategies.

The first concept is based on catalogues. A catalogue contains similar objects, e.g., web-sites about machine learning. Hence, a query to such a catalogue system is answered with a certain set of catalogues. Each of them ideally carries objects relevant to the query. Search engines in libraries and web directories like Yahoo![1]

---

[1] http://www.yahoo.com

K.P. Jantke et al. (Eds.): Federation over the Web, LNAI 3847, pp. 1–24, 2006.
© Springer-Verlag Berlin Heidelberg 2006

are based on this approach. The quality depends on the quality of the catalogues. Producing good catalogues is still time consuming and expensive.

The second strategy is to perform a full-text search over all available documents. Common web search engines like Google[2] and AltaVista[3] are based on this concept. The disadvantage of a full-text search is the large number of matches. Therefore, a ranking is introduced and only the top ranked documents are returned. Google's main ranking criterion is the linkage rate of a web-site, that is, the more pages link to the document or web-site the higher the rank.

AltaVista uses a syntactical concept. It ranks the results depending on criteria like the positions of and distances between the queried words in the document. So, the alignment of the words should reflect the relevance of the document.

Both strategies have their advantages and disadvantages. Moreover, both approaches fail, for example, if the query allows ambiguities (cf. [13]). And the ranking criteria may overlook relevant documents or give them a low ranking, since simple queries do not allow a fine-grained ranking of relevance.

Now, the idea is to combine the advantages of both approaches. Our search engine takes a set of documents as query, classifies them, and ranks all the documents known by the search engine according to their relevance. To receive a ranking based on semantical relevance we use a model, which can keep more of the meaning of a document than common *data representation models*.

Following Ron *et al.* [18], we tried to use the *variable memory Markov model* defined as a *prediction suffix tree* (abbr. PST). So, we arrive at a *Markov model with variable memory*, or *n-gram VMM model* for short which is used for text representation. The *n-gram VMM model* is learned by statistical inference, a special form of inductive learning. Then we combine text retrieval and text classification.

We shortly outline the underlying mathematical background, describe the workflow of the resulting search engine, and report experimental results.

2   Preliminaries

Natural language is the most common form to exchange information between human beings, e.g., news stories are published in natural language as well as scientific papers. These documents often contain additional information encoded in structured text, like tables or formulas, or in graphical form. However, we shall only use the text in a document. Such a reduction may waste information. But for the particular setting we study within this paper, i.e., the Reuters Data set, it is sufficient. Additionally, all documents in this data set are written in English. Therefore, we restrict ourselves to deal with English texts.

We assume familiarity with formal language theory (cf., e.g., [9]). The word is used as smallest unit. In the literature, one also finds many other possible atomic units. Research has been done using sub-word units like letters or morphemes on the one hand and multi-word units, i.e., combinations of one or more words, on the other hand, e.g., see [13], [10], and [19].

---

[2] http://www.google.com
[3] http://www.av.com

We continue with technical notations. $\mathbb{N} = \{0, 1, 2, \ldots\}$ denotes the set of all natural numbers, and $\mathbb{N}^+ = \mathbb{N} \setminus \{0\}$. By Σ we denote a fixed finite alphabet, Σ^* denotes the free monoid over Σ, and $\Sigma^+ = \Sigma^* \setminus \{\epsilon\}$, where ϵ is the empty word. An n-gram is a string of $n \in \mathbb{N}^+$ concatenated letters. The set of all n-grams over Σ is denoted by Σ^n, where $\Sigma^0 = \{\epsilon\}$. We use $\Sigma^{\leq n}$ to denote $\bigcup_{i=1}^n \Sigma^i$.

Our alphabet is the set of all English words, i.e., a suitable subset of the English vocabulary which we denote by $\mathbb{V}$. Thereby we have to assure that $\mathbb{V}$ is a set of indivisible symbols such that there exist an one-to-one mapping between the symbols in $\mathbb{V}$ and the words in the English dictionary. The words of the vocabulary are written in another alphabet which we denote by $\mathbb{A}$. The relation between a word symbol in $\mathbb{V}$ and its representation in $\mathbb{A}^+$ is expressed by a mapping $\omega : \mathbb{V} \to \mathbb{A}^+$, where $\omega(\cdot)$ is injective. This can be easily achieved by introducing a delimiter symbol β such that $\beta \notin \mathbb{A}$.

Note that we use the term *word* to refer to member of $\mathbb{V}$. Therefore, an n-gram $s = \sigma_1 \ldots \sigma_n$, $\sigma_i \in \mathbb{V}$, $1 \leq i \leq n$, is a concatenation of n words and a string refers to any n-gram, $n \in \mathbb{N}$. A phrase is a meaningful concatenation of two or more words; technically any n-gram, $n > 1$, occurring in a document is a phrase. And finally, a term is either a word or a phrase. A document is then a sequence of sentences, where a sentence is a concatenation of words from $\mathbb{V}$.

For dealing with document classification and retrieval we use probabilistic language models. The idea is that documents dealing with different subjects also use a different subset of the vocabulary $\mathbb{V}$ and even different phrases over these subsets. For example, a document about stock exchange might contain words like "hausse" and "baisse", which will almost never appear in a text about machine learning. So, the observation is that texts about different subjects differ in the used words. Furthermore, terms like "machine learning" or "conditional mutual information" are surely not part of texts about stock markets, but the single words "machine", "learning", "conditional", "mutual", and "information" may occur in such a text. Moreover, the idea is to look at how likely a word is, if the previous words are known. In a text about machine learning it is very likely that "machine" is followed by "learning", where in a text about stock market exchange it is probably followed by "manufacture" or "supplier", but not by "learning".

The task of predicting the next word given the previous words is called *language modeling task* and a model solving the task is called a *generative model*, see [13] and [8]. Therefore, we continue with the following definitions.

Definition 1 (Stochastic model). *A stochastic model or process is a sequence of random variables* $(X_t)_{t \in \mathbb{N}}$.

Let us assume every random variable in $(X_t)_{t \in \mathbb{N}}$ has the same range $\mathcal{X}$. Thus, the statistical properties of $(X_t)_{t \in \mathbb{N}}$ are completely determined by the nth-order probability distribution $p(x_0, x_1, \ldots, x_n) := P(X_0 = x_0, X_1 = x_1, \ldots, X_n = x_n)$, $x_i \in \mathcal{X}$, $0 \leq i \leq n$, $n \in \mathbb{N}$, see [16].

Moreover, we use $\mathcal{L}$ to denote the language used by subject S, i.e., $\mathcal{L} \subset \mathbb{V}^*$. We then expect two documents to be about the same subject and hence semantically related, if the subjects of the documents use the same language. But we shall use probabilities instead of absolute statements. That is, we do not wish to decide whether or not a string or a sentence is in $\mathcal{L}$. Instead the language model we are aiming at returns for every string $s \in \mathbb{V}^*$ the probability for s to be in $\mathcal{L}$.

Let S be a subject, let $\mathcal{L}$ be the language of S, and let p_S be the probability distribution underlying $\mathcal{L}$. Furthermore, let M be a *generative model* for S. Thus, M solves the *language modeling task* for S, if $p_S(\sigma|s) = p_M(\sigma|s)$ for every $\sigma \in \mathbb{V}$ and for every $s \in \mathbb{V}^*$, where s is the sequence of all preceding words. Obviously, if M solves the *language modeling task* for S, the strings generated by M are distributed according to p_S and hence M is a probabilistic language model for S.

How many of the previous words are necessary for making a good prediction for the next word? The surprising answer is: most often only a few. For example, if we see the word "machine" in a text about machine learning, "learning" is very likely to be the next word, and knowing the words previous to "machine" does not provide much additional information about the likeliness. Manning *et al.* [13] claim that it takes quite a big effort to beat a *generative model* for natural language, which predicts the next word on the previous two words.

In general, good estimations for the next word in natural language are context dependent. An example is provided by this text. As mentioned before, the word "machine" is very likely to be followed by "learning"; but what about "Markov"? In the following, the words "model" and "chain" occurs after "Markov", but the 3-*gram* "variable memory Markov" is always followed by "model". Hence, we want a model, which can capture this property of natural language.

The model which has the desired properties, is an *n-gram Markov model with variable memory*, *n-gram VMM model* for short, which is defined by a *variable memory Markov model*, *VMM model* for short. A *VMM model* in turn is a special kind of the well-known *Markov model*. So, first *Markov models* are shortly repeated, followed by the definition of the *VMM model*, from which we derive the *n-gram VMM model*. In addition, the classical *n-gram Markov model* is presented and compared to our model, which proves to be superior.

If we regard *generative models* as stochastic processes, any random variable of the process has the property of only depending on the previous variables. A special kind of those dependencies is captured by the *Markov model*, where a random variable depends only on its direct predecessor. We shall see that, despite this restriction, the *Markov model* is a suitable base for a *generative model* for a language. In terms of a *Markov model* we call the value of a random variable a *state* and its range *state space*.

Definition 2 (Markov model). *Let $(X_t)_{t \in \mathbb{N}}$ be a stochastic model and let $\mathcal{X}$ be the state space for all random variables $X_t, t \in \mathbb{N}$. $(X_t)_{t \in \mathbb{N}}$ is a Markov model, iff it meets the Markov assumption*

$$P(X_{t+1} = x_{t+1}|X_0 = x_0, \ldots, X_t = x_t) = P(X_{t+1} = x_{t+1}|X_t = x_t) . \quad (1)$$

Let $p(\cdot|\cdot)$ be a function $p : \mathcal{X} \times \mathcal{X} \to [0,1]$. The Markov model $(X_t)_{t \in \mathbb{N}}$ is homogeneous, iff it fulfills the time invariance assumption

$$P(X_{t+1} = x_{t+1}|X_t = x_t) = p(x_{t+1}|x_t), \quad \text{for every } t \in \mathbb{N}. \quad (2)$$

p is the Markov core, where $p(x|y) \geq 0$ and $\sum_{x \in \mathcal{X}} p(x|y) = 1$ for all $x, y \in \mathcal{X}$.

If a random variable depends only on its predecessor, the question remains of how to predict the *state* of the initial random variable X_0. This is done by a special initial distribution. A *Markov model* together with an initial distribution for X_0 leads to the definition of a *Markov chain*. We follow the definition given by [4], because it fits our purpose best. Other definitions do not restrict *Markov chains* to be homogeneous, e.g., see [2].

Definition 3 (Markov chain). *A Markov chain is a homogeneous Markov model $(X_t)_{t \in \mathbb{N}}$ with state space $\mathcal{X}$, Markov core p and initial probability distribution π, where X_0 is distributed according to π.*

Before we continue with the definition of the *variable memory Markov model*, we use the *Markov chain* to define a first probabilistic language model, the classical *n-gram Markov model*. It shows how to use a *Markov model* to derive a language model; the *n-gram VMM model* will be defined analogously. We shall also use it to point to the advantages of our model.

The *n-gram Markov model* is a *generative model* predicting the next word in dependence on the previous n words. Since a *Markov chain*, by its definition, predicts the value of a random variable only on the value of its direct predecessor the following construction is necessary which uses overlapping random variables.

Let $(\Sigma_t)_{t \in \mathbb{N}}$ be a sequence of random variables, where each random variable in $(\Sigma_t)_{t \in \mathbb{N}}$ has range $\mathbb{V}$. We define a second sequence of random variables $(S_t)_{t \in \mathbb{N}}$, where each random variable in $(S_t)_{t \in \mathbb{N}}$ has range $\mathbb{V}^n$, $n \in \mathbb{N}^+$. The relation between $(\Sigma_t)_{t \in \mathbb{N}}$ and $(S_t)_{t \in \mathbb{N}}$ is given by the definition of the following equivalence. Let s be an *n-gram* and let $s = \sigma_0 \sigma_1 \ldots \sigma_{n-1}$, $\sigma_i \in \mathbb{V}$, $0 \le i < n$. Then,

$$S_t = s \quad \overset{def}{\Longleftrightarrow} \quad \Sigma_t = \sigma_0, \Sigma_{t+1} = \sigma_1, \ldots, \Sigma_{t+n-1} = \sigma_{n-1}, \tag{3}$$

for every $t \in \mathbb{N}$. Thus, the random variables S_t overlap, i.e., S_t depends on its predecessors, where the dependency is completely described by the direct predecessor S_{t-1}, $t \in \mathbb{N}^+$.

S_t contains the information about n words and hence, for predicting the value of Σ_{t+n} given the previous n words, the knowledge of the value of S_t is sufficient. We express the probability of the value of Σ_{t+n} in terms of S_t and S_{t+1} as follows. Let $S_t = s_0$, let $S_{t+1} = s_1$, and let $s_0 = \sigma_0 \sigma_1 \ldots \sigma_{n-1}$, where s_0 and s_1 in $\mathbb{V}^n$, $\sigma_i \in \mathbb{V}$, $0 \le i < n$. From (3) it follows that $s_1 = \sigma_1 \ldots \sigma_{n-1} \sigma_n$, $\sigma_n \in \mathbb{V}$, and hence

$$
\begin{aligned}
P(&S_{t+1} = s_1 | \, S_t = s_0) \\
=&P(\Sigma_{t+1} = \sigma_1, \ldots, \Sigma_{t+n-1} = \sigma_{n-1}, \Sigma_{t+n} = \sigma_n \\
&| \Sigma_t = \sigma_0, \Sigma_{t+1} = \sigma_1, \ldots, \Sigma_{t+n-1} = \sigma_{n-1}) \\
=&P(\Sigma_{t+n} = \sigma_n | \, \Sigma_t = \sigma_0, \Sigma_{t+1} = \sigma_1, \ldots, \Sigma_{t+n-1} = \sigma_{n-1}) \\
=&P(\Sigma_{t+n} = \sigma_n | \, S_t = s_0), \quad \text{for every } t \in \mathbb{N} \, .
\end{aligned}
\tag{4}
$$

Obviously, $(S_t)_{t \in \mathbb{N}}$ fulfills the *Markov assumption* and thus we see how a *Markov chain* can be used to predict a word in dependence on the previous n words. Thus, we arrive at the following definition.

Definition 4 (n-gram Markov model). *Let S denote a subject and let p_S be the probability distribution of the language of S. Furthermore, let $(S_t)_{t \in \mathbb{N}}$ be a Markov chain with state space $\mathbb{V}^n$, Markov core p and initial probability distribution π. $(S_t)_{t \in \mathbb{N}}$ is called n-gram Markov model for S, iff*

$$p_S(\sigma_0 \sigma_1 \ldots \sigma_{m-1}) = \pi(s_0)p(s_1|s_0)p(s_2|s_1) \ldots p(s_{m-n}|s_{m-n-1}), \qquad (5)$$

where $s_i \in \mathbb{V}^n$, $s_i = \sigma_i \sigma_{i+1} \ldots \sigma_{i+n-1}$, $0 \le i \le m - n$, for all m-grams $\sigma_0 \sigma_1 \ldots \sigma_{m-1} \in \mathbb{V}^m$, $m \in \mathbb{N}$, $m \ge n$.

Because p_S is to fulfill Kolmogorov's consistency condition the initial probability distribution π must have the following property, see [1].

Let $s = \sigma_1 \sigma_2 \ldots \sigma_n$, $\sigma_i \in \mathbb{V}$, $1 \le i \le n$, be an n-gram. Furthermore, let suff(s) denote the longest proper suffix of s, i.e., suff(s) $= \sigma_2 \ldots \sigma_n$. Then π must fulfill the equation

$$\pi(\text{suff}(s)\,\sigma) = \sum_{\sigma' \in \mathbb{V}} p(\sigma|\sigma'\text{suff}(s))\,\pi(\sigma'\text{suff}(s)),$$

for every $s \in \mathbb{V}^n$, where $\sigma \in \mathbb{V}$. We get the desired property, if we define $\pi(\sigma_1 \ldots \sigma_n)$ as $P(S_1 = s)$, where $s = \sigma_1 \ldots \sigma_n$ for all n-grams $\sigma_1 \ldots \sigma_n \in \mathbb{V}^n$.

Now, we have a first probabilistic language model. But the size of the *state space* is by definition $|\mathbb{V}|^n$. This will lead to problems if $n \ge 2$ when one wants to learn such a model and the documents are too short (cf., e.g., [2]). For seeing the problem, note that a normal vocabulary of natural language has a size of more than 20.000 words. So, in order to estimate all probabilities described above for an 2-*gram Markov model* one needs a sample of more than $20.000^3 = 8 \times 10^{12}$ words. Obviously, we normally do not possess such a large sample.

Therefore, we want to use the *variable memory Markov model* which has been defined in a different context by Ron *et al.* [18]. A variable memory Markov model is defined as a *prediction suffix tree(PST)*.

Definition 5 (suffix tree). *Let Σ be an alphabet, let $\mathcal{T}$ be a tree and let $\mathbf{E}$ denote the set of edges between the nodes in $\mathcal{T}$. Furthermore, let each edge be labeled by a symbol $\sigma \in \Sigma$ and each node by a string $s \in \Sigma^*$. The two functions $l_{\mathbf{E}} : \mathbf{E} \to \Sigma$ and $l_{\mathcal{T}} : \mathcal{T} \to \Sigma^*$ return the label of an edge and of a node, respectively. $\mathcal{T}$ is a suffix tree over Σ, iff it has the following properties:*

i) *$\mathcal{T}$ has degree $|\Sigma|$.*
ii) *The root node n_0 of $\mathcal{T}$ has label ϵ.*
iii) *For every node $n_l \in \mathcal{T}$, $l \in \mathbb{N}$, and $n_0 \to n_1 \to \ldots \to n_{l-1} \to n_l$, the walk from the root node n_0 to node n_l, the label of n_l equals the concatenated labels of the passed edges, i.e., $l_{\mathcal{T}}(n_l) = l_{\mathbf{E}}(e_{0,1})\, l_{\mathbf{E}}(e_{1,2}) \ldots l_{\mathbf{E}}(e_{l-1,l})$*
iv) *Neither two edges of one node nor two nodes have the same label.*

Definition 6 (next symbol probability function). *Let Σ be an alphabet and let $\gamma_s, s \in \Sigma^*$, be a function. The function γ_s is called next symbol probability function over Σ, iff it defines a probability distribution over Σ.*

Definition 7 (prediction suffix tree). *Let Σ be an alphabet and let $\mathcal{T}$ be a suffix tree over Σ. $\mathcal{T}$ becomes a prediction suffix tree by expanding the label of every node in $\mathcal{T}$ to (s, γ_s), where s is the label of the node in the suffix tree and γ_s is a next symbol probability function over Σ.*

For the sake of readability, we use the string $s \in \Sigma^*$ synonymously for the label of a node and for the node itself. Ron *et al.* [18] proved the following for *VMM* models. Every *VMM* model can be described by a *Markov chain*, whose size grows exponentially in the maximum depth of the *VMM* model. And almost every *Markov chain* can be described by an *VMM* model. In particular, an *n-gram Markov model* can be simulated by a *VMM* model.

Let $\mathcal{T}$ be a *VMM* model over Σ with maximal depth n. A similar *VMM* model $\tilde{\mathcal{T}}$ over Σ with maximal depth n can be learned with arbitrary precision from an example generated by $\mathcal{T}$ in linear time in the length of the example. The sufficient length of the example is bounded by a polynomial function, which depends on the number of nodes $|\mathcal{T}|$, where we assume $|\mathcal{T}| \geq |\Sigma|$ and $|\mathcal{T}| \geq n$, and on the desired precision.

Using the terminology of *Markov models*, we call the set of nodes in an *VMM* model *state space* and a single node *state*.

Now we have the desired model, which uses a variable amount of memory. The last step is to define a language model, the *n-gram VMM model*, which is based on a *VMM* model.

Definition 8 (n-gram Markov model with variable memory). *Let S denote a subject and let p_S be the probability distribution of the language of S. Furthermore, let $\mathcal{T}$ be a VMM model over $\mathbb{V}$ having maximal depth n.*

$\mathcal{T}$ is called n-gram Markov model with variable memory, or n-gram VMM model for short, for S iff

$$p_S(\sigma_0 \sigma_1 \ldots \sigma_{m-1}) = \gamma_{s^0}(\sigma_0) \gamma_{s^1}(\sigma_1) \gamma_{s^2}(\sigma_2) \ldots \gamma_{s^{m-1}}(\sigma_{m-1}), \qquad (6)$$

where s^i, $0 \leq i \leq m-1$, is the longest suffix of $\sigma_0 \sigma_1 \ldots \sigma_i$ labeling a node in $\mathcal{T}$, for all m-grams $\sigma_0 \sigma_1 \ldots \sigma_{m-1} \in \mathbb{V}^m$, $m \in \mathbb{N}$, $m \geq n$.

So, the *state space* of the *n-gram VMM model* is a subset of $\mathbb{V}^n$, whereas, by Definition 4, the *state space* for the *n-gram Markov model* is the full set $\mathbb{V}^n$.

Here again, we can derive a special property, which $\mathcal{T}$ must have for p_S to fulfill Kolmogorov's consistency condition.

Lemma 1. *Let $\mathcal{T}$ be an n-gram VMM model over $\mathbb{V}$. Then the next probability function γ_s must fulfill the equation*

$$\gamma_{\mathit{suff}(s)}(\sigma) = \sum_{\sigma' \in \mathbb{V}} \gamma_{\sigma' \mathit{suff}(s)}(\sigma), \qquad (7)$$

for each $s \in \mathbb{V}^+$ labeling a node in $\mathcal{T}$ and for every $\sigma \in \mathbb{V}$.

From the definition of the conditional probability it follows that $p(\sigma|s)$ equals $\gamma_{s'}(\sigma)$ for every $\sigma \in \mathbb{V}$ and every $s \in \mathbb{V}^n$, $n \in \mathbb{N}$, where s' is the longest suffix of s labeling a node in $\mathcal{T}$, and $p(s) > 0$. This notation immediately shows that we have a probabilistic language model, where the prediction of the next word depends on a variable number of previous words.

Let us assume that we want to learn the n-gram VMM model $\mathcal{T}_S$, which describes the probability distribution of the language of the subject S. Learning is done from sample strings, where a sample string t for S, $t \in \mathbb{V}^*$, is just a finite string generated by $\mathcal{T}_S$. According to Definition 8, the value $\gamma_s(\sigma)$ equals $p_S(\sigma|s)$, which in turn equals approximately $\tilde{P}_t(\sigma|s)$ for every $\sigma \in \mathbb{V}$ and every $s \in \mathbb{V}^{\leq n}$, if only t is sufficiently large. $\tilde{P}_t(\sigma|s)$ denotes the conditional empirical probability of σ given s achieved from t.

In order to derive the conditional empirical probabilities we need to count $(n+1)$-grams. The function $\#_t^{n+1}(\cdot)$ counts the number of occurrences of a certain $(n+1)$-gram in the sample string t and is defined as

$$\#_t^{n+1}(s) := \text{the number of occurrences of } s \text{ in } t \ ,$$

where $s \in \mathbb{V}^{n+1}$. Furthermore, let N_t be the number of all $(n+1)$-grams in t. Now, we are able to define the empirical probabilities for $(n+1)$-grams and from there we derive the desired conditional empirical probabilities:

$$\tilde{P}_t(s\sigma) := \frac{\#_t^{n+1}(s\sigma)}{N_t}, \quad \tilde{P}_t(\sigma|s) = \frac{\tilde{P}_t(s\sigma)}{\sum_{\sigma' \in \mathbb{V}} \tilde{P}_t(s\sigma')} = \frac{\#_t^{n+1}(s\sigma)}{\sum_{\sigma' \in \mathbb{V}} \#_t^{n+1}(s\sigma')},$$

where $s \in \mathbb{V}^n$ and $\sigma \in \mathbb{V}$. The conditional empirical probabilities of lower order are derived by the following recursion:

$$\tilde{P}(\sigma|\text{suff}(s)) = \sum_{\sigma' \in \mathbb{V}} \tilde{P}(\sigma|\sigma'\text{suff}(s))$$

So, $\sum_{s \in \mathbb{V}^{n+1}} \tilde{P}_t(s) = 1$ holds and therefore Lemma 1 is fulfilled by construction.

A catalogue or class is a collection of related subjects, e.g., if the subject of a document is "pruning algorithms for decision tree learning", it might be part of the classes "decision tree learning" and "machine learning". Obviously, most classes can be divided into subclasses yielding a hierarchy of classes, e.g., "decision tree learning" is a subclass of "machine learning". Hence, a subject can be viewed as the indivisible element on the bottom of a class hierarchy.

A class c is a set of documents, i.e., $c = \{d_0, d_1, \ldots, d_q\}$, $q \in \mathbb{N}$. Let S_i be the subject of document d_i, let $\mathcal{L}_{S_i}$ be the language of S_i, and let p_{S_i} be the probability distribution underlying $\mathcal{L}_{S_i}$, $0 \leq i \leq q$. So, the language of c is given by $\mathcal{L}_c = \bigcup_{i=0}^q \mathcal{L}_{S_i}$. We denote the probability distribution underlying $\mathcal{L}_c$ by p_c.

Obviously, if each probability distribution p_{S_i} can be described by an n-gram VMM model, p_c can be described by an n-gram VMM model, too.

The problem of finding the class a document is part of is known as the *text classification* task. The *text classification* task consists of a set of classes $\mathbf{C} = \{c_0, c_1, \ldots, c_r\}$, $r \in \mathbb{N}$, a set of documents $\mathbf{D}$, and a function $k : \mathbf{D} \to \{0, 1, \ldots, r\}$ called classification rule. $\mathbf{D}$ is the set all documents such that each document

$d \in \mathbf{D}$ belongs to exactly one class in $\mathbf{C}$. Then, one wants to find a classification rule k_{opt} approximating k_{true} best, where k_{true} returns the correct class label for each document in $\mathbf{D}$, i.e., if $d \in \mathbf{D}$ belongs to $c_i \in \mathbf{C}$, then $k_{true}(d) = i$.

The definition of the best approximation varies; often one tries to minimize the *error rate* defined as the ratio of misclassifications to the total number of classifications. We follow this definition, because there exists a classification rule known as *Bayes' classification rule* that achieves the minimal *error rate*, if $p(c|d)$ is known for every $c \in \mathbf{C}$ and for every $d \in \mathbf{D}$.

Normally, the classification rule does not work on the documents and classes themselves, but on a model for either the classes or for both, classes and documents. A *text classifier* is defined as a 3-tuple $(\mathbf{C}, M, k)$ consisting of a set of classes $\mathbf{C}$, a model M, and a classification rule k, where k is performed on M. If k is *optimal* for every set of classes with respect to M, $(\mathbf{C}, M, k)$ is called an *optimal text classifier*. If k is *optimal* on the documents and classes themselves, i.e., k does not use a model, then k is called a *perfect text classifier*, see [5].

Finally, we formalize a search engine. In general, a search engine works as follows. The users states a query, the search engine estimates the relevance of each document to the query, the documents are sorted according to the estimates, and finally the list of the sorted documents are returned to the user. In practice, the list is usually truncated but it should contain the maximal possible number of relevant documents. We use the key concepts of *text retrieval* for the definition of a search engine. Note that our search engine uses queries consisting of documents.

Let $\mathbf{Q}$ be a nonempty, finite set of documents, we call $\mathbf{Q}$ a *query*. Let $\mathbf{D}$ be a finite, nonempty set of documents, where $\mathbf{D}$ is split into two sets $\mathbf{R}$ and $\mathbf{N}$. $\mathbf{R}$ is the set of all documents in $\mathbf{D}$ being relevant to query $\mathbf{Q}$ and $\mathbf{N} = \mathbf{D} \setminus \mathbf{R}$ is the set of all irrelevant documents. A *text retrieval* system is an algorithm which assigns a rank $r \in \{1, 2, \ldots, |\mathbf{D}|\}$ to each document in $\mathbf{D}$ such that no two documents get the same rank, where we refer to 1 as the highest rank. A search engine is just a *text retrieval* system.

Let $\mathbf{D}_n \subset \mathbf{D}$ be the set of the n documents having the highest ranks. A *text retrieval* system is called *optimal*, if

$$|\mathbf{R}_n| \text{ is maximal for all } n \in \{1, 2, \ldots, |\mathbf{D}|\} \text{ for every query } \mathbf{Q} .$$

Similar to *text classification*, we distinguish between an *optimal* and a *perfect* *text retrieval* system. An *optimal text retrieval* system performs the ranking task on models of the documents in $\mathbf{D}$. A *perfect text retrieval* system achieves the *optimal* result on the documents themselves. Since we use *n-gram VMM model* as a model for a document we have *probabilistic text retrieval* system. For a *probabilistic text retrieval* system the optimum criterion becomes

$$E[|\mathbf{R}_n|] = \sum_{d \in \mathbf{D}_n} P(\mathbf{R}|d) \text{ is maximal for all } n \in \{1, 2, \ldots, |\mathbf{D}|\},$$

where $P(\mathbf{R}|d)$ is called *probability of relevance*. Robertson [17] has shown that such an *optimal probabilistic text retrieval* system exists and that it can be derived by the *probability ranking principle*(*PRP*). A short definition of the *PRP* is given in [13], p. 538.

Probability Ranking Principle. Ranking documents in order of decreasing probability of relevance is optimal.

Therefore, our goal in a *probabilistic text retrieval* system is to find a suitable model for estimating the *probabilities of relevance*.

We use the following two observations. First, if d and the documents in $\mathbf{Q}$ are about the same subject, d is with high probability relevant to $\mathbf{Q}$. Note that we model d and each document in $\mathbf{Q}$ by a *n-gram VMM model* and compare these *n-gram VMM models*. If the *n-gram VMM models* are similar, we expect d to be in $\mathbf{R}$.

Second, normally d and the documents in $\mathbf{Q}$ belong to the same class, if d is relevant to $\mathbf{Q}$ and vice versa. We shall use a *text classifier* based on *n-gram VMM models* to determine whether or not d and $\mathbf{Q}$ belong to the same class.

3   Learning the N-Gram VMM Model

A *language learner* is an algorithm learning the probability distribution underlying a language. We define it as 5-tuple $(\mathbf{T}_S, \mathbb{V}, n, \mathcal{H}, L)$. $\mathbf{T}_S = \{d_0, d_1, \ldots, d_q\}$, $q \in \mathbb{N}$, is a set of documents called training set for S. $\mathbb{V} = \{w_0, w_1, \ldots, w_k\}$, $k \in \mathbb{N}$, is an alphabet; in our setting we use the English vocabulary. $n \in \mathbb{N}^+$ is the order of the model to be learned, i.e., we will learn *n-gram VMM models*, and $\mathcal{H} = \{\mathcal{T} : \mathcal{T}$ is an *n-gram VMM model*$\}$ is the hypothesis space.

$L : \mathbf{T}_S \to \mathcal{H}$ is the learning algorithm. Let $\mathcal{L} \subset \mathbb{V}^*$ be the language of subject S and let p the probability distribution underlying $\mathcal{L}$. The aim of L is to map the training set $\mathbf{T}_S$ to the *n-gram VMM model* $\tilde{\mathcal{T}}_S \in \mathcal{H}$ approximating p best. Often, $\mathbf{T}_S$ consists only of a single document d. In that case, we denote the outcome of L equally as $\tilde{\mathcal{T}}_d$. We present two algorithms for learning $\tilde{\mathcal{T}}_S$, the *CPR-principle* and the *LLR-principle*. Both algorithms define different success criteria.

Next, we define a *discriminative learner* for a *multiclass model*. In terms of natural language processing *discriminative learning* consists of solving the *text classification* task, i.e., to find that *multiclass model* having most discriminative power among $\mathbf{C}$, where $\mathbf{C}$ is a set of classes.

In particular, we use a collection of *n-gram VMM models*, one for each class in $\mathbf{C}$, as *multiclass model*. *Bayes' classification rule* is used for classification (cf. Mitchell [15]). The learner is called *multiclass learner*. We define it as a 6-tuple $(\mathbf{C}, \mathbf{T_C}, \mathbb{V}, n, \mathcal{H}, L)$. Here $\mathbf{C} = \{c_0, c_1, \ldots, c_r\}$, $r \in \mathbb{N}$ is a set of classes or categories. Furthermore, $\mathbf{T_C} = \{\mathbf{T}_{c_0}, \mathbf{T}_{c_1}, \ldots, \mathbf{T}_{c_r}, \}$ is the training set for $\mathbf{C}$ and consists of a training set for each class in $\mathbf{C}$, where $\mathbf{T}_{c_i} = \{d_0, d_1, \ldots, d_{q_i}\}$, $q_i \in \mathbb{N}$, is a training set for class c_i, $c_i \in \mathbf{C}$.

$\mathbb{V}$, n, and $\mathcal{H}$ are defined in the same way as for the *language learner*.

$L : \mathbf{T_C} \to \mathcal{H}^r$ is the learning algorithm. The result of L is an *n-gram VMM model* for each class in $\mathbf{C}$. That is, L maps $\mathbf{T_C}$ to $(\tilde{\mathcal{T}}_{c_0}, \tilde{\mathcal{T}}_{c_1}, \ldots, \tilde{\mathcal{T}}_{c_r})$, $\tilde{\mathcal{T}}_{c_i} \in \mathcal{H}$, $0 \leq i \leq r$, where $\tilde{\mathcal{T}}_{c_i}$ is the model for class c_i. We refer to $\tilde{\mathcal{T}}_{c_i}$ as *discriminative class model* or just as *class model*.

Both, the *language learner* and the *multiclass learner*, learn by statistical inference. Here we have to approximate the probability distribution of a language.

Let $\mathcal{L} \subset \mathbb{V}^*$ be a language and let p be the probability distribution underlying $\mathcal{L}$. Let $\mathbf{T} = \{d_0, d_1, \ldots, d_q\}$, $q \in \mathbb{N}$, be a sample or training set for $\mathcal{L}$. Therefore, each document $d_i \in \mathbf{T}$, $0 \leq i \leq q$, consists of samples taken from $\mathcal{L}$. Formally, a document $d_i = (t_{ij})_{j=0}^o$, $o \in \mathbb{N}$, is a list of sentences, where each sentence is in $\mathcal{L}$, i.e., $t_{ij} \in \mathcal{L}$ for every $i \in \{0, 1, \ldots, q\}$ and for every $j \in \{0, 1, \ldots, o\}$.

Furthermore, we assume that the sentences are mutually independent. The goal is to learn p from the samples in $\mathbf{T}$. Without prior knowledge the relative frequencies in $\mathbf{T}$, i.e., the empirical probability distribution, are most likely to equal p. We gain the empirical probability $\tilde{P}(s)$ for an n-$gram$ $s \in \mathbb{V}^n$ by computing the ratio between the number of occurrences of s in $\mathbf{T}$ and the total number of n-$grams$ in $\mathbf{T}$. The number of occurrences of s in training set $\mathbf{T}$ is denoted by $\#_{\mathbf{T}}(s)$, where

$$\#_{\mathbf{T}}(s) := \sum_{i=0}^q \#_{d_i}(s), \qquad \mathbf{T} = \{d_0, d_1, \ldots, d_q\},$$

$$\#_{d_i}(s) := \sum_{j=0}^o \#_{t_{ij}}(s), \qquad d_i = (t_{ij})_{j=0}^o, \tag{8}$$

$$\#_{t_{ij}}(s) := \text{the number of occurrences of } s \text{ in } t_{ij}, \; t_{ij} \in \mathbb{V}^*.$$

The number of all n-$grams$ is denoted by $N_{\mathbf{T}} = \sum_{s \in \mathbb{V}^n} \#_{\mathbf{T}}(s)$.

With the help of the counts we can calculate the empirical probabilities for all l-$grams$, $1 \leq l \leq n$. Let $\sigma_i \in \mathbb{V}$, $1 \leq i \leq n$, the empirical probabilities are calculated as

$$\tilde{P}(\sigma_i \sigma_{i+1} \ldots \sigma_n) = \begin{cases} \dfrac{\#_{\mathbf{T}}(\sigma_1 \sigma_2 \ldots \sigma_n)}{N_{\mathbf{T}}}, & \text{if } i = 1, \\ \displaystyle\sum_{\sigma \in \mathbb{V}} \tilde{P}(\sigma \sigma_i \sigma_{i+1} \ldots \sigma_n), & \text{if } 1 < i \leq n, \end{cases} \tag{9}$$

where $\tilde{P}(\epsilon) := 1$.

Unfortunately, the empirical probability distribution is not a good estimator for the distribution of natural language, because of the sparse data problem. To overcome the problem we smooth the empirical probabilities, i.e., we assign a probability greater than zero to every l-$gram$, $1 \leq l \leq n$. We use a common smoothing technique known as *Lidstone's law*, see [13]. The smoothed empirical probability $P_{Lid}(s)$ for an l-$gram$ s, $1 \leq l \leq n$, is calculated as

$$P_{Lid}(s) := \mu \tilde{P}(s) + (1 - \mu)\frac{1}{|\mathbb{V}|^l}, \qquad \mu = \frac{N_{\mathbf{T}}}{N_{\mathbf{T}} + \lambda|\mathbb{V}|}, \tag{10}$$

where $P_{Lid}(\epsilon) := 1$. The parameter $\lambda \in (0, \infty)$ is a constant, which is most often set to 0.5. Obviously, $\tilde{P}(s)$ equals $P_{Lid}(s)$ for $n \to \infty$.

For learning an n-$gram$ *VMM model* we need to estimate conditional probabilities. We derive the estimate for the conditional probability $\sigma \in \mathbb{V}$ given $s \in \mathbb{V}^{\leq n}$ in the following way. Let $\sigma_i \in \mathbb{V}$, $1 \leq i \leq n + 1$. The conditional empirical probabilities of σ_{n+1} given the previous up to n words is computed as

$$P_{Lid}(\sigma_{n+1} | \sigma_i \sigma_{i+1} \ldots \sigma_n) = \frac{P_{Lid}(\sigma_i \sigma_{i+1} \ldots \sigma_n \sigma_{n+1})}{\sum_{\sigma \in \mathbb{V}} P_{Lid}(\sigma_i \sigma_{i+1} \ldots \sigma_n \sigma)}, \tag{11}$$

where $P_{Lid}(\sigma_{n+1} | \epsilon) = P_{Lid}(\sigma_{n+1})$.

Now, we are ready to present the learning algorithms. We use two already known algorithms and a new one. The existing algorithms are the *CPR-principle* and the *MMI-principle*. The *CPR-principle* has been introduced for learning the probability distribution of a language and the *MMI-principle* has been introduced for learning class models.

The new one is the *LLR-principle*. There are two instances of the *LLR-principle*, one for learning the probability distribution of a language and one for learning class models.

3.1   The CPR-Principle

The *CPR-principle* was introduced by Ron *et al.* [18] for learning a probabilistic language model. The learner consists of $(\mathbf{T}_S, \mathbb{V}, n, \mathcal{H}, L_{CPR})$. The goal is to approximate p, the probability distribution of $\mathcal{L} \subset \mathbb{V}^*$, where $\mathcal{L}$ is the language used by subject S.

Ron *et al.* [18] make the simplifying assumption that p can be described by an *n-gram VMM model* $\mathcal{T}_S \in \mathcal{H}$. Henceforth, let $\tilde{\mathcal{T}}_S \in \mathcal{H}$ denote the *n-gram VMM model* learned by L_{CPR} from training set $\mathbf{T}_S$. L_{CPR} aims to minimize the divergence between $\mathcal{T}_S$ and $\tilde{\mathcal{T}}_S$, where the divergence is measured in terms of the *Kullback-Leibler (KL) divergence* defined as

$$D(p\|q) = \sum_{x \in \mathcal{X}} p(x) \, \log \frac{p(x)}{q(x)}, \text{ where } p \text{ and } q \qquad (12)$$

are two probability distributions defined over the finite, nonempty set $\mathcal{X}$.

Ron *et al.* [18] proved that the *KL divergence* between $\mathcal{T}_S$ and $\tilde{\mathcal{T}}_S$ converges to zero for sufficient large training sets.

The main idea of the algorithm introduced by [18] is to add a node $s \in \mathbb{V}^{\leq n}$ into $\tilde{\mathcal{T}}_S$, if $\tilde{P}(\sigma|s) > \tilde{P}(\sigma|\text{suff}(s))$ for any $\sigma \in \mathbb{V}$. More precisely, s is added if

$$\frac{\tilde{P}(\sigma|s)}{\tilde{P}(\sigma|\text{suff}(s))} \geq \varepsilon_2, \qquad s \in \mathbb{V}^{\leq n}, \ \varepsilon_2 \in [1, \infty), \qquad (13)$$

for any $\sigma \in \mathbb{V}$. Because of the equation, we termed the algorithm the *conditional probability ratio (CPR) principle*.

The *next symbol probabilities* for each node in $\tilde{\mathcal{T}}_S$ are set to the corresponding smoothed conditional empirical probabilities. If we would use the unsmoothed probabilities, the divergence between $\mathcal{T}_S$ and $\tilde{\mathcal{T}}_S$ would not converge to zero. This is caused by the fact that the *KL divergence* between $\mathcal{T}_S$ and $\tilde{\mathcal{T}}_S$ becomes infinite if $\mathcal{T}_S$ assigns a probability greater than zero to an *n-gram* s, while $\tilde{\mathcal{T}}_S$ assigns zero probability to s; see [18] for further details.

3.2   The MMI-Principle

The *MMI-principle* has been introduced by Slonim *et al.* [19]. In contrast to the *CPR-principle* the *MMI-principle* aims to learn class models. Therefore, the learner consists of $(\mathbf{C}, \mathbf{T_C}, \mathbb{V}, n, \mathcal{H}, L_{MMI})$.

The result of L_{MMI} is a *multiclass model* consisting of an *n-gram VMM model* for each class in **C**. The class model for class $c \in$ **C** is used to calculate the probability that a document belongs to c. Thus, the goal is to learn those class models minimizing the classification error rate. More precisely, the algorithm proposed by [19] aims to minimize *Bayes' error rate*. For information about *Bayes' classification rule* and *Bayes' error rate* see e.g., [15].

Let D be a random variable whose range is the set of all documents and let C be a random variable with range **C**. From the definition of *Bayes' classification rule* it follows that *Bayes' error rate* decreases, if the uncertainty in $p(C|D)$ is reduced, for details see [7].

The uncertainty of the probability distribution underlying a random variable is measured in terms of the entropy, see e.g., [16]. Let X and Y be two random variables. Henceforth, we denote the entropy of X by $H(X)$ and the mutual information between X and Y by $I(X;Y)$, where $I(X;Y) := H(X) - H(X|Y)$. Thus, what we need is a way to minimize $H(C|D)$. We can model a document as a sequence of random variables $(S_i)_{i=1}^o$, $o \in \mathbb{N}^+$, where each S_i, $1 \leq i \leq o$, has range $\mathbb{V}^+$. We assume the random variables S_i, $1 \leq i \leq o$, to be equally distributed and mutually independent.

Let us assume that every sentence has exactly length m. Consequently, $S_i = \Sigma_1, \Sigma_2, \ldots, \Sigma_m$ for every $i \in \{1, 2, \ldots, o\}$, where Σ_j, $1 \leq j \leq m$, is a random variable with range $\mathbb{V}$.

If we assume that all documents have exactly o sentences, we derive the following equation, see [16].

$$
\begin{aligned}
H(D) &= H((S_i)_{i=1}^o) \\
&= o\, H(\Sigma_1, \Sigma_2, \ldots, \Sigma_m) \\
&= mo\, H(\Sigma_{n+1} | \Sigma_1, \Sigma_2, \ldots, \Sigma_n),
\end{aligned}
\tag{14}
$$

where the last step follows from the fact that $\Sigma_1, \Sigma_2, \ldots, \Sigma_m$ is distributed according to an *n-gram VMM model* which in turn fulfills the *Markov assumption*. We simplify the notation by introducing two extra random variables, $\Sigma := \Sigma_{n+1}$ and $S := (\Sigma_1, \Sigma_2, \ldots, \Sigma_n)$. Now, we obtain our main result.

$$
\begin{aligned}
H(C|D) &= H(D|C) + H(C) - H(D) \\
&= H(C) - mo\,(H(\Sigma|S) - mo\, H(\Sigma|S, C)) \\
&= H(C) - mo\, I(\Sigma; C|S),
\end{aligned}
\tag{15}
$$

where the equality of $H(D)$ and $mo\, H(\Sigma|S)$ as well as the equality of $H(D|C)$ and $mo\, H(\Sigma|S, C)$ follows from (14).

We conclude, maximizing $I(\Sigma; C|S)$ minimizes $H(C|D)$ and therefore minimizes *Bayes' error rate*, too.

We call the resulting algorithm the *maximum mutual information (MMI) principle*, as it tries to maximize $I(\Sigma; C|S)$. Further details are omitted due to the lack of space.

3.3   The LLR-Principle

The *LLR-principle* is a new way either to learn an *n-gram VMM model* for a subject or to learn *n-gram VMM models* serving as class models. The main motivation of the *LLR-principle* is a common drawback of the *CPR-* and the *MMI-principle*. Both make the assumption that the training set is always sufficiently large in order to get reliable estimates for the unknown probability distribution. Let p be an unknown probability distribution and let us assume p is described by the *n-gram VMM model* $\mathcal{T}$. Furthermore, $|\mathcal{T}|$ denotes the number of nodes in $\mathcal{T}$. The size of the needed sample set for achieving reliable results for p is bounded by a polynomial function over $|\mathcal{T}|$, for details see [18]. In our setting we have no knowledge about $|\mathcal{T}|$, besides the fact that $|\mathcal{T}|$ is upper-bounded by $|\mathbb{V}|^n$, but in general we do not possess a sample set larger than $|\mathbb{V}|^n$. Hence, we normally cannot determine, whether or not the training set is sufficiently large.

So, what can happen if the training set is not large enough? Dependencies might be preserved, which are true for the training set, but not for p, i.e., the learned *n-gram VMM model* overfits. Overfitting in turn can reduce classification and retrieval performance, see e.g., [15] and [12].

Thus, the idea of the *LLR-principle* is to add a node s only, if there is strong evidence that s is an indispensable node in $\mathcal{T}$. In particular, we use a statistical test to determine whether or not s is indispensable.

First, we use the idea to learn the probability distribution of the language of a subject S. Let $(\mathbf{T}_S, \mathbb{V}, n, \mathcal{H}, L_{LLR})$ be the learner and let $L_{LLR}(\mathbf{T}_S) = \tilde{\mathcal{T}}_S$. Furthermore, let p be the probability distribution of the language used by subject S. Thus, our goal is to approximate p.

Formally, we want to add a node $s \in \mathbb{V}^{\leq n}$ into $\tilde{\mathcal{T}}_S$, if $p(\sigma|s) > p(\sigma)$ for any $\sigma \in \mathbb{V}$. In other words, we add s into $\tilde{\mathcal{T}}_S$, if the probabilities of some of the words following s are not independent of s.

Since we do not know $p(\sigma|s)$, we use the conditional empirical probability achieved from $\mathbf{T}_S$ as estimator for $p(\sigma|s)$. Furthermore, we use a statistical test to decide whether or not a dependency occurring in $\mathbf{T}_S$ exists in p. Thus, we use the following two hypotheses for the test:

$$
\begin{aligned}
H_0\colon & p(\sigma|s) = p = p(\sigma) \\
H_1\colon & p(\sigma|s) = p_1 > p_2 = p(\sigma)
\end{aligned}
\tag{16}
$$

If the null hypotheses H_0 is rejected for any $\sigma \in \mathbb{V}$, we add s to $\tilde{\mathcal{T}}_S$.

As statistical test we use the *log-likelihood ratio (LLR) test* proposed in [3].

Dunning [3] applied the *LLR-test* on the task of finding dependencies between words in texts written in natural language and compared it to *Pearson's χ^2-test*. Especially for small word counts, i.e., for short samples, the *LLR-test* performed superior to *Pearson's χ^2-test*.

The *LLR-test* seems to be the statistical test fitting best for finding dependencies between words when dealing with small word counts (cf. [13, 20]).

[3] used $p(\sigma|s) = p(\sigma|\neg s)$ as null hypothesis, where $p(\neg s) := 1 - p(s)$. However, Dunning's null hypothesis is equal to H_0:

$$p(\sigma|s) = p(\sigma|\neg s)$$
$$\Longleftrightarrow \quad p(\sigma|s) = \frac{p(\neg s\ \sigma)}{p(\neg s)}$$
$$\Longleftrightarrow \quad p(\sigma|s) = \frac{\sum_{s' \in \mathbb{V}^{|s|}} p(s'\ \sigma) - p(s\ \sigma)}{1 - p(s)}$$
$$\Longleftrightarrow (1 - p(s))p(\sigma|s) = p(\sigma) - p(s\ \sigma)$$
$$\Longleftrightarrow \quad p(\sigma|s) = p(\sigma)$$

Computing the test statistic proposed in [3] for H_0, is done using the counts:

$$k_1 := \#_{\mathbf{T}_S}(s\sigma), \quad n_1 := \#_{\mathbf{T}_S}(s), \quad k_2 := \#_{\mathbf{T}_S}(\sigma) - k_1, \quad n_2 := N_{\mathbf{T}_S} - n_2$$

As estimates for the tested probabilities we simply use the empirical probabilities. In terms of the above counts the estimates can be expressed as

$$\tilde{p}_1 = \frac{k_1}{n_1}, \quad \tilde{p}_2 = \frac{k_2}{n_2}, \quad \tilde{p} - \frac{k_1 + k_2}{n_1 + n_2}.$$

Now, the test statistic for hypothesis H_0 is calculated as

$$\xi = -2\log\lambda = 2\,(\log L(\tilde{p}_1, k_1, n_1) + \log L(\tilde{p}_2, k_2, n_2)$$
$$- \log L(\tilde{p}, k_1, n_1) - \log L(\tilde{p}, k_2, n_2)), \quad (17)$$

where $L(p, k, n) := p^k(1 - p)^{(n-k)}$. For further details about the *LLR-test* and the derivation of the *LLR-test* statistic, see [3].

The value λ is the ratio between the likelihood of H_0 and the likelihood of H_1. So, λ decreases and thus ξ increases, if H_1 is more likely than the null hypothesis H_0. Moreover, ξ approximates the χ^2-distribution with one degree of freedom.

Putting it all together, we add $s \in \mathbb{V}^{\le n}$ to $\tilde{T}_S$, if $\xi_{\sigma|s} \ge (\chi_1^2)^{-1}(1 - \alpha)$, $\alpha \in (0, 1)$, for any $\sigma \in \mathbb{V}$. $\xi_{\sigma|s}$ denotes the value of the *LLR-test* statistic computed for σ and s. The complete algorithm is given in Figure 1.

In the algorithm, the parameter ε is the critical value for the χ_1^2-distribution for a chosen significance level $\alpha \in (0, 1)$, i.e., $\varepsilon = (\chi_1^2)^{-1}(1 - \alpha)$.

The advantage of the *LLR-principle* is that a node is only added, if it is with high probability an indispensable node in an *n-gram VMM model* describing p. Unfortunately, some nodes may not be added even when they are necessary for modeling a dependency in p. So, the question is if the learned *n-gram VMM model* still fits for solving the *text retrieval* and *text classification* task, respectively.

In the worst case the learned *n-gram VMM model* $\tilde{T}_S$ consists only of the root node, i.e., words are regarded as to be independent to one another. Hence, $\tilde{T}_S$ can be described by a 0-*gram VMM model*. *Bayes' classification rule* applied to the 0-*gram VMM model* yields the *naive Bayes classifier*, which shows an excellent performance for the *text classification* task, see e.g., [14, 15].

In fact, other classifiers and text retrieval systems assuming independence between words got good results in *text classification* and *text retrieval*, see [10, 12, 13]. So, we expect the *n-gram VMM model* $\tilde{T}_S$ learned by the *LLR-principle* to yield good results, even if some dependencies in p are not modeled by $\tilde{T}_S$.

First step (prediction suffix tree)

```
// initialize the prediction suffix tree T̃_S
T̃_S := {ε};
// build the prediction suffix tree T̃_S
for (i = 1 to n) {
    foreach (s ∈ V^i) {
        ξ_max := 0;
        foreach (σ ∈ V) {
            // test for a dependency in the language of S
            k_1 := #_T_S(sσ); n_1 := #_T_S(s);
            k_2 := #_T_S(σ) − k_1; n_2 := N_T_S − n_1;
            p̃ := (k_1 + k_2)/(n_1 + n_2); p̃_1 := k_1/n_1; p̃_2 := k_2/n_2;
            ξ := llr_test(p̃, p̃_1, p̃_2; k_1, n_1, k_2, n_2);
            // find the maximal value for ξ
            ξ_max := max{ξ, ξ_max};
        }
        // add only those nodes, which pass the test
        if (ξ_max ≥ ε) {
            add s into T̃_S;
        }
    }
}
```

Second step (next symbol probabilities)

```
// compute the next symbol probabilities
foreach (s ∈ T̃_S) and (σ ∈ V) {
    γ̃_s(σ) := P_Lid(σ|s);
}
```

Fig. 1. Pseudo-code for the LLR-principle (subject case)

Next, we apply the *LLR-test* to the task of learning class models. The learner consists of $(\mathbf{C}, \mathbf{T_C}, \mathbb{V}, n, \mathcal{H}, L_{MMI})$. Similar to the *MMI-principle* we aim to find the suffix tree $\tilde{\mathcal{T}}$ containing all the nodes, which have discriminative power among $\mathbf{C}$. Thus, we add a node $s \in \mathbb{V}^{\le n}$ to $\tilde{\mathcal{T}}$, if s fulfills the following two requirements.

First, for some class $c \in \mathbf{C}$ there exist a dependency between s and the words following s. This requirement yields the following hypotheses for a statistical test:

$$H_0^1: p(\sigma|s, c) = p = p(\sigma|c)$$
$$H_1^1: p(\sigma|s, c) = p_1 > p_2 = p(\sigma|c) \tag{18}$$

Therefore, the first requirement is fulfilled, if the null hypotheses H_0^1 is rejected for any $\sigma \in \mathbb{V}$ and $c \in \mathbf{C}$.

For testing the null hypotheses we apply the *LLR-test* on the training set $\mathbf{T_C}$. Concretely speaking, for testing H_0^1 for $s \in \mathbb{V}^{\le n}$, $\sigma \in \mathbb{V}$, and $c \in \mathbf{C}$ the training set $\mathbf{T}_c$ is used. From $\mathbf{T}_c$ we get the following counts needed for calculating the *LLR-test* statistic:

$$k_1 := \#_{\mathbf{T}_c}(s\sigma), \quad n_1 := \#_{\mathbf{T}_c}(s), \quad k_2 := \#_{\mathbf{T}_c}(\sigma) - k_1, \quad n_2 := N_{\mathbf{T}_c} - n_2$$

The value of the *LLR-test* statistic is computed by (17).

The second requirement is that a node s has discriminative power among $\mathbf{C}$. That is, a dependency between s and the words following s depends on $\mathbf{C}$, too. In other words, if $p(\sigma|s,c)$ is equal for every $c \in \mathbf{C}$ and for every $\sigma \in \mathbb{V}$, s has no discriminative power among $\mathbf{C}$.

We formalize the second requirement by the following hypotheses for a statistical test:

$$\begin{aligned} H_0^2 &: p(\sigma|s,c) = p = p(\sigma|s) \\ H_1^2 &: p(\sigma|s,c) = p_1 > p_2 = p(\sigma|s) \end{aligned} \tag{19}$$

Thus, if H_0^2 is rejected for any $\sigma \in \mathbb{V}$ and $c \in \mathbf{C}$, then the second requirement is fulfilled.

For computing the *LLR-test* statistic for $s \in \mathbb{V}^{\leq n}$, $\sigma \in \mathbb{V}$, and $c \in \mathbf{C}$ we need counts over the training set $\mathbf{T}_c$ and over $\mathbf{T_C}$. The number of occurrences of an *n-gram* $s \in \mathbb{V}^n$ in the training set $\mathbf{T_C}$ is defined as

$$\#_{\mathbf{T_C}}(s) := \sum_{i=0}^{r} \#_{\mathbf{T}_{c_i}}(s), \quad \mathbf{T_C} = \{\mathbf{T}_{c_0}, \mathbf{T}_{c_1}, \ldots, \mathbf{T}_{c_r}\}, \tag{20}$$

and hence $N_{\mathbf{T_C}} := \sum_{i=0}^{r} N_{\mathbf{T}_{c_i}}$. Consequently, the *LLR-test* is performed on:

$$k_1 := \#_{\mathbf{T}_c}(s\sigma), \quad n_1 := \#_{\mathbf{T}_c}(s), \quad k_2 := \#_{\mathbf{T_C}}(\sigma) - k_1, \quad n_2 := N_{\mathbf{T_C}} - n_2$$

If a node $s \in \mathbb{V}^{\leq n}$ fulfills both requirements, then s is added to $\tilde{\mathcal{T}}$. We omit further details.

4   Text Classification and Text Retrieval

The *text classification* task consists of a set of classes $\mathbf{C} = \{c_0, c_1, \ldots, c_r\}$, $r \in \mathbb{N}$, a set of documents $\mathbf{D}$, and a function $k : \mathbf{D} \to \{0, 1, \ldots, r\}$ called classification rule. $\mathbf{D}$ is the set of all documents d such that each $d \in \mathbf{D}$ belongs to exactly one class in $\mathbf{C}$. The aim of the *text classification* task is to find that classification rule that approximates k_{true} best, where k_{true} returns the correct class label for each document in $\mathbf{D}$, i.e., if $d \in \mathbf{D}$ belongs to $c_i \in \mathbf{C}$, then $k_{true}(d) = i$.

Function k only relies on the knowledge about $\mathbf{C}$ and hence, if the knowledge about $\mathbf{C}$ is not sufficient for certain classifications, k is expected to make some misclassifications. The classification rule theoretically making the least number of misclassifications is called *Bayes' classification rule* and it is denoted by k_{Bayes}. The ratio of misclassifications made on average by *Bayes' classification rule* is called *Bayes' error rate*. For further details see e.g., [15].

Let $(\mathbf{C}, \mathbf{T_C}, \mathbb{V}, n, \mathcal{H}, L)$ be an *n-gram VMM model* learner for class models, where $L(\mathbf{T_C}) = (\tilde{\mathcal{T}}_{c_i})_{i=0}^{r}$, $\tilde{\mathcal{T}}_{c_i} \in \mathcal{H}$, $c_i \in \mathbf{C}$, $0 \leq i \leq r$. Furthermore, let $\tilde{k}_{Bayes}$ be *Bayes' classification rule* for $\mathbf{C}$, where $\tilde{k}_{Bayes}$ uses $\tilde{\mathcal{T}}_{c_i}$ to estimate the value of $p(d|c_i)$ for every $c_i \in \mathbf{C}$, $0 \leq i \leq r$, and for every $d \in \mathbf{D}$. We call the triple $(\mathbf{C}, (\tilde{\mathcal{T}}_{c_i})_{i=0}^{r}, \tilde{k}_{Bayes})$ nst order *naive Bayes classifier*, where the 0st order *naive Bayes classifier* is a member of the family of the common *naive Bayes classifiers*.

Following McCallum *et al.* [14] we also look at the commonly used *multivariate naive Bayes classifier* and the *multinomial naive Bayes classifier*. Both classifiers use the vector space model of $\mathbb{V} = \{w_0, w_1, \ldots, w_k\}$, $k \in \mathbb{N}$, to represent each document in $\mathbf{D}$. In the multinomial model the likelihood of $d \in \mathbf{D}$, $d = (t_l)_{l=0}^o$, $t_l \in \mathbb{V}^+$, $0 \leq l \leq o$, given class $c \in \mathbf{C}$ is

$$p(d|c) = N_d! \prod_{i=0}^{k} \frac{p(w_i|c)^{v_i}}{v_i!}, \qquad N_d = \sum_{i=0}^{k} \#_d(w_i), \qquad (21)$$

which is just the multinomial distribution. Let $\mathbf{T}_c$ be a training set for c. The parameter $p(w_i|c)$, $0 \leq i \leq k$, of the multinomial distribution are estimated by the smoothed conditional empirical probabilities achieved from $\mathbf{T}_c$.

Additionally, we shall use two classification rules relying on the vector space model over $\mathbb{V}$ for comparative reasons, the *k-nearest-neighbor (k-nn)-classifier* and the *centroid based classifier*(cf., e.g., [8] and [13]). The most common similarity measure used in *text classification* and *text retrieval* is the cosine of the angel between two vectors v and u in $\mathcal{V}$. Therefore, we also use it. For further details on the cosine function as similarity measure see e.g., [8,13].

A drawback of the vector space model over $\mathbb{V}$ is its limited representation power, as it only regards single words, i.e., 1-*grams*. There exist two commonly used ways for improving the representation power: either to use the vector space over all *n-grams* for an $n \in \mathbb{N}$, $n > 1$, or the vector space over all *l-grams*, $1 \leq l \leq n$. Both kind of vector spaces have been tested in practical experiments, see e.g., [12,6]. The results indicate that classification performance increases for small n, but decreases for larger n; the reason is overfitting caused by the high dimensionality of the vector space. The way to overcome the problem of high dimensionality is to build the vector space only over those *l-grams*, $1 \leq l \leq n$, having relevance for classification. Many different approaches for measuring the relevance of a single *l-gram*, $1 \leq l \leq n$, have been proposed, see e.g., [6,20].

Here, we examine two approaches, one based on mutual information, which we derive from the *MMI-learning-principle*. The other one is based on statistical tests and it is derived from the *LLR-learning-principle*.

The measures used for evaluating classification results are micro-averaged precision/recall.

Last but not least, we use a probabilistic text retrieval system. Recall that a query $\mathbf{Q}$ as a set of documents. For every query $\mathbf{Q}$ we split $\mathbf{D}$ into two sets, $\mathbf{R}$ (the relevant documents) and $\mathbf{N}$ (the irrelevant ones). A *text retrieval system* is an algorithm that assigns a rank $r \in \{1, 2, \ldots, |\mathbf{D}|\}$ to each document in $\mathbf{D}$ such that no two documents get the same rank, where 1 is referred to as the highest rank. Informally speaking, an *optimal text retrieval* system makes at any time and for every query the least number of wrong assignments of ranks. A wrong assignment has happened, if a document in $\mathbf{N}$ gets a higher rank than any document in $\mathbf{R}$. $\mathbf{D}_n \subset \mathbf{D}$ is the set of the n documents having the highest ranks, i.e., the ranks 1 to n, and $\mathbf{R}_n = \mathbf{D}_n \cap \mathbf{R}$. A probabilistic *text retrieval* system is called *optimal*, if

$$E[|\mathbf{R}_n|] = \sum_{d \in \mathbf{D}_n} P(\mathbf{R}|d) \text{ is maximal for all } n \in \{1, 2, \ldots, |\mathbf{D}|\}, \qquad (22)$$

where $P(\mathbf{R}|d)$ is called *probability of relevance*. Robertson [17] has shown that such an *optimal probabilistic text retrieval* system exists and can be derived by the *probability ranking principle(PRP)*. Thus, the performance of the system relies on the reliability of our estimates for $P(\mathbf{R}|d)$.

In Section 2 we already presented two observations about d, $\mathbf{Q}$, $\mathbf{R}$, and hence about $P(\mathbf{R}|d)$. First, d is probably in $\mathbf{R}$, if d and the documents in $\mathbf{Q}$ are about the same subject. Second, if d and the documents in $\mathbf{Q}$ belong to the same class, we expect d to be in $\mathbf{R}$, too. Both observation can be quantified and the results are used to get an estimate for $P(\mathbf{R}|d)$. We omit details.

5   Implementation

Next, we outline the workflow of our search engine and take a short look at the core algorithms used within the single steps of the workflow. Figure 2 shows the workflow of the search engine and the single steps making up the workflow. Every document processed by the search engine passes these steps with exception of documents used for learning a class model, which pass only the first six steps.

We distinguish three levels of representation of a document. First, the document is a collection of bits. In this step we extract the text of a document. Then it has to be split into words and sentences for further processing.

On the multi-word level the computer has a more advanced view of the document. Instead of single words, it regards *l-grams*, $1 \leq l \leq n$, i.e., words are regarded within their local context. In order to be able to receive *l-grams* we need the sentences boundaries as we do not want to regard *l-grams* across multiple sentences.

The next level is the *n-gram VMM model* itself. Actually, our hope is to gain a representation capturing the meaning of the document. However, we do not aim to represent the semantic of a document in an operational form. That is, we cannot answer the question "What subject do you deal with?", but our hope is that we are able to answer the question "Do you deal with the same subject as document x?".

Next, we take a short look at the steps presented in Figure 2. The first task is text extraction. In this step, we extract the parts of natural language within a document. For documents published in HTML format, we use a simple HTML-filter. The filter just removes all HTML-tags and all the text between HTML-tags, which are known to mark structured text.

Scientific papers published in the Internet are normally encoded as postscript-files or as PDF-files. The postscript- and the PDF-format are strongly related and were invented to provide a good, platform independent readability of natural and structured text for an human reader. The result is a format, which makes automatic text extraction quite complicated.

Here, we use a two-step-process for *text extraction*. First, the `ps2ascii` tool delivered with the `ghostscript` package[4] is used to interpret the postscript-

---

[4] http://www.ghostscript.com

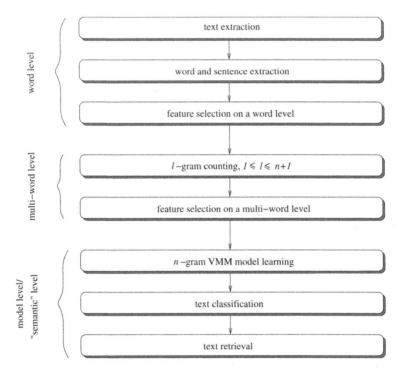

Fig. 2. Workflow of the search engine

document and to get a list of word fragments. The second step is done by a self-written filter, which combines the fragments into words, finds paragraphs of natural text, and removes words belonging to structures like formulas, etc.

In the next step, the extracted text is converted into unicode. Then we cut the text into words and sentences. In English words are normally separated by spaces. Hence, we regard every sequence of characters flanked by spaces as a word. Finding sentences is not trivial mainly due to the fact that a period does not necessarily mark the end of a sentence. We use an algorithm based on the sentence boundary detection algorithm proposed in [13]. The algorithm uses an heuristic approach, is fast and on common texts very reliable. After finding sentence boundaries, all punctuation marks are removed.

Up to this point we used the English dictionary as vocabulary. Note that the large size large size of the vocabulary and the resulting huge number of l-grams, $1 \leq l \leq n$, can cause serious problems with respect to time and memory requirements. In order to overcome the problem there exist a variety of techniques to select those l-grams, $1 \leq l \leq n$, being somehow relevant for learning the desired n-gram VMM models and to discard all irrelevant ones. The general task is called *feature selection* and is done as a pre-processing step before inferring any models, see e.g., [13, 10]. In the workflow *feature selection* occurs on two levels, on the word and on the multi-word level. At both levels, we use *stopword elimination* and *word frequency thresholding* among others.

Then, we count all l-grams, $1 \leq l \leq n$, in a sample set. After counting, l-gram frequency thresholding is applied at the result list in order to remove all l-grams occurring less than two times. The remaining frequencies are used to compute the normal and the smoothed conditional empirical probabilities. The probabilities and the counts are required for learning the n-gram VMM model.

Counting is probably the most important step in the workflow of the search engine. It is most expensive in time and the structure build up over all l-grams during the counting step is later on used for a fast find, calculation, and comparison of l-gram frequencies and probabilities. Word counting is done by applying a hash function which uses the single words as key and stores the counts in a hash map. The resulting algorithm runs in time $O(m)$ and uses $O(m)$ memory, where m is the number of words in the training set.

We can easily extend the approach for counting all l-grams, $1 \leq l \leq n$. That is, we count the number of occurrences of each l-gram, $1 \leq l \leq n$, separately. The resulting algorithm has a runtime of $O(mn^2)$ and needs $O(mn^2)$ memory, but we can do better. We omit the details here.

The data structure developed for counting fits in general for a prediction suffix tree(PST), too. With this in mind the objects stored in the array of hash maps will serve as nodes and next symbol probabilities at the same time. This design allows us to store a PST in a very compact manner. For learning, we use the principles described in Section 3.

6   Experimental Results

We have used the Reuters-21578 data set for testing[5]. The data set consists of 21578 Reuters newswire stories from the year 1987 all related to financial topics. In order to support retrieval and routing, Reuters defined a set of 135 category labels. The stories have been manually indexed using these labels, where each story may be indexed by zero, one, or several category labels.

Lewis was the first making extensive use of the Reuters data set for evaluating text classification systems, e.g., see [11]. Henceforth, the data set has become a standard benchmark for text classifiers, e.g., see [19, 10].

In general, we use the newswire stories as documents and the categories as classes for our search engine. However, it is difficult to make a selection of documents for a training set and a test set, respectively, because many of the stories are only of limited use or completely unusable. The most common way to split the data set is the so called modified Apte split[6], which we will use, too. It defines a training set of 9603 documents and a test set of 3299 documents. The remaining 8676 documents are not used, because of one or several of the following reasons. They have no class label assigned, the assigned class label is obviously false, or the document contains no text. Furthermore, Reuters allowed multi-classification. Our text classification system is restricted to single-classification. Thus, we only use the documents belonging exactly to one class.

---

[5] http://www.daviddlewis.com/resources/testcollections/reuters21578/
[6] http://www.daviddlewis.com/resources/testcollections/reuters21578/readme.txt

A single newswire story is often very short and consists only of one or a few sentences; a story is on average 152 words long. Therefore, we normally cannot learn an *n-gram VMM model* from a single or a few stories, because the limitedness of training data does not allow reliable statistical inference. Therefore, we use only those Reuters categories as classes, where the training set provides a sufficient large number of training documents. In particular, we only use the ten most populous categories yielding a minimum number of 90 documents per category. This approach follows several other studies like [10, 14, 19].

The ten categories are listed in the following table. Additionally, the number of documents and words per category are given. Word counting is done without prior *feature selection*, but every word was converted to lowercase.

category	topic	number of documents	number of words
earn	Earnings and Earnings Forecasts	2840	221992
acq	Mergers/Acquisitions	1596	192130
crude	Crude Oil	253	50376
trade	Trade	251	57693
money-fx	Money/Foreign Exchange	206	35014
interest	Interest Rates	190	22471
money-supply	Money Supply	123	12605
ship	Shipping	108	16488
sugar	Sugar	97	17012
coffee	Coffee	90	18757

So, we get a training set of 5754 documents and a test set of 2254 documents. Without any kind of *feature selection* the vocabulary of the training set consists of 37965 words and 2051584 different *l-grams*, $1 \leq l \leq 6$, where we will not use larger *l-grams* for testing.

The second consequence of the shortness of the newswire stories directly concerns our *text retrieval* system. A single document is too small to be used for learning an *n-gram VMM model* and hence we cannot use the *KL divergence* based similarity measure to predict the similarity between two documents. Therefore, we compute the vector space representation for each document and use the cosine function as similarity measure. The following example shows the difficulties in using such short documents as contained in the Reuters data set. The example is taken from the used test set and belongs to "interest".

Bundesbank's Schlesinger says no plan to cut discount rate - Nihon Keizai newspaper
Blah blah blah.
(Reuters-21578, NEW_ ID=17445)

We present here only some text classification results due to lack of space. We compare the *n*st order *naive Bayes classifier* learned by the *MMI-principle* with the one learned by the *LLR-principle*. Additionally, for both principles we let the nst order *naive Bayes classifier* compete against the *centroid based* and the *k-nn-classifier*, where both use the vector space $\mathcal{V}^n_{MMI(LLR)}$.

We evaluate the general improvement gained by applying a learning algorithm. Thus, we run *Bayes' classification rule* without prior learning, i.e., we build a *prediction suffix tree* containing a node s for each $s\sigma$ occurring in the training set, $s \in \mathbb{V}^{\leq n}$, $\sigma \in \mathbb{V}$.

We use the following *feature selection* techniques on a word level. Every word is converted to lowercase, every number is replaced by the word <NUMBER>, word frequency thresholding is applied, and stopwords are eliminated. On a multi-word level l-*gram* frequency thresholding, $1 \leq l \leq n$, is applied. We used this set-up for every *text classification* and *text retrieval* task reported here.

Table 1. Classification results. The values inside the table are micro-averaged *precision/recall*, where the column determines the used n-*gram VMM model* and the row determines the used combination of decision rule and learning principle. Here, "*Bayes*" is short for nst order *naive Bayes classifier*, "*centroid*" is short for *centroid based classifier*, and "*1-nn*" is short for *k-nn-classifier*, where k is set to 1.

	$n = 0$	1	2	3	4	5
no learning						
Bayes	0.95874	0.95209	0.9512	0.95164	0.95075	0.9512
MMI-principle						
Bayes	0.95874	0.95874	0.95918	0.9543	0.95386	0.9543
centroid	0.48048	0.93966	0.93478	0.9299	0.9339	0.93256
1-nn	0.92902	0.92902	0.93523	0.93833	0.93789	0.937
LLR-principle						
Bayes	0.95874	0.95608	0.95519	0.95608	0.95608	0.95563
centroid	0.48048	0.92414	0.90816	0.90595	0.90639	0.90639
1-nn	0.91926	0.92014	0.92103	0.9197	0.92014	0.92014

Furthermore, we use the micro-averaged *precision/recall* to measure the classification performance of a single combination of classification rule, learning principle, and memory depth n. The micro-averaged *precision* and *recall* are equal because of the *single classification* setting. However, for a single class *precision* and *recall* are normally different.

Table 1 summarizes the results for all combinations of classification rule and learning principle. All combinations were evaluated for $n = 0$ to 5.

References

[1] J. L. Doob. *Stochastic Processes*. Wiley, 1990.
[2] L. Dümbgen. *Stochastik für Informatiker*. Springer, 2003.
[3] T. E. Dunning. Accurate methods for the statistics of surprise and coincidence. *Computational Linguistics*, 19(1):61–74, 1994.

[4] W. Feller. *An Introduction to Probability Theory and Its Applications*, volume 1. Wiley, third edition, 1968.

[5] N. Fuhr. Probabilistic models in information retrieval. *The Computer Journal*, 35(3):243–255, 1992.

[6] J. Fürnkranz. A study using n-gram features for text categorization. Technical report, Austrian Institute for Artificial Intelligence, 1998.

[7] A. Garg and D. Roth. Understanding probabilistic classifiers. In L. D. Raedt and P. A. Flach, editors, *Machine Learning: EMCL 2001, 12th European Conference on Machine Learning, Freiburg, Germany, September 5-7, 2001, Proceedings*, volume 2167 of *Lecture Notes in Computer Science*, pages 179–191. Springer, 2001.

[8] D. Hand, H. Mannila, and P. Smyth. *Principles of Data Mining*. MIT Press, 2002.

[9] M. A. Harrison. *Introduction to Formal Language Theory*. Addison Wesley, 1978.

[10] T. Joachims. *Learning to Classify Text using Support Vector Machines: Methods, Theory, and Algorithms*. Kluwer Academic Publishers, 2002.

[11] D. D. Lewis. Feature selection and feature extraction for text categorization. In *Proceedings of Speech and Natural Language Workshop*, pages 212–217, San Mateo, California, 1992. Morgan Kaufmann.

[12] D. D. Lewis and K. S. Jones. Natural language processing for information retrieval. *Communications of the ACM*, 39(1):92–101, 1996.

[13] C. D. Manning and H. Schütze. *Foundations of Statistical Natural Language Processing*. MIT Press, 2002.

[14] A. McCallum and K. Nigam. A comparison of event models for naive bayes text classification. In *Proceedings of the AAAI-98 Workshop on Learning for Text Categorization*, 1998.

[15] T. M. Mitchell. *Machine Learning*. WCB/McGraw-Hill, 1997.

[16] A. Papoulis. *Probability, Random Variables, and Stochastic Processes*. WCB/McGraw-Hill, third edition, 1991.

[17] S. E. Robertson. The probability ranking principle in ir. *Journal of Documentation*, 33:294–304, 1977.

[18] D. Ron, Y. Singer, and N. Tishby. The power of amnesia: Learning probabilistic automata with variable memory length. *Machine Learning*, 25(2–3):117–149, 1996.

[19] N. Slonim, G. Bejerano, S. Fine, and N. Tishby. Discriminative feature selection via multiclass variable memory markov model. In C. Sammut and A. G. Hoffmann, editors, *Machine Learning, Proceedings of the Nineteenth International Conference (ICML 2002), University of New South Wales, Sydney, Australia, July 8-12, 2002*, pages 578–585. Morgan Kaufmann, 2002.

[20] Y. Yang. An evaluation of statistical approaches to text categorization. *Information Retrieval*, 1(1/2):69–90, 1999.

Faster Pattern Matching Algorithm
for Arc-Annotated Sequences

Takuya Kida*

Hokkaido University, Kita 14, Nishi 9, Kita-ku, Sapporo 060-0814, Japan
kida@ist.hokudai.ac.jp

Abstract. We present an improvement of pattern matching algorithm for arc-annotated sequences. Arc-annotated sequences are used for representing the structural information, *e.g.*, RNA and protein sequences in molecular biology. Given two sequences with arcs, a text of length n and a pattern of length m, the problem is to determine whether the pattern is an arc-preserving subsequence of the text. Although it is NP-complete in a general case, an $O(mn)$ algorithm has been proposed if the given sequences have no crossing-arcs. Our contribution is to revise it and to obtain more simple one. We also present our experimental results of the running time.

1 Introduction

Knowledge look-up and matching is a key topic for knowledge federation over the web. Information retrieval, document clustering, and data mining for knowledge extraction are used as fundamental techniques for such purposes, and pattern matching problem is among the most basic and important topics of them.

Although many researchers have tackled the problem and developed some efficient algorithms so far [3, 7, 12], simple pattern matching algorithms are not enough for such purposes, e.g., discovering a knowledge from large text databases, connecting with a knowledge to another on the web, and so on. Traditionally, however, the study of pattern matching has concentrated on simple and fast search. From this viewpoint texts are treated as just a sequence of characters, where any background knowledges and semantics of the texts are ignored, and therefore we could obtain efficient algorithms.

In future, we need to do pattern matching with considering explicit or implicit structures of the text in order to do more powerful and intelligent searching in practical use. For example, semi-structured data such as XML and HTML files have tree structures implicitly, where each tag in them corresponds to a node. In such case, they are usually converted to explicit tree structures (DOM trees) and then processed. On the other hand, a significant amount of domain knowledge for textual information is becoming available online in the form of thesaurus or taxonomy [2, 8] recently, and demands for searching that can incorporate with

---

* This research is supported by JSPS under Grant-in-Aid for Young Scientists (B) (17700024).

K.P. Jantke et al. (Eds.): Federation over the Web, LNAI 3847, pp. 25–39, 2006.

Fig. 1. Arc-annotated sequence

Fig. 2. A tRNA(tRNAPhe) secondary structure

these knowledge are also increased [13]. For the former demand, we have already developed a pattern matching algorithm to deal with semi-structured data without constructing any DOM trees [14]. For the latter demand, we have tackled the pattern matching problem incorporating with taxonomic information [10].

In this paper, we study the pattern matching problem for *arc-annotated* sequences, which are strings with information about relationships between characters on the strings, which are represented by arcs (see Fig. 1). Such a string, for example, can represent a text with phrase dependency in a Japanese sentence. Pattern matching for those texts may enable us to find a pair of sentences similar in meaning to each other, and to extract articles or essays which has a similar outline from the web. This will be useful for knowledge federation.

The main motivation of this problem comes from computational biology, doing pattern matching transfer RNA (tRNA) data (see Fig. 2) with considering their structures [15]. That is, given a text and a pattern with arc information, the problem is to answer whether the pattern can match a subsequence of the text with preserving the arc shape. Gramm et al. [6] define this matching problem as *Arc-Preserving-Subsequence* (APS for short) problem. The complexity of the problem depends on the types of the arc annotations: Table 1 shows the summary of the complexity for different versions of this problem [6]. Although it is proved as NP-complete in a general case [5], they presented an algorithm which can solve the problem in $O(nm)$ time if both the text and the pattern contain no crossing arcs and any two arcs do not share a character at the same position,

Table 1. Summary of the complexity for different versions of the APS problem. The row corresponds to the arc-annotation type of the text. The column corresponds to arc-annotation type of the pattern. The class "unlimited" allows that some arcs share the same endpoints. In this paper, however, we do not consider such case. This table is based on Gramm et al. [6]. For APS(crossing, nested) and APS(crossing, chain), they claimed that the complexities of them can be easily proved from [5], but the details are omitted in [6].

APS(.,.)	unlimited	crossing	nested	chain	plain
unlimited	NP-complete [5]				
crossing	—	NP-complete [5]	NP-complete		?
nested	—	—	$O(nm)$ [6]		

where n, m are the text length and the pattern length, respectively. However, their algorithm has an error. Moreover, experimental results to estimate the efficiency of the algorithm have not been given so far.

In this paper, we present the revised version of Gramm et al.'s algorithm and propose more simple one. We also present our experimental results of the running time of them.

Related works. To measure the similarity between two RNA sequences, several researchers tackled the more general problem, which is to compute the *longest arc-preserving common subsequence* (LAPCS). Evans [5] presented that the problem is NP-complete in a general case, and also presented that there exist polynomial-time algorithms in some special cases. Jiang et al. [9] answered an open problem mentioned in [5], and improve the hardness result in [5]. Alber et al. [1] studied LAPCS restricted to nested arcs, and presented efficient approximation algorithms. Vialette [15] mentioned the complexity of LAPCS in detail. Ma, Wang, and Zhang [11], and El-Mabrouk and Raffinot [4] studied the similarity of RNA sequences based on the other models, considering with their secondary structures. Although almost all works mentioned above are from the theoretical viewpoint, only [4] showed the experimental results of their algorithm.

2   Preliminaries

Although we follow most definitions in [6], note that some are different from the original one.

Let Σ be a finite alphabet. The length of a *sequence (string)* $S \in \Sigma^*$ is denoted by $|S|$. A sequence whose length is 0 is denoted by ε, that is, $|\varepsilon| = 0$. The ith character of $S \in \Sigma^*$ is denoted by $S[i]$ for $1 \leq i \leq |S|$, and $S[i:j]$ denotes the interval from $S[i]$ to $S[j]$ for $1 \leq i \leq j \leq |S|$. For convenience, let $S[i:j] = \varepsilon$ for $i > j$. For two sequence S and T ($|S| \leq |T|$), if T becomes the same sequence as S by eliminating $|T| - |S|$ characters from T, S is called a *subsequence* of T.

An *arc annotation* A of a sequence S is a set of pairs of $\{1, 2, \ldots, |S|\}$. An element of A is called an *arc*. We assume below that it holds $i_L < i_R$ for any arc $(i_L, i_R) \in A$, and that any two arcs do not contain the same integer. An arc

$(i_L, i_R) \in A$ of a sequence S represents that $S[i_L]$ is connected with $S[i_R]$ by the arc. $S[i_L]$ and $S[i_R]$ are called *left endpoint* and *right endpoint*, respectively. Note that any two arcs do not share the same endpoint from the above assumption. We also denote by $|A|$ the cardinality of a set A.

If a sequence S has no arcs, we call such arc structure *plain*. If any two arcs of S are not nested or crossed, we call it *chain*. If any two arcs of S are not crossed but may be nested, we call it *nested*. If some arcs of S are crossed, we call it *crossing*. That is, for any two arcs $(i_L^1, i_R^1), (i_L^2, i_R^2) \in A$, it holds that $i_R^1 < i_L^2$ or $i_R^2 < i_L^1$ if S is chain, and it holds that $i_L^2 < i_L^1 < i_R^2 \Leftrightarrow i_L^2 < i_R^1 < i_R^2$ if S is nested.

Let S_1 and S_2 be two sequences with arcs A_1 and A_2, respectively. We say *base match* if $S_1[i] = S_2[j]$ for $1 \le i \le |S_1|$ and $1 \le j \le |S_2|$. We also say *arc match* if $S_1[i_L^1] = S_2[i_L^2]$ and $S_1[i_R^1] = S_2[i_R^2]$ for $(i_L^1, i_R^1) \in A_1$ and $(i_L^2, i_R^2) \in A_2$. If S_2 is a subsequence of S_1, there exists a one-to-one mapping M from $\{1, 2, \ldots, |S_2|\}$ to a subset of $\{1, 2, \ldots, |S_1|\}$, given by $M = \{(j, i_j) \mid 1 \le j \le |S_2|, 1 \le i_j \le |S_1|\}$, and it holds that $S_2[j] = S_1[i_j]$ for $(j, i_j) \in M$. If S_2 is mapped into a subsequence of S_1 by M and the subsequence preserves the shape of the arcs of S_2, we call S_2 *arc-preserving subsequence* of S_1. That is, for any $(j_L, i_L), (j_R, i_R) \in M$, it holds that $(j_L, j_R) \in A_2 \Leftrightarrow (i_L, i_R) \in A_1$.

We define a set $I_1^{(k,\ell)}$ for a sequence $S_1 = S_1[1:n]$ and $1 \le k \le \ell \le n$, as

$$I_1^{(k,\ell)} = \{i \mid k \le i \le \ell\} - \bigcup_{\substack{(i_L, i_R) \in A_1 \\ \wedge k \le i_L < i_R \le \ell}} \{i' \mid i_L \le i' \le i_R\},$$

and also define $I_2^{(k,\ell)}$ in the same manner. That is, $I_1^{(k,\ell)}$ is a set of character positions except for those covered by arcs within $S_1[k:\ell]$. We define a function $\mathrm{maxaps}(S_1[i_1:i_2], S_2[j_1:j_2])$ as to return the largest j' for $j_1 \le j' \le j_2$ such that $S_2[j_1:j']$ is an arc-preserving subsequence of $S_1[i_1:i_2]$, or to return $j_1 - 1$ if such j' does not exist.

Arc-Preserving Subsequence problem. Given two sequences $S_1 = S_1[1:n]$ and $S_2 = S_2[1:m]$ with arc-annotation A_1 and A_2, respectively, the *Arc-Preserving Subsequence* (APS) problem is to answer if S_2 is an arc-preserving subsequence of S_1. For convenience, we call the sequence S_1 *text* and S_2 *pattern*. The complexity of the problem changes according to each arc structure of the text and the pattern. Therefore, we denote the combination of them by APS(TYPE1, TYPE2), where TYPE1 is the text structure and TYPE2 is the pattern structure. For example, APS(nested, chain) indicates the arc-preserving subsequence problem for a text with nested arc-annotation and a pattern with chain arc-annotation.

3 Algorithms

In this section we make brief sketches of the revised version of [6] and our algorithm.

3.1 GGN Algorithm

Gramm et al.[6] proposed an $O(nm)$ algorithm which solves APS(nested, nested). Their idea is to calculate maxaps for each subsequences inside the most inner arcs of the text S_1 and the pattern S_2 at first, and then calculate maxaps for subsequences outer the arc with dynamic programming. Finally, the value of maxaps($S_1[1 : n], S_2[1 : m]$) is computed. In [6], they introduced the algorithm for APS(nested, chain) at first from the observation of APS(nested, plain) and APS(chain, plain), and then extended it into the algorithm for APS(nested, nested). Roughly estimating the complexity of their algorithm for APS(nested, nested), it runs $O(nm)$ time since $S_1[i]$ must be compared to $S_2[j]$ for any i, j ($1 \le i \le n, 1 \le j \le m$). The space needed for storing the table for dynamic programming is $O(|A_1|m)$.

Let $S_1[1 : n]$ be the text with arc-annotation A_1 and $S_2[1 : m]$ be the pattern with arc-annotation A_2. Consider we now compute maxaps($S_1[i_L : i_R], S_2[j_L : j_R]$). If $S_1[i_L : i_R]$ and $S_2[j_L : j_R]$ have no arcs, namely in case of APS(plain, plain), the values of maxaps for them can be easily computed in $O(|S_1[i_L : i_R]|)$ time since we have only to check if the characters can match each other by sliding pointers over $S_1[i_L : i_R]$ and $S_2[j_L : j_R]$.

Next we consider the case of APS(chain, plain) such as Fig. 3. We cannot

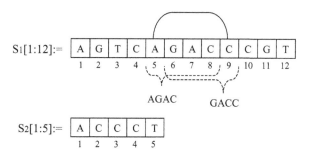

Fig. 3. Example of APS(chain, plain)

take both of two endpoints of the arc on S_1 because of the definition of the APS problem. Thus, we consider the part inside the arc as that two different sequences are in parallel, and take the maximum of the values of maxaps for them. For the running example,

$$\text{maxaps}(S_1[5 : 9], S_2[1 : 5]) = \max \left\{ \begin{matrix} \text{maxaps}(S_1[5 : 8], S_2[1 : 5]), \\ \text{maxaps}(S_1[6 : 9], S_2[1 : 5]) \end{matrix} \right\}$$
$$= \max\{2, 3\} = 3.$$

How to compute the value of maxaps in case of APS(nested, plain) can be derived from the case of APS(chain, plain). Assuming that the values of maxaps for each subsequence of any inner arcs and each suffix of the pattern are computed, then we can compute it for the most outer arc in the same manner as

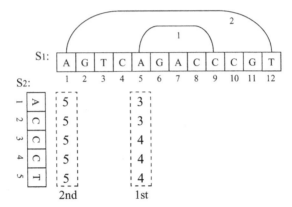

Fig. 4. Example of APS(nested, plain). The figures under arcs indicate the order of processing. The figures inside the dashed squares indicate $\mathrm{maxaps}(S_1[i_L : i_R], S_2[j, 5])$ for each arc $(i_L, i_R) \in A_1$ and $1 \leq j \leq 5$. The values of maxaps for the inner arc are firstly computed, and then those for the outer arc are computed.

APS(chain, plain). Namely, we avoid computing values of maxaps for the parts inside the inner arcs twice by using dynamic programming technique. For the example of Fig. 4, $\mathrm{maxaps}(S_1[1 : 12], S_2[1 : 5])$ is computed as follows:

$$\mathrm{maxaps}(S_1[1 : 12], S_2[1 : 5])$$

$$= \max \left\{ \begin{array}{l} \mathrm{maxaps}(S_1[1 : 11], S_2[1 : 5]), \\ \mathrm{maxaps}(S_1[2 : 12], S_2[1 : 5]) \end{array} \right\}$$

$$= \max \left\{ \begin{array}{l} \mathrm{maxaps}(S_1[10 : 11], S_2[\mathrm{maxaps}(S_1[5 : 9], S_2[\mathrm{maxaps}(S_1[1 : 4], \\ \hspace{6cm} S_2[1 : 5]) + 1 : 5]) + 1 : 5]), \\ \mathrm{maxaps}(S_1[10 : 12], S_2[\mathrm{maxaps}(S_1[5 : 9], S_2[\mathrm{maxaps}(S_1[2 : 4], \\ \hspace{6cm} S_2[1 : 5]) + 1 : 5]) + 1 : 5]) \end{array} \right\}$$

$$= \max \left\{ \begin{array}{l} \mathrm{maxaps}(S_1[10 : 11], S_2[\mathrm{maxaps}(S_1[5 : 9], S_2[3 : 5]) + 1 : 5]), \\ \mathrm{maxaps}(S_1[10 : 12], S_2[\mathrm{maxaps}(S_1[5 : 9], S_2[1 : 5]) + 1 : 5]) \end{array} \right\}$$

$$= \max \left\{ \begin{array}{l} \mathrm{maxaps}(S_1[10 : 11], S_2[4 + 1 : 5]), \\ \mathrm{maxaps}(S_1[10 : 12], S_2[3 + 1 : 5]) \end{array} \right\}$$

$$= \max\{4, 5\} = 5.$$

In case of APS(nested, chain), computing the values of maxaps is rather complicated. Although the approach is similar to the way of APS(nested, plain), we must pay much attention to the order of the computation of maxaps in this case. In the original algorithm of [6], the arcs are processed in increasing order of their right endpoints. For example, in Fig. 5, $\mathrm{maxaps}(S_1[i_L : i_R], S_2[1 : 2])$ for any $(i_L, i_R) \in A_1$ is computed at first, and then $\mathrm{maxaps}(S_1[i_L : i_R], S_2[3 : 4])$ for any $(i_L, i_R) \in A_1$ is computed. Finally, it for whole sequences is computed. However, this algorithm may touch undefined entries of maxaps in this order. Considering the computation of $\mathrm{maxaps}(S_1[2 : 9], S_2[1 : 2])$, since the arc $(1, 2) \in A_2$ can arc-match $(3, 5) \in A_1$ and thus $S_1[3 : 5]$ is APS of $S_2[1 : 2]$, namely

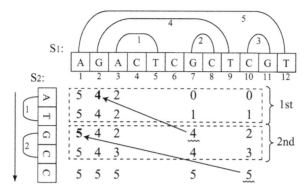

Fig. 5. Computation order of the original way in case of APS(nested, chain). The figures under arcs indicate the order of processing. The values of maxaps inside the upper dashed square are firstly computed, and then those inside the lower dashed square are computed. However, computing each value indicated as a bold figure needs for each value underlined with the waved-line which has not computed yet at the time.

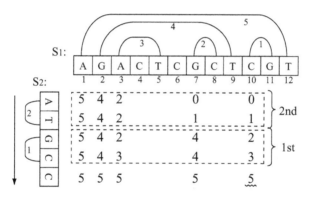

Fig. 6. Modified version of the computation order in case of APS(nested, chain). The order of the processing must be in the reverse way of the original one. However, the value underlined with the waved-line remains as a special case.

maxaps($S_1[2 : 9], S_2[1 : 2]$) must be larger than 2. It must be equal to maxaps for $S_2[3 : 5]$ and the rest part inside the arc $(2, 9)$, namely $S_1[6 : 9]$. In fact, the original algorithm computes maxaps($S_1[6 : 9], S_2[3 : 5]$) in the such case, where the value of maxaps($S_1[7 : 8], S_2[3 : 4]$) is required, while it has not been computed yet. The similar case occurs when maxaps($S_1[1 : 12], S_2[3 : 4]$) is computed. To avoid this problem we must process the arcs in descending ordered by left endpoints, and treat some undefined cases specially(Fig. 6).

The computation in case of APS(nested, nested) is derived as a natural extension of the case of APS(nested, chain) in a similar manner of the extension from APS(chain, plain) to APS(nested, plain).

Fig. 7 and Fig. 8 show the revised version of Gramm et al.'s algorithm (GGN algorithm).

function $\mathrm{maxaps_{np}}(S_1[i_1 : i_2], S_2[j_1 : j_2])$ {
  if $(S_1[i_1 : i_2] = \varepsilon$ or $S_2[j_1 : j_2] = \varepsilon)$ return $j_1 - 1$;
  else if $(i_1 = i_2)$ {
    if $(S_1[i_1] = S_2[j_1])$ return j_1;
    else return $j_1 - 1$;
  } else if $(j_1 = j_2$ and $i_1 < i_2)$ {
    if $(S_1[i_1] = S_2[j_1])$ return j_1;
    else return $\mathrm{maxaps_{np}}(S_1[i_1 + 1 : i_2], S_2[j_1 : j_1])$;
  } else if $(i_1 < i_2$ and $j_1 < j_2)$ {
    if $(S_1[i_1]$ is a left endpoint of $(i_L, i_R) \in A_1)$ {
      return $\mathrm{maxaps_{np}}(S_1[i_R + 1 : i_2], S_2[T(i_1, j_1) + 1 : j_2])$;
    } else if $(S_1[i_1] = S_2[j_1])$ {
      return $\mathrm{maxaps_{np}}(S_1[i_1 + 1 : i_2], S_2[j_1 + 1 : j_2])$;
    } else {
      return $\mathrm{maxaps_{np}}(S_1[i_1 + 1 : i_2], S_2[j_1 : j_2])$;
    }
  }
}

function $\mathrm{maxaps_{nc}}(S_1[i_1 : i_2], S_2[j_1 : j_2])$ {
  if $(S_1[i_1 : i_2] = \varepsilon$ or $S_2[j_1 : j_2] = \varepsilon)$ return $j_1 - 1$;
  else if $(i_1 = i_2)$ {
    if $(S_1[i_1] = S_2[j_1]$ and $S_2[j_1]$ is not endpoint) return j_1;
    else return $j_1 - 1$;
  } else if $(i_1 < i_2$ and $j_1 = j_2)$ {
    if $(S_2[j_1]$ is not endpoint) return $j_1 - 1$;
    else if $(S_1[i_1] = S_2[j_1])$ return j_1;
    else return $\mathrm{maxaps_{nc}}(S_1[i_1 + 1 : i2], S_2[j_1 : j_1])$;
  } else if $(i_1 < i_2$ and $j_1 < j_2$ and
        $S_1[i_1]$ and $S_2[j_1]$ are not endpoints) {
    if $(S_1[i_1] = S_2[j_1])$ return $\mathrm{maxaps_{nc}}(S_1[i_1 + 1 : i_2], S_2[j_1 + 1 : j_2])$;
    else return $\mathrm{maxaps_{nc}}(S_1[i_1 + 1 : i_2], S_2[j_1 : j_2])$;
  } else if $(i_1 < i_2$ and $j_1 < j_2$ and
        $S_2[j_1]$ is endpoint but $S_1[i_1]$ is not endpoint) {
    return $\mathrm{maxaps_{nc}}(S_1[i_1 + 1 : i_2], S_2[j_1 : j_2])$;
  } else if $(i_1 < i_2$ and $j_1 < j_2$ and
        $S_1[i_1]$ is a left endpoint of $(i_L, i_R) \in A_1)$ {
    if $(T(i_1, j_1)$ is not defined) {
      $T(i_1, j_1) = \max(\mathrm{maxaps_{nc}}(S_1[i_1 : i_R - 1], S_2[j_1 : j_2]),$
                 $\mathrm{maxaps_{nc}}(S_1[i_1 + 1 : i_R], S_2[j_1 : j_2]))$;
    }
    return $\mathrm{maxaps_{nc}}(S_1[i_R + 1 : i_2], S_2[T(i_1, j_1) + 1 : j_2])$;
  }
}

Fig. 7. Functions for GGN algorithm

procedure GGNalgorithm(S_1, A_1, S_2, A_2) {
  for each $(j_L, j_R) \in A_2$ (descending ordered by their left endpoints) {
    for each $j \in I_2^{(j_L+1, j_R-1)}$ {
      for each $(i_L, i_R) \in A_1$ (descending ordered by their left endpoints) {
        if $((j_L, j_R) \in A_2$ is the most inner arc) {
          $T(i_L, j) = \max(\text{maxaps}_{\text{np}}(S_1[i_L : i_R - 1], S_2[j : j_R - 1]),$
                  $\text{maxaps}_{\text{np}}(S_1[i_L + 1 : i_R], S_2[j : j_R - 1]));$
        } else {
          $T(i_L, j) = \max(\text{maxaps}_{\text{nc}}(S_1[i_L : i_R - 1], S_2[j : j_R - 1]),$
                  $\text{maxaps}_{\text{nc}}(S_1[i_L + 1 : i_R], S_2[j : j_R - 1]));$
        }
      }
    }
    for each $(i_L, i_R) \in A_1$ (descending ordered by their left endpoints) {
      if $((i_L, i_R) \in A_1$ is the most inner arc
        such that $\text{maxaps}_{\text{nc}}(S_1[i_L : i_R], S_2[j_L : j_R]) = j_R)$ {
        $T(i_L, j_L) = j_R;$
      } else {
        $T(i_L, j_L) = \text{maxaps}_{\text{nc}}(S_1[i_L + 1 : i_R], S_2[j_L : m]);$
      }
    }
  }
  for each $j \in I_2^{(1,m)}$ (in descending order) {
    for each $(i_L, i_R) \in A_1$ (descending ordered by their left endpoints) {
      $T(i_L, j) = \max(\text{maxaps}_{\text{nc}}(S_1[i_L + 1 : i_R], S_2[j : m]),$
            $\text{maxaps}_{\text{nc}}(S_1[i_L : i_R - 1], S_2[j : m]));$
    }
  }
  if $(\text{maxaps}_{\text{nc}}(S_1[1 : n], S_2[1 : m]) = m)$ {
    print 'S_2 is an aps of S_1';
  } else {
    print 'S_2 is an aps of S_1';
  }
}

Fig. 8. GGN algorithm for APS(nested, nested)

3.2 Proposed Algorithm

GGN algorithm uses a kind of bottom-up dynamic programming. It must calculate for any combination of i and j ($1 \leq i \leq n, 1 \leq j \leq m$). However, in practice, the great part of calculations tends to be useless when we need to know only if $\text{maxaps}(S_1[1 : n], S_2[1 : m]) = m$ or not. We can omit the useless calculations by using a kind of top-down dynamic programming any by storing values which are actually needed. We can also reduce the calculations by using the property that arc matches are followed by base matches. Moreover, while GGN algorithm utilizes maxaps$_{np}$ for APS(nested, plain) and maxaps$_{nc}$ for APS(nested, chain), note that it can be combined into one because maxaps$_{nc}$ contains maxaps$_{np}$ essentially.

Let $S_1[1:n]$ be the text with arc-annotation A_1 and $S_2[1:m]$ be the pattern with arc-annotation A_2. Now assume that $S_1[1:i-1]$ is an APS of $S_2[1:j-1]$ for some $1 \leq i < n$ and $1 \leq j < m$, namely maxaps$(S_1[1:i-1], S_2[1:m])$ $= j - 1$. Then $S_1[1:n]$ is an APS of $S_2[1:m]$ if maxaps$(S_1[i:n], S_2[j:m]) =$ m. Our proposed algorithm computes maxaps by left-to-right manner basically as follows.

We check if $S_1[i]$ base-matches with $S_2[j]$ at first. If $S_1[i]$ does not match with $S_2[j]$, then we increase i by 1 and continue the base-match check. If $S_1[i]$ matches with $S_2[j]$, then two cases are considered. One is the case that $S_2[j]$ is not an endpoint, and another is that $S_2[j]$ is an endpoint of an arc $(j_L, j_R) \in A_2$. In the former case, $S_1[i]$ is an APS of $S_2[j]$ if $S_1[i]$ is not an endpoint, thus we increase i and j by 1 and continue the base-match check. Otherwise, we must compute maxaps$(S_1[i:i_R], S_2[j:m])$ for $(i, i_R) \in A_1$ recursively. In the latter case, we check if $S_1[i]$ arc-matches with $S_2[j]$. If maxaps$(S_1[i:i_R], S_2[j:m])$ has already computed for $(i, i_R) \in A_1$, we proceed the pointers as $i = i_R + 1$ and $j = $ maxaps$(S_1[i:i_R], S_2[j:m])+1$. Otherwise, next we check if maxaps$(S_1[i+1:i_R-1], S_2[j+1:j_R-1])$ for $(i, i_R) \in A_1$ and $(j, j_R) \in A_2$ is equals to $j_R - 1$ or not. If it is equal to or larger than j_R, there may be another arc inside (i, i_R) that arc-matches with (j, j_R), and then we must compute maxaps$(S_1[i:i_R], S_2[j:m])$ recursively.

During above processing, if the pointer j reaches to m before the pointer i becomes larger than n, we can say maxaps$(S_1[1:n], S_2[1:m]) = m$, namely $S_1[1:n]$ is an APS of $S_2[1:m]$. For example, the process of the algorithm is as Fig. 9.

From the above observation, we can obtain a more simple algorithm showed in Fig. 10.

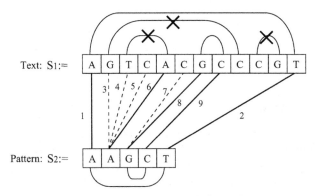

Fig. 9. Computation of the proposed algorithm. Solid lines between S_1 and S_2 indicate matches, and dashed lines indicate mismatches. The figures followed by the lines indicates the order of the comparisons. Crosses over the arcs indicate that they could not arc-match.

```
function maxaps(S₁[i₁ : i₂], S₂[j₁ : j₂]) {
  if (S₁[i₁ : i₂] = ε or S₂[j₁ : j₂] = ε) {
    return j₁ − 1;
  }
  for (i = i₁, j = j₁; i ≤ i₂ and j ≤ j₂; i + +) {
    if (S₁[i] ≠ S₂[j]) {
      continue;
    }
    if (S₂[j] is not endpoint) {
      if (S₁[i] is not a left endpoint of (i_L, i_R) ∈ A₁) {
        j + +;
      } else {
        if (T(i, j) is not defined) {
          T(i, j) = max(maxaps(S₁[i : i_R − 1], S₂[j : j₂]),
                        maxaps(S₁[i + 1 : i_R], S₂[j : j₂]));
        }
        j = T(i, j) + 1;
        i = i_R;
      }
    } else {
      if (S₂[j] is a left endpoint of (j_L, j_R) ∈ A₂) {
        if (S₁[i] is a left endpoint of (i_L, i_R) ∈ A₁ and S₁[i_R] = S₂[j_R]) {
          if (T(i, j) is not defined) {
            t₁ = maxaps(S₁[i + 1 : i_R − 1], S₂[j + 1 : j_R − 1]);
            t₂ = maxaps(S₁[i + 1 : i_R], S₂[j : j₂]);
            if (t₁ = j_R − 1 and t₁ > t₂) {
              T(i, j) = t₁ + 1;
            } else {
              T(i, j) = t₂;
            }
          }
          j = T(i, j) + 1;
          i = i_R;
        }
      }
    }
  }
  return j − 1;
}
procedure FGGNalgorithm(S₁, A₁, S₂, A₂) {
  if (maxaps(S₁[1 : n], S₂[1 : m]) = m) {
    print 'S₂ is an aps of S₁';
  } else {
    print 'S₂ is an aps of S₁';
  }
}
```

Fig. 10. Faster GGN(FGGN) algorithm

4   Experimental Results

We implemented two algorithms mentioned above in C, and tested them for some data which generated randomly on $\Sigma = \{A, C, G, U\}$. We used DELL Precision650 (Intel Xeon 3.06GHz dual-CPU and 3.5GB memory) running Cygwin on Windows XP, and used Gcc version 3.3.1. For each experiment, we prepared 1000 sequences as texts which are generated in the same condition, and carried out on them for 5 different patterns. We measured the total CPU time for the patterns and calculated the average.

Fig. 11 shows the result where we changed text lengths $n = |S_1|$ from 100 to 1000 and we set $|A_1|$ equal to 20% of n, for patterns whose length $m = |S_2| = 20$ and $|A_2| = 4$. Fig. 12 shows the result where we changed pattern lengths $m = |S_2|$ from 10 to 100 and we set $|A_2|$ equal to 20% of m, for texts whose length $n = |S_1| = 1000$ and $|A_1| = 100$. Fig. 13 shows the result where we changed

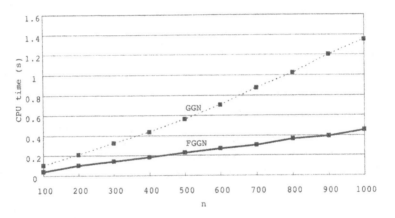

Fig. 11. Changes in running time with n

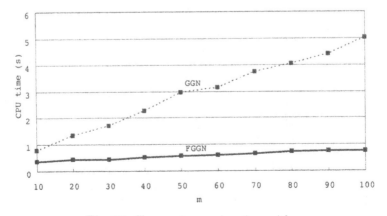

Fig. 12. Changes in running time with m

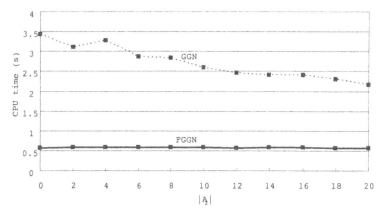

Fig. 13. Changes in running time with $|A_2|$

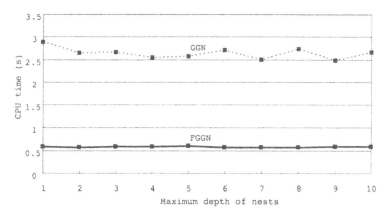

Fig. 14. Changes in running time with the max-depth of nests

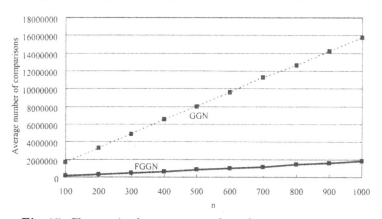

Fig. 15. Changes in the average number of comparisons with n

$|A_2|$ of patterns from 0 to 20 and we set $m = |S_2| = 50$, for texts whose length $n = |S_1| = 1000$ and $|A_1| = 100$. Fig. 14 shows the result where we changed the maximum depth of nests of patterns from 1 to 10 and we set $m = |S_2| = 50$ and $|A_2| = 20$, for texts whose length $n = |S_1| = 1000$ and $|A_1| = 100$.

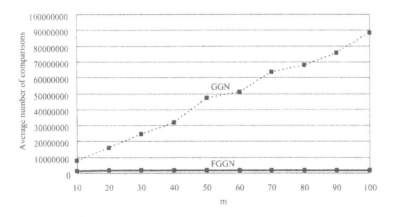

Fig. 16. Changes in the average number of comparisons with m

In addition to the above, we also measured the average number of comparisons between characters of S_1 and S_2 in order to remove the influence on the environment of implementation and so on. Fig. 15 shows the result where the conditions are the same as Fig. 11. Fig. 16 shows the result where the conditions are the same as Fig. 12. We can see that the results tend to be similar to those for running time.

5   Conclusion

From the experimental results, our algorithm runs $2 \sim 5$ times faster than the revised version of GGN algorithm. Moreover, note that the running time of our algorithm is little affected by the length, the number of arcs, and the depth of nests of a given pattern, which is especially desirable in practical uses.

It is not obvious whether APS(crossing, plain) is NP-complete or not. A polynomial time algorithm for the problem is expected. Since n, m tend to be rather small in real data, there may exist an algorithm that solves in reasonable time even if APS(crossing, crossing). Such a practically efficient algorithm will be useful for real applications. To carry out an experiment for real data is our future work.

Pattern matching with arc-annotation where each arc has attributes is also a challenging problem.

References

1. J. Alber, J. Gramm, J. Guo, and R. Niedermeier. Computing the similarity of two sequences with nested arc annotations. *Theoretical Computer Science*, 312(2-3):337–358, January 2004.
2. G. O. Consortium. Gene ontology: Tool for the unification of biology. *Nature Genetics*, 25:25–29, 2000. http://www.geneontology.org/.
3. M. Crochemore and W. Rytter. *Jewels of Stringology*. World Scientific Publishing, 2002.
4. N. El-Mabrouk and M. Raffinot. Approximate matching of secondary structures. In *Proc. RECOMB*, pages 156–164. ACM Press, 2002.
5. P. A. Evans. Finding common subsequences with arcs and pseudoknots. In *Proc. 10th CPM*, volume 1645 of *LNCS*, pages 270–280. Springer, 1999.
6. J. Gramm, J. Guo, and R. Niedermeier. Pattern matching for arc-annotated sequences. In *Proc. 22nd FSTTCS*, volume 2556 of *LNCS*, pages 182–193. Springer, 2002.
7. D. Gusfield. *Algorithms on Strings, Trees, and Sequences: Computer Science and Computational Biology*. Cambridge University Press, 1997.
8. L. Japan Electronic Dictionary Research Institute. Edr electronic dictionary technical guide (2nd edition). Technical Report TR-045, 1995. http://www.iijnet.or.jp/edr.
9. T. Jiang, G.-H. Lin, B. Ma, and K. Zhang. The longest common subsequence problem for arc-annotated sequences. *Journal of Discrete Algorithms*, 2(2):257–270, June 2004.
10. T. Kida and H. Arimura. Pattern matching with taxonomic information. In *Proc. Asia Information Retrieval Symposium*, pages 265–268, October 2004.
11. B. Ma, L. Wang, and K. Zhang. Computing similarity between rna structures. *Theoretical Computer Science*, (276):111–132, 2002.
12. G. Navarro and M. Raffinot. *Flexible Pattern Matching in Strings: Practical on-line search algorithms for texts and biological sequences*. Cambridge University Press, 2002.
13. R. Stevens, I. Horrocks, C. Goble, and S. Bechhofer. Building a reson-able bioinformatics ontology. *IEEE Transactions on Information Technology and Biomedicine*, 6(2):136–41, 2002.
14. M. Takeda, S. Miyamoto, T. Kida, A. Shinohara, S. Fukamachi, T. Shinohara, and S. Arikawa. Processing text files as is: Pattern matching over compressed texts, multi-byte character texts, and semi-structured texts. In *Proc. 9th International Symposium on String Processing and Information Retrieval*, volume 2476 of *LNCS*, pages 170–186. Springer, September 2002.
15. S. Vialette. On the computational complexity of 2-interval pattern matching problems. *Theoretical Computer Science*, 312(2-3):223–249, January 2004.

VSOP (Valued-Sum-of-Products) Calculator for Knowledge Processing Based on Zero-Suppressed BDDs

Shin-ichi Minato

Graduate School of Information Science and Technology, Hokkaido University,
Sapporo, 060-0814 Japan

Abstract. Recently, Binary Decision Diagrams (BDDs) are widely used for efficiently manipulating large-scale Boolean function data. BDDs are also applied for handling combinatorial item set data. Zero-suppressed BDDs (ZBDDs) are special type of BDDs which are suitable for implicitly handling large-scale combinatorial item set data. In this paper, we present *VSOP* program developed for calculating combinatorial item set data specified by symbolic expressions based on ZBDD techniques. Our program supports not only combinatorial set operations but also numerical arithmetic operations based on *Valued-Sum-Of-Products* algebra, such as addition, subtraction, multiplication, division, numerical comparison, etc. We discuss the data structures and algorithms in our program, and show some typical applications. VSOP calculator will be useful for solving many problems in Computer Science. We show one of the promising application to find a hidden data group related each other under the huge amount of web space. Our method will facilitates knowledge federation over the web, and also useful for many other applications in computer science.

1 Introduction

Manipulation of Boolean functions is a fundamental techniques for handling various problems in computer science. Binary Decision Diagrams(BDDs)[4] are efficient graph-based representation of Boolean functions, intensively studied in 1990's, and now widely used in digital system design and many other areas. Zero-suppressed BDDs (ZBDD)[10, 15] are a special type of BDDs for efficient manipulation of combinatorial item set data. ZBDD-based method have been applied for many algorithmic problems such as minimizing sum-of-products forms[14], database analysis[16], and many kinds of graph optimization problems[6].

In this paper, we present *VSOP* calculator developed for calculating combinatorial item sets specified by symbolic expressions. Based on ZBDD techniques, VSOP can efficiently handle large-scale sum-of-products expressions with a number of item symbols. Our program supports not only Boolean set operations but also numerical arithmetic operations based on *Valued-Sum-Of-Products* algebra, such as addition, subtraction, multiplication, division, numerical comparison, etc.

The author has a past result of developing an arithmetic Boolean expression manipulator "BEM-II"[9] based on (ordinary) BDDs, and the program was

K.P. Jantke et al. (Eds.): Federation over the Web, LNAI 3847, pp. 40–58, 2006.

utilized for many works[17, 18, 8]. VSOP deal with the arithmetic and numerical operations as well as BEM-II, and extends the data model from Boolean functions to combinatorial sets. The interface of VSOP is very flexible and customizable for solving many kinds of combinatorial problems, and it will facilitate research and development for knowledge processing.

As one of the promising applications, this paper shows that our VSOP calculator facilitates "knowledge federation over the web". Usually, the knowledge on the web consists of a number of distributed data, and one important task is to find a hidden data group strongly related each other over a huge amount of web space. We will show the experimental results to extract combinations of web pages which are frequently appearing together in a session of web transactions.

The paper is organized as follows: First, we briefly review BDDs and ZBDDs in Section 2. We then describe the representation method of Valued-Sum-Of-Products forms based on ZBDDs in Section 3. We present algorithms of arithmetic operations in Section 4, and several display formats of VSOP are shown in Section 5. Finally we show some typical applications of VSOP calculator followed by concluding remarks.

2   BDDs and ZBDDs

BDD is a directed graph representation of the Boolean function, as illustrated in Fig. 1(a). It is derived by reducing a binary tree graph representing recursive *Shannon's expansion*, indicated in Fig. 1(b). The following reduction rules yield a *Reduced Ordered BDD (ROBDD)*, which can efficiently represent the Boolean function. (see [4] for details.)

– Delete all redundant nodes whose two edges point to the same node. (Fig. 2(a))
– Share all equivalent sub-graphs. (Fig. 2(b))

ROBDDs provide canonical forms for Boolean functions when the variable order is fixed. Most research on BDDs are based on the above reduction rules.

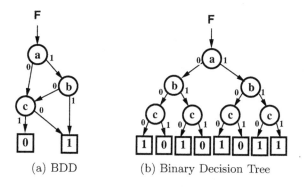

(a) BDD   (b) Binary Decision Tree

Fig. 1. Reduced and non-reduced BDDs for $F = (a \land b) \lor \bar{c}$

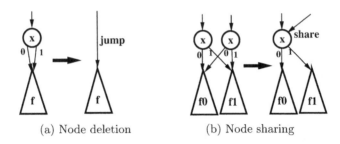

(a) Node deletion   (b) Node sharing

Fig. 2. Conventional BDD reduction rules

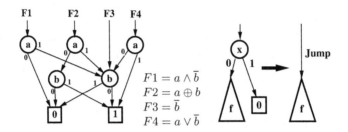

$$F1 = a \wedge \bar{b}$$
$$F2 = a \oplus b$$
$$F3 = \bar{b}$$
$$F4 = a \vee \bar{b}$$

Fig. 3. Shared BDD   **Fig. 4.** ZBDD reduction rule

In the following sections, ROBDDs will be referred to as BDDs (or ordinary BDDs) for the sake of simplification.

As shown in Fig. 3, a set of multiple BDDs can be shared each other under the same fixed variable ordering. In this way, we can handle a number of Boolean functions simultaneously in a monolithic memory space.

Using BDDs, we can uniquely and compactly represent many practical Boolean functions including AND, OR, parity, and arithmetic adder functions. Using Bryant's algorithm[4], we can efficiently construct a BDD for the result of a binary logic operation (i.e. AND, OR, XOR), for given a pair of operand BDDs. This algorithm is based on hash table techniques, and the computation time is almost linear to the data size unless the data overflows the main memory. (see [13] for details.)

BDDs are originally developed for handling Boolean function data, however, they can also be used for implicit representation of combinatorial sets. Here we call "combinatorial item set" for a set of elements each of which is a combination out of n items. This data model often appears in real-life problems, such as combinations of switching devices, Boolean item sets in the database, and combinatorial sets of edges or nodes in the graph data model.

A combinatorial item set can be mapped into Boolean space of n input variables. If we choose any one combination of items, a Boolean function determines whether the combination is included in the combinatorial item set. Such Boolean functions are called *characteristic functions*. The set operations such as union, intersection, and difference can be performed by logic operations on characteristic functions.

By using BDDs for characteristic functions, we can manipulate combinatorial item set efficiently. They can be generated and manipulated within a time roughly proportional to the BDD size. When we handle many combinations including similar patterns (sub-combinations), BDDs are greatly reduced by node sharing effect, and sometimes an exponential reduction benefit can be obtained.

Zero-suppressed BDD (ZBDD)[10, 15] is a special type of BDDs for efficient manipulation of combinatorial item set. ZBDDs are based on the following special reduction rules.

- Delete all nodes whose 1-edge directly points to the 0-terminal node, and jump through to the 0-edge's destination, as shown in Fig. 4.
- Share equivalent nodes as well as ordinary BDDs.

Notice that we do not delete the nodes whose two edges point to the same node, which used to be deleted by the original rule. The zero-suppressed deletion rule is asymmetric for the two edges, as we do not delete the nodes whose 0-edge points to a terminal node. It is proved that ZBDDs are also gives canonical forms as well as ordinary BDDs under a fixed variable ordering.

Here we summarise the features of ZBDDs.

- In ZBDDs, the nodes of irrelevant items (never chosen in any combination) are automatically deleted by ZBDD reduction rule. In ordinary BDDs, irrelevant nodes still remain and they may spoil the reduction benefit of sharing nodes. (An example is shown in Fig. 5.)
- ZBDDs are especially effective for representing sparse combinations. For instance, sets of combinations selecting 10 out of 1000 items can be represented by ZBDDs up to 100 times more compact than ordinary BDDs.
- Each path from the root node to the 1-terminal node corresponds to each combination in the set. Namely, the number of such paths in the ZBDD

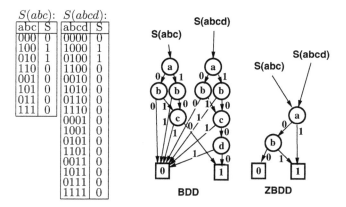

Fig. 5. Effect of ZBDDs

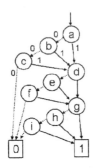

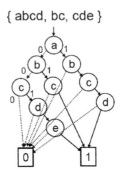

Fig. 6. ZBDD for $(a + b + c)(d + e + f)(g + h + i)$

Fig. 7. Explicit representation with ZBDD

equals to the number of combinations in the set. In ordinary BDDs, this property does not always hold.

– When no equivalent nodes exist in a ZBDD, that is the worst case, the ZBDD structure explicitly stores all items in all combinations, as well as using an explicit linear linked list data structure. Namely, (the order of) ZBDD size never exceeds the explicit representation. An example is shown in Fig. 7. If more nodes are shared, the ZBDD is more compact than linear list. Ordinary BDDs have larger overhead to represent sparser combinations while ZBDDs have no such overhead.

Figure 8 shows the most of primitive operations of ZBDDs. In these operations, $\emptyset$, **1**, $P.top$ are executed in a constant time, and the others are almost linear to the size of graph. We can describe various processing on combinatorial item sets by composing of these primitive operations.

"$\emptyset$"	Returns empty set. (0-termial node)
"**1**"	Returns the set of only null-combination. (1-terminal node)
$P.top$	Returns the item-ID at the root node of P.
$P.offset(v)$	Selects the subset of combinations each of which does not include item v.
$P.onset(v)$	Selects the subset of combinations including item v, and then delete v from each combination.
$P.change(v)$	Inverts existence of v (add / delete) on each combination.
$P \cup Q$	Returns union set.
$P \cap Q$	Returns intersection set.
$P - Q$	Returns difference set. (in P but not in Q.)
$P.count$	Counts number of combinations.

Fig. 8. Primitive ZBDD operations

3   VSOP Expressions Using ZBDDs

In this paper, we call VSOP (Valued-Sum-Of-Products) for a combinatorial item set (or a sum-of-products form) such that each product term has a value. This value can also be considered as a coefficient or a weight for each term. So far, we deal with only integer values. We define the value as zero for a product term not included in the VSOP.

For example, the formula $(5abc + 3ab + 2bc + c)$ represents a VSOP with four terms abc, ab, bc, and c, each of which is valued as $5, 3, 2$, and 1, respectively. This meas that a pattern abc appears five times in a same database. Another meaning is that five times cost is needed to obtain a pattern abc in a certain process.

Not only enumerating combinations but also assigning such values (coefficients or weights) for each product term, we can represent a simple but fundamental knowledge data, which can be used for various problems in computer science. That is a motivation for us to develop a program to efficiently calculate VSOP expressions based on ZBDD techniques.

In the VSOP algebra, the addition follows the ordinary rule: $1 + 1 = 2$ and $x + x = 2x$. However, multiplication rule is not conventional: $2 \times 2 = 4$, $x \times y = xy$, but $x \times x = x$, because we only handle combinatorial item sets, not considering higher degree of item symbols. Notice that the same algebra is also used in calculating expressions of probabilistic variables.

Here we discuss the way to compactly represent VSOP data by using ZBDDs. Since ZBDDs are representation of combinatorial item sets, a simple ZBDD distinguishes only existence of each product term in the set. Thus we need some extended data structure to represent numerical numbers using ZBDDs. Two methods are known on this issue, the one is using BMDs (Binary Moment Diagrams)[5] handling not only 0- and 1-terminal nodes but also numerical valued terminal nodes. The other method is using vector of ordinary ZBDDs to represent binary coding of numerical values[12]. In our program, we use the latter method. We decompose the integer number into m-digits of ZBDD vector $\{F_0, F_1, \ldots, F_{m-1}\}$ to represent integers up to $(2^m - 1)$, as shown in Fig. 9. Namely, F_0 represents a set of terms whose values are odd numbers, F_1 represents a set of terms whose values have '1' at the second digit of binary coding, and listing such ZBDDs until F_{m-1}, we can implicitly represent a VSOP data.

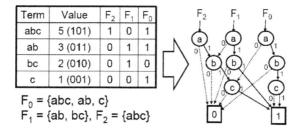

Term	Value	F_2	F_1	F_0
abc	5 (101)	1	0	1
ab	3 (011)	0	1	1
bc	2 (010)	0	1	0
c	1 (001)	0	0	1

$F_0 = \{abc, ab, c\}$
$F_1 = \{ab, bc\}$, $F_2 = \{abc\}$

Fig. 9. ZBDD vector for $(5abc + 3ab + 2bc + c)$

When dealing with integer values in binary coding, we have to consider the expression of negative numbers. There are two well-known methods, one of which is using 2's complement representation, and the other is using the absolute value with sign; however, both method have drawbacks. When using 2's complement, it yields many non-zero digits for small negative numbers (typically, -1 is "all one"), and the ZBDD reduction rule is not effective to those non-zero bits. On the other hand, when using absolute value, the operation of addition become complicated since we have to classify the product terms to choose addition or subtraction depending on magnitude of values.

To solve the above problems, we adopted another binary coding[12] based on (-2), namely, each bit represents $1, -2, 4, -8, 16, \ldots$. For example, -12 can be decomposed into $(-2)^5 + (-2)^4 + (-2)^2 = -2 \cdot 2^4 + 2^4 + 2^2$. In this encoding we can also uniquely represent the integer numbers. Using binary coding with (-2), the higher digits become zero both for positive and negative numbers, and the ZBDD reduction rule works effectively to eliminate the meaningless nodes of higher digits.

In our implementation, we define the special item symbols to combine the ZBDD vector into a single ZBDD. By using 20 special item symbols with higher variable order (near to the root node), up to 2^{20} (about one million) digits of ZBDD vector can be combined into one ZBDD. This means that practically unlimited long digital numbers are representable in our program.

4   Algorithms for Arithmetic Operations

VSOP expressions are manipulated by arithmetic operations, such as addition, subtraction, multiplication, and division. We first generate ZBDDs for trivial VSOP expressions which are single item symbols or integer constants, and then apply those arithmetic operations to construct more complicated VSOP expressions. In this section, we present efficient algorithms for the arithmetic operations of VSOPs based on ZBDDs.

(Multiplication by an item). Multiplication of a VSOP F and an item symbol v can be done by simply attach v to all product terms in F. This is easily written by the basic operations *Onset, Offset*, and *Change* of ZBDDs. Computation time is linear to the number of nodes which are ordered lower than v in the ZBDD.

(Multiplication by a constants). Multiplication of F by an integer constant c means that each value of term is multiplied c times. If c is exactly exponential number of (-2), this operation is just shifting each digits of ZBDD vectors, so computation time is linear to the number of digits, not depending on the number of ZBDD nodes. For general integer c, we decompose c into a bit-vector $c_0, c_1, \ldots, c_m$ and compute $F \times (-2)^i c_i$ for each i. After that we calculate total of them by using addition operation, described as follows.

```
procedure (F + G)                 procedure (F − G)
{ C ← (F ∩ G) ;                   { B ← (F̄ ∩ G) ;
  S ← (F ∪ G) − C ;                 D ← (F ∩ Ḡ) ;
  if (C = 0) return S ;             if (B = 0) return D ;
  else return S − (−2 · C);        else return D + (−2 · B);
}                                 }
```

Fig. 10. Algorithm for addition and subtraction

(**Addition and Subtraction**). Addition of the two VSOPs $F + G$ is defined as generating a new VSOP expression such that each value of product term is sum of values of the same item combinations in F and G. For example, When $F = ab + 2bc − 3c$ and $G = 3ac − 2bc + c$, then $(F + G) = ab + 3ac − 2c$.

Figure 10 shows the algorithms for addition and subtraction based on ZBDD operations. If $(F ∩ G)$ is empty, that means there are no common combinations at any digit, in such case we do not need any carry up, so the addition $(F + G)$ can be completed by just merging them $(F ∪ G)$. On the other hand, if $(F ∩ G)$ contains some common combinations, it represents the set of carries of respective digits. We then make twice of the set of carries and call addition operation again to sum up the carries. By repeating this process, common combinations are eventually exhausted and the procedure is completed.

Since we use the binary coding based on $(−2)$, the one-bit shift corresponds to not twice, but $(−2)$ times, so the carry up formula becomes $S − (−2 · C)$. Namely, we call a subtraction from the addition procedure. Similarly, a borrow of subtraction calls an addition operation. We can implement the both operations with a dual structure.

(**Multiplication of two VSOPs**). Here we define the multiplication (or product) of two VSOPs $(F × G)$ as generating all possible concatenations of two product terms in respective F and G.

Using the multiplication by items or constants, we can compose the multiplication algorithm for the general VSOPs, as shown in Fig. 11. This algorithm is based on the divide-and-conquer idea. Suppose v is the highest-ordered item, F and G are then factored into two parts: $F = v·F_1 ∪ F_0$, $G = v · G_1 ∪ G_0$.

Under this factorization, the product $(F × G)$ can be written as:

$$((F_1 × G_1) + (F_1 × G_0) + (F_0 × G_1)) × v + (F_0 × G_0).$$

Each sub-product term can be computed recursively. The expressions are eventually broken down into trivial ones and the result is obtained. In the worst case, this algorithm would require exponential number of recursive calls for the number of items; however, we can accelerate them by using a hash-based cache memory which stores the results of recent operations. By referring to the cache before each recursive call, we can avoid duplicate executions for equivalent sub-formulas. Consequently, the execution time depends on ZBDD size, not on the number of terms.

```
procedure(F × G)
{  if (F.top < G.top) return (G × F) ;
    if (G = 0) return 0 ;
    if (G = 1) return F ;
    H ← cache("F × G") ;
    if (H exists) return H ;
    v ← F.top ; /* the highest item in F */
    (F₀, F₁) ← factors of F by v ;
    (G₀, G₁) ← factors of G by v ;
    H ← ((F₁ × G₁) + (F₁ × G₀) + (F₀ × G₁)) × v
        +(F₀ × G₀) ;
    cache("F × G") ← H ;
    return H ;
}
```

Fig. 11. Algorithm for multiplication

(Division by an item). Division of a VSOP by an item, the quotient (F/v) and the remainder $(F\%v)$ are defined as classification of the product terms into the two subset, including or excluding v in the item combinations. These operations are exactly same as *Onset* and *Offset* operations of ZBDDs.

(Division by a constant). Division of a VSOP by a constant, (F/c) and $(F\%c)$, are simply defined as integer division (quotient and reminder) for each value of product terms in F. For example, computing $(F/30)$ can delete all product terms whose values are less than 30. Oppositely, $(F\%30)$ extracts such product terms valued less than 30. We can implement this numerical operation by using arithmetic shift and addition/subtraction operations.

(Division of VSOPs). In the VSOP algebra, we have the non-linear multiplication rule $v \times v = v$, and this rule leads that the result of arithmetic division (F/G) is not decided uniquely in general. Thus, we must define our division rule to make a unique result.

In the model of "Boolean" sum-of-products expressions without integer values, *Weak-division method*[3] has been known for long time and widely used in VLSI logic optimization problems. This division method is based on the following rule:

If the divisor G consists of multiple product terms T_i, the quotient $Q(= F/G)$ is defined as the sum of product terms included in every $Q_i = F/T_i$ for all i. Now we propose here the new division method, named *Valued weak division*, which is natural extension of (boolean) weak division. This new method is the same as conventional one until calculating Q_i. After that, we do not extract common product terms, but calculating values absolutely minimum in all Q_i. For example, assume that $F = 2ab + 4ac + ad - 2bc + 3bd$ and $G = a + b$, then

$Q_1 = (F/a) = 2b + 4c + d,$
$Q_2 = (F/b) = 2a - 2c + 3d$

and we obtain $Q = -2c + d$.

```
procedure(F/G)
{      if (G =constant:c) return (F/c) ;
       if (F =constant:c) return 0 ;
       Q ← cache("F/G") ;  if (Q exists) return Q ;
       v ← G.top ; /* the highest variable in G */
       (F₀, F₁) ← factors of F by v ;
       (G₀, G₁) ← factors of G by v ;
       Q ← F₁/G₁ ;
       if (G₀ ≠ 0 and Q ≠ 0 )
            Q₀ ← F₀/G₀ ;
            Q ← (choose value from Q or Q₀
               absolutely smaller one) ;
       cache("F/G") ← Q ;
       return Q ;
}
```

Fig. 12. Algorithm for division

If the given F and G have only boolean values in every terms, our division method gives completely same results as conventional weak division, so it is a natural extension of conventional method.

Figure 12 shows the algorithm of this division methods using ZBDDs. This is an extension of *ZBDD-based fast weak division method*[11] to the VSOP model. As well as the multiplication algorithm, we can accelerate the execution by using a hash-based cache memory to avoid duplicate executions for equivalent sub-formulas, and the computation time depends on ZBDD size, not on the number of terms.

The remainder of division ($F\%G$) can be obtained by computing $F - (F/G) \times G$.

(**Comparison**). VSOP program supports the operators (== != > >= < <=) to compare the numerical values of the two VSOPs. Each of those operators extracts all the product terms included at least in the left or the right expressions and satisfying the arithmetic relation of the operator. For example, suppose $F = 3ab + 2bc - c$ and $G = 2ab - 2b + 3c$, and then we can get $(F > G) = ab + bc + b$. On the same case, $(F$!= $0)$ becomes $ab + bc + c$, and this is regarded as the regularization of all non-zero values to 1 (Boolean). Those comparison operations can be executed in almost same computation time as addition/subtraction operations.

(**Other operations**). We also implemented the *If-Then-Else* operator $(F ? G : H)$, which extracts the product terms from G such that the item combinations included in F, and also extracts the terms from H for the item combinations not included in F. Using this operations with arithmetic comparisons, we can specify various nonlinear functions. For instance, $(F > G)$? $F : G$ generates a VSOP choosing the terms with larger values between F and G.

In addition, we implemented *Restrict* and *Permit* operations proposed in [19], which are basically same as *SupSet* and *Subset* operations in [6]. F.Restrict(G) extracts the product terms from F such that the item combination is a superset of at least one item combination in G. On the other hand, F.Permit(G) extracts the product terms from F such that the item combination is a subset of at least one item combination in G. The computation time is almost linear to ZBDD size. These two operations are useful for solving constraint satisfaction problems[19] by describing restrictive or permissive conditions with VSOP expressions.

5   Display Formats for Computation Results

VSOP program provides several helpful display formats to show the calculation results to the user. We explain typical formats as follows.

(Sum-of-products form with coefficients). The most basic method is to enumerate all product terms with their values. For example, the formula $3abc + 2bc - c$ shows all product terms with coefficients. The order of product terms is a lexicographical manner of item combinations. This format is easy to see if the number of terms is not so many. In our program, one VSOP data may have millions of terms, and in such cases, we cannot finish the output in a practical time.

(Integer Karnaugh map). As shown in Fig. 13, using a matrix indexing item combinations, and display the integer value on each element. We call this an *Integer Karnaugh map*. It is useful to understand the behavior of the VSOP data, but they are practical only for fewer than five or six items.

(Sorting by values). In some cases, it is useful to make sorting of the product terms in terms of their values. For example, the expression $2ab + 3ac + 2b - bc + 3$ can be listed as follows.

$\quad$ 3: $ac + 1$
$\quad$ 2: $ab + b$
-1: bc

(Bit-wise listing). We can list the respective digits of the internal ZBDD vector representation. It is used for observing the relationship of VSOP data and the internal data structures.

(Statistical information). To know the total number of product terms in a VSOP expression corresponds to compute the number of solutions for a

```
a b : c d
    |    00      01      11      10
00 |    0       0       0       3
01 |    1       25      2       0
11 |    0       0       -4      -2
10 |    1       0       -1      0
```

Fig. 13. Integer Karnaugh map

combinatorial problem. Although the number may become an exponential to the number of items, we can quickly count it only in a linear time to the ZBDD size. In addition, we can get other statistical information such as the density of the solutions, and the number of ZBDD nodes.

(**Any satisfiable solutions**). Sometimes we do not have to display all the solutions, just needed to see any one solution (or a counter example). If a ZBDD for the VSOP data has been constructed, it is easy (in a time linear to number of items) to show any one product term, even if the VSOP data is too complicated to display all at once.

When each item has a cost to use in a combination, we can also find the minimum (or maximum) cost combinations in the VSOP data. This operation can be executed in a linear time to the ZBDD size.

Our program can also display the maximum (or minimum value) in the VSOP data. In addition, the set of items used in the given VSOP data can be listed.

6   Applications

Based on ZBDD techniques, we developed an arithmetic calculator to handle large-scale sum-of-products expressions with a number of item symbols. Here we briefly present the specification of VSOP and some typical applications.

6.1   VSOP Calculator

This program, called VSOP, has a C-shell-like interface, both for interactive keyboard inputs and batch style execution from a script file. The program is written in C, C++, and yacc, executable on 32bit Linux PCs.

In VSOP scripts, we can use two kind of symbols, *item symbols* and *program variables*. Item symbols, denoted by strings starting with a lower-case letter, represent the items used in the set of combinations. Program variables, starting with an upper-case letter, are used to identify the memory to which a computation result to be stored temporarily. We can describe multi-level expressions by using these two type of symbols. Calculation results are displayed in expressions of including item symbols only, not using program variables. VSOP allows up to 65,510 different item symbols to be used, and no limit for program variables, as long as the ZBDD nodes are handled in the main memory.

VSOP calculator supports not only set operations but also numerical arithmetic operations based on *Valued-Sum-Of-Products* algebra, as presented in the previous sections. The program parses the script only from left to right. Neither branches nor loop controls are supported. However, using another script processor such as C-shell or Perl, we can generate a straight VSOP script file by unrolling the complicated control structures, and feed it to the VSOP calculator by pipelined manner.

Our program need a few seconds to calculate VSOP expressions which are the size of human-readable or writable. More than ten millions of ZBDD nodes can be handled according to main memory capacity. Our ZBDD package uses about 30 byte memory per node. Calculation results are displayed in various formats as shown previously. Figure 14 shows a simple execution example.

```
***** VSOP calculator <v0.95> *****
vsop> symbol a b c d e
vsop> F = (a + 2 b)(c + d)
vsop> print F
  a c + a d + 2 b c + 2 b d
vsop> print /rmap F
  a b : c d
      |    00    01    11    10
  00 |     0     0     0     0
  01 |     0     2     0     2
  11 |     0     0     0     0
  10 |     0     1     0     1
vsop> G = (2 a - d)(c - e)
vsop> print G
  2 a c - 2 a e - c d + d e
vsop> H = F * G
vsop> print H
  4 a b c d - 4 a b c e + 4 a b c - 4 a b d e + a c d e -
    2 a c e + 2 a c - a d e + 2 b c d e - 4 b c d + 2 b d e
vsop> print /count H
    11
vsop> print /size H
    24 (35)
vsop> quit
```

Fig. 14. Example of execution

6.2   Basic Performances

To evaluate our method, we constructed VSOP expressions of large number of product terms with large values. In this experiments, we used a Pentium-4 PC (800MHz, 512MB, SuSE Linux 9). We can deal with up to about 10,000,000 ZBDD nodes in this machine.

We first generated ZBDDs for large constant numbers. 100 !, which becomes as much as a 160 digits of decimal number, can be represented with only 121 nodes of ZBDD, in 0.2 second to compute it. Next we tried calculating $\Pi_{k=1}^{n}(x_k + k)$. As shown in Table 1, within a feasible time and space, we can generate ZBDDs for extremely large-scale expressions, some of which consist of millions of terms.

Table 1. Generating VSOPs for $\Pi_{k=1}^{n}(x_k + k)$

n	#Terms	Max.value	#Nodes	Time(s)
4	16	24	16	0.002
8	256	40,320	199	0.007
12	4,096	479,001,600	1,866	0.108
16	65,536	20,922,789,888,000	9,383	0.689
20	1,048,576	(2.43×10^{18})	76,705	14.399
24	16,777,216	(6.20×10^{23})	530,308	276.993

6.3   Database Analysis (Application for Knowledge Federation over the Web)

As one of the promising applications, we will show that the VSOP calculator facilitates "knowledge federation over the web". Usually, the knowledge on the web consists of a number of distributed data, and one important task is to find a hidden data group strongly related each other over a huge amount of web space. We will show the experimental results to extract combinations of web pages which are frequently appearing together in a session of web transactions.

Here we consider one of the popular benchmark data of web data mining, "BMS-WebView1" and "BMS-WebView-2"[20]. These datasets contain several months worth of clickstream data from two e-commerce web sites. Each transaction in these datasets is a web session consisting of all the product detail pages viewed in that session. That is, each product detail view is an item. The goal for both of these datasets is to find associations between products viewed by visitors in a single visit to the web site.

Here we show the way to applying VSOP calculator. The basic structure of the dataset is as follows. One line corresponds to one record, and the numbers represents IDs of items included in the record.

```
1 3 9 13 23 25 34 36 38 40 52 54 59 63 67
2 3 9 14 23 26 34 36 39 40 52 55 59 63 67
. . .
```

In this database, the similar item combinations (sub patterns) appear many times in multiple records. To count the frequency (number of appearances) of the patterns is an important and fundamental problem in data mining techniques[2], which is regarded as the basis of knowledge processing. Using VSOP calculator, we can efficiently construct the pattern histogram and applying various analysis operations to the histogram data. At first, we transform the above database file into the following VSOP script.

```
P = 0
P = P + (1+x1)(1+x3)(1+x9)(1+x13)(1+x23)(1+x25)(1+x34)(1+x36)
        (1+x38)(1+x40)(1+x52)(1+x54)(1+x59)(1+x63)(1+x67)
P = P + (1+x2)(1+x3)(1+x9)(1+x14)(1+x23)(1+x26)(1+x34)(1+x36)
        (1+x39)(1+x40)(1+x52)(1+x55)(1+x59)(1+x63)(1+x67)
P = P + ...
```

Each line represents the set of all sub-patterns contained in one record. After execution of this script for all records, the variable P holds the histogram for all sub-patterns included in the database.

Once the histogram is generated, various queries can be applied as a sequence of VSOP operations. For example,

```
print /count (P/30)
```

Table 2. Pattern-histogram generation for web transaction database

Name	#Items	ZBDD nodes	Time(s)	#Patterns
BMS-WebView1	263	68,103	2.48	155,120,368,024,193,688,104,957,723
BMS-WebView2	1,287	22,643	3.02	36,893,635,521,153,518,271

displays the number of product terms with the values more than 29, which mean the number of frequent patterns included in more than 29 records in the database. For another example,

```
print /count (P/(x1 x2))
```

shows the number of patterns including both x1 and x2.

We applied VSOP calculator to generate pattern-histograms for "BMS-WebView1" and "BMS-WebView-2". Both two dataset consists of more than 10,000 records of transactions, but due to the limitation of memory capacity, we selected only 1,000 records from the top of the database. The results are shown in Table 2. In this table, #Items means a number of items used in the 1,000 records we selected. #Patterns shows the total number of sub-patterns included in the histogram generated by VSOP calculator.

After generating a pattern-histogram, we can easily extract frequent pattern sets from the histogram. For example, we can see that "BMS-WebView-2" includes 108 patterns that appears at least 10 times in the 1,000 records. Here is the output data of VSOP calculator that shows those frequent patterns.

```
x86055 + x84839 + x78687 + x203733 x203729 + x203733 +
x55899 x55891 + x55899 + x84159 + x222351 + x222319 + x55563 +
x55891 + x55535 + x84727 + x222439 + x55543 + x83547 + x84759 +
x83719 + x55275 + x203729 + x55555 + x56769 x56761 + x56769 +
x55843 + x222471 + x222335 + x55531 + x197025 + x55887 + x55871 +
x55855 + x222615 + x222459 + x222395 + x222339 x55351 +
x222339 x55271 + x222339 x55267 + x222339 + x56761 x55267 +
x56761 + x56037 + x55875 + x55559 + x55551 + x55487 + x55483 +
x55463 + x55351 x55271 x55267 x55295 + x55351 x55271 x55267 x55287 +
x55351 x55271 x55267 + x55351 x55271 x55295 + x55351 x55271 x55287 +
x55351 x55271 + x55351 x55267 x55295 + x55351 x55267 x55287 +
x55351 x55267 + x55351 x55319 + x55351 x55323 + x55351 x55295 +
x55351 x55287 + x55351 + x55315 x55267 + x55315 + x55291 +
x55271 x55267 x55295 + x55271 x55267 x55287 + x55271 x55267 +
x55271 x55283 + x55271 x222331 + x55271 x55323 + x55271 x55295 +
x55271 x55287 + x55271 + x55267 x55323 + x55267 x55295 +
x55267 x55287 + x55267 + x82719 + x55367 + x55319 + x55859 +
x55343 + x88683 + x84731 + x89453 + x55283 + x222331 + x222323 +
x55327 x55323 + x55327 + x55323 x55295 + x55323 + x55295 x55287 +
x55295 + x55287 + x222607 + x56765 + x55895 + x55863 + x55847 +
x55839 + x55835 x55831 + x55835 + x55831 + x55403 + x55455 + 1
```

From this output data, we can find a hidden data group related each other over a large amount of web transaction data.

Such ZBDD-based database analysis method is presented in [16] for more detail.

6.4   Solving Constraint Satisfaction Problems

Okuno et al.[19] presented the way to solve various constraint satisfaction problems (CSP) using BDDs or ZBDDs. In this paper, they consider N-queens problems and magic square problems as examples of CSPs. Those problems can be described by arithmetic Boolean expressions handling logic variables and numerical numbers.

Previously, there is an arithmetic Boolean expression manipulator "BEM-II"[9] based on (ordinary) BDDs, and the program was utilized for many works[17, 18, 8]. However, there have not been a good arithmetic calculator based on ZBDDs, so the research of ZBDD applications for CSPs have not been active as well as ordinary BDDs. Our VSOP calculator will extend the data model from Boolean functions to combinatorial sets toward applications of knowledge processing.

For example, to describe constraints for a magic square, we can write the number for each square $A, B, C \ldots$ as:

```
A = a1 + 2 a2 + 3 a3 + 4 a4 + ...
B = b1 + 2 b2 + 3 b3 + 4 b4 + ...
C = ...
```

We then compute the following formula.

```
S = A (B != 0) + B (A != 0)
```

This result becomes as:

```
2 a1 b1 + 3 a1 b2 + 4 a1 b3 + 5 a1 b4 +
3 a2 b1 + 4 a2 b2 + 5 a2 b3 + 6 a2 b4 +
4 a3 b1 + 5 a3 b2 + 6 a3 b3 + 7 a3 b4 ...
```

We can see this expression enumerates the sum of two numbers at A and B for all possible combinations. Next, the formula

```
S = S (C != 0) + C (S != 0)
```

produces the total number of A, B, and C for all possible combinations, and it is stored in S. After that, the formula

```
C = (S == 15 (S != 0))
```

generates the constraint C such that the total S equals to 15. In similar manner, we can generate VSOP data representing the constraints of all horizontal, vertical, and diagonal lines.

In this way, we can describe various CSPs by using VSOP scripts, and easily try solving it by VSOP calculator.

6.5 Probabilistic Symbolic Simulation

VSOP calculator is based on the arithmetic operation rules as $x + x = 2x$, $x \times x = x$, and $x \times y = xy$. These rules are the same as the probabilistic calculation that the variables x and y represent probabilities. If the two events occur independently, the logical AND becomes arithmetic products of two variables, but if the two event are based on a same probabilistic variable, the logical AND does not become x^2 but just x. Consequently, VSOP calculator can be used for probabilistic analysis of systems in various areas.

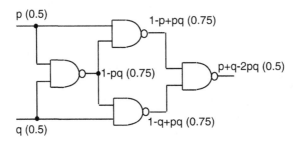

Fig. 15. Probabilistic symbolic logic simulation

One good application is computing signal probability in logic circuits. As illustrated in Fig. 15, on each primary input of the circuit, we assign a variable representing the probability that the signal is '1'. Then, the probability at primary outputs and internal nets can be expressed exactly in VSOP expressions using those probabilistic variables. On each logic gate with input A, B and output Y, we can compute $Y = A \times B$ for AND gate, $Y = A + B - (A \times B)$ for OR gate, and $Y = 1 - A$ for NOT gate.

This technique is applicable for various kinds of statistic analysis, such as probabilistic fault simulation, estimating power consumption, and timing hazard analysis.

7   Conclusion

We have presented a method of computing combinatorial item sets with numerical values. This method consists of an efficient data structure, manipulation algorithms, and helpful display formats. VSOP calculator, implemented based on the above techniques, is customizable for various applications. We expect it to be utilized as a helpful tool in solving many problems in computer science. In future, we will release our program as open software to facilitate research and development of knowledge processing.

We have presented a method of computing combinatorial item sets with numerical values. This method consists of an efficient data structure, manipulation algorithms, and helpful display formats. VSOP calculator, implemented based on the above techniques, is customizable for various applications. We have shown one of the promising application to find a hidden data group related each other over a huge amount of web space. This is one of the basic and important task for knowledge federation over the web. We have also shown some other useful applications such as solving CSPs and executing probabilistic simulation. In future, we will release our program as open software to facilitate research and development for various area.

Acknowledgment

The author thanks Prof. Arimura and Prof. Zeugmann of Hokkaido Univ. for their technical comments. This study is partly supported by Grant-in-Aid Scientific Research on Priority Area "Informatics", 2004 (Area #006) and Scientific Research (B), 2005, 17300041.

References

1. Akers, S. B., Binary decision diagrams, IEEE Trans. Comput., C-27, 6 (1978), 509–516.
2. R. Agrawal, H. Mannila, R. Srikant, H. Toivonen and A. I. Verkamo, Fast Discovery of Association Rules, In *Advances in Knowledge Discovery and Data Mining*, MIT Press, 307–328, 1996.
3. R. K. Brayton, R. Rudell, A. Sangiovnni-Vincentelli, and A. R. Wang, "MIS: A multiple-level logic optimization system," IEEE Trans. on CAD, vol. CAD-6, pp. 1062–1081, Nov. 1987.
4. Bryant, R. E., Graph-based algorithms for Boolean function manipulation, IEEE Trans. Comput., C-35, 8 (1986), 677–691.
5. R. E. Bryant and Y.-A. Chen, "Verification of arithmetic functions with binary moment diagrams," Proc. of 32nd ACM/IEEE Design Automation Conference (DAC'95), session 32.1, June. 1995.
6. O. Coudert, "Solving graph optimization problems with ZBDDs", In Proc. of IEEE The European Design and Test Conference (ED&TC'97), pp. 244-248, Mar. 1997.
7. B. Goethals, M. Javeed Zaki (Eds.), Frequent Itemset Mining Dataset Repository, Frequent Itemset Mining Implementations (FIMI'03), 2003. http://fimi.cs.helsinki.fi/data/
8. Y. Hayashi and J. Matsuki, "Determination of Optimal System Configuration in Japanese Secondary Power Systems," IEEE Trans. on Power Systems, VOL. 18, NO. 1, pp. 394–399, Feb. 2003
9. S. Minato: "BEM-II: An Arithmetic Boolean Expression Manipulator Using BDDs", IEICE Trans. Fundamentals, Vol. E76-A, No. 10, pp. 1721-1729, Oct. 1993.
10. Minato, S., Zero-suppressed BDDs for set manipulation in combinatorial problems, In Proc. 30th ACM/IEEE Design Automation Conf. (DAC-93), (1993), 272–277.
11. S. Minato: "Calculation of Unate Cube Set Algebra Using Zero-Suppressed BDDs", In Proc. of 31st ACM/IEEE Design Automation Conference (DAC'94), pp. 420-424, Jun. 1994.

12. S. Minato: "Implicit Manipulation of Polynomials Using Zero-Suppressed BDDs", In Proc. of IEEE The European Design and Test Conference (ED&TC'95), pp. 449-454, Mar. 1995.
13. S. Minato: "Binary Decision Diagrams and Applications for VLSI CAD", Kluwer Academic Publishers, November 1996.
14. S. Minato: "Fast Factorization Method for Implicit Cube Set Representation", IEEE Trans. on Computer-Aided Design of Integrated Circuits and Systems, VOL. 15, No. 4, pp. 377-384, Apr. 1996.
15. Minato, S., Zero-suppressed BDDs and Their Applications, International Journal on Software Tools for Technology Transfer (STTT), Springer, Vol. 3, No. 2, pp. 156–170, May 2001.
16. S. Minato and H. Arimura: "Efficient Combinatorial Item Set Analysis Based on Zero-Suppressed BDDs", IEEE/IEICE/IPSJ International Workshop on Challenges in Web Information Retrieval and Integration (WIRI-2005), pp. 3–10, Apr., 2005.
17. T. Miyazaki, Boolean-based formulation for data path synthesis, IEEE Asia-Pasific Conference on Circuits and Systems 'APCCAS'92), pp. 201–205, Dec. 1992.
18. H.G. Okuno, "Reducing Combinatorial Explosions in Solving Search-Type Combinatorial Problems with Binary Decision Diagram," Trans of Information Processing Soc. Japan (IPSJ), (in Japanese), vol. 35, no. 5, pp 739-753, May 1994.
19. H.G. Okuno, S. Minato, and H. Isozaki, On the properties of combination set operations, Information Processing Letters, Vol. 66, pp. 195–199, May 1998.
20. Z. Zheng, R. Kohavi, and L. Mason, Real World Performance of Association Rule Algorithms, In Proc. of ACM SIGKDD conference KDD-2001, pp. 401–406, 2001.

A Method for Pinpoint Clustering of Web Pages with Pseudo-Clique Search

Makoto Haraguchi and Yoshiaki Okubo

Division of Computer Science,
Graduate School of Information Science and Technology, Hokkaido University,
N-14 W-9, Sapporo 060-0814, Japan
{mh, yoshiaki}@ist.hokudai.ac.jp

Abstract. This paper presents a method for *Pinpoint Clustering* of web pages. We try to find useful clusters of web pages which are significant in the sense that their contents are similar to ones of higher-ranked pages. Since we are usually careless of lower-ranked pages, they are unconditionally discarded even if their contents are similar to some pages with high ranks. Such hidden pages together with significant higher-ranked pages are extracted as a cluster. As the result, our clusters can provide new valuable information for users.

In order to obtain such clusters, we first extract semantic correlations among terms by applying *Singular Value Decomposition* (SVD) to the term-document matrix generated from a corpus. Based on the correlations, we can evaluate potential similarities among web pages to be clustered. The set of web pages is represented as a weighted graph G based on the similarities and their ranks. Our clusters can be found as *pseudo-cliques* in G. An algorithm for finding Top-N weighted pseudo-cliques is presented. Our experimental result shows that a quite valuable cluster can be actually extracted according to our method.

We also discuss an idea for improvement on meanings of clusters. With the help of *Formal Concept Analysis*, our clusters, called FC-based clusters, can be provided with clear meanings. Our preliminary experimentation shows that the extended method would be a promising approach to finding meaningful clusters.

1 Introduction

The *World Wide Web* is one of the most useful resources of information and knowledge. We often try to obtain desired information or knowledge from web pages on the Internet with an information retrieval (IR) engine, such as *Google*. It is, however, not so easy to efficiently find useful pages because of the hugeness of the web space. For example, Google often gets a number of web pages with the order of hundred thousands for given keywords.

In general, only some of the higher-ranked pages are actually browsed and the others are discarded as less important ones, since the list given by the IR system contains a large number of pages. However, there might exist many pages which are unfortunately lower-ranked but are significant in the sense that their contents

K.P. Jantke et al. (Eds.): Federation over the Web, LNAI 3847, pp. 59–78, 2006.

are similar or closely related to higher-ranked pages. They can be considered *implicitly significant pages*. By making such hidden but valuable pages visible, our chance to get valuable information or knowledge from web pages can be enhanced. As the result, we can enjoy the Web as a more useful and abundant knowledge resource.

From this point of view, we discuss in this paper a method for *Pinpoint Clustering* of web pages retrieved by an IR system. In order to make hidden lower-ranked but valuable pages visible, extracting *clusters* of web pages will be an important task. In a word, our method tries to extract clusters consisting of higher and lower-ranked pages with similar contents. Such clusters of web pages compactly tell us what page contents the IR system has retrieved for the given keywords. As the result, we would roughly understand the contents of the pages retrieved by the system.

Several clustering methods for web pages have been already investigated (e.g. refer to [2]). Many of them are based on the traditional *hierarchical* or *partitional* clustering methods. In these methods, the whole set of retrieved web pages is divided into several clusters. This means that each page always belongs to some cluster. Although the number of clusters to be obtained is usually controlled by a user-defined parameter, it is well known that providing an adequate value for the parameter is quite difficult. If the number is too large, we will often obtain many useless clusters. Furthermore, in the computational point of view, the cost of constructing useless clusters is quite wasteful. On the other hand, if it is too small, interesting clusters will be missed.

These observations motivate us to investigate a new clustering method, *Pinpoint Clustering*, by which we can efficiently extract *only* nice clusters whose evaluation values are in the top-N, where N can be given arbitrarily. By such a method, we will never suffer from quite useless clusters. Furthermore, extracting only nice clusters has also an advantage in the computation. We can enjoy a branch-and-bound search in order to extract them. In our search, we do not have to examine many branches concerning clusters not in the top N. Therefore, it is expected that our method can extract nice clusters with reasonable time even for a large data set.

In order to realize it, we first extract semantic correlations among terms by applying *Singular Value Decomposition*(SVD) [3] to the term-document matrix generated from a corpus with a specific topic. Given a set of ranked web pages to be clustered, we can evaluate potential similarities among them based on the semantic correlations of terms. In previous approaches [2], similarities among web pages are often determined based on the link structure of web pages. More concretely speaking, it has been considered that web pages with similar topical contents have dense links among them. Such a link structure might roughly reflects similarities among relatively *mature* pages. However, many interesting pages are newly released day by day and it is often difficult to expect a dense link structure of *fresh* pages. As the result, based on the link-based approach, we will fail in finding similarities among such new pages even if they have similar contents. On the other hand, we try to capture similarities among web pages independently of their link structure. With the help of SVD, we take some semantic correlations among terms into account. Based on the correlations, potential similarities among contents of web pages can be captured.

The set of web pages to be clustered is then represented as a weighted undirected graph G based on the (potential) similarities and their ranks. If a pair of pages have a similarity higher than a given threshold, they are connected by an edge. Moreover, each vertex (i.e. a web page) is assigned a weight so that higher-ranked pages have higher weights. Our clusters can be extracted by finding *pseudo-cliques* in the graph G. The notion of pseudo-cliques has been first introduced in [13, 14] to address an issue of overlapping exact cliques. A pseudo-clique is defined as a union of several exact maximal cliques in G with a required degree of overlap. In the strict sense, therefore, it is no longer a clique and is regarded as an approximation of exact cliques.

Simple theoretical properties of pseudo-cliques are presented. Based on the properties, we can obtain some pruning rules for pseudo-clique search. We design a depth-first branch-and-bound algorithm for finding pseudo-cliques whose weights are in the top N, where the weight of a pseudo-clique is evaluated as the sum of the vertex weights in it. Our preliminary experimental result shows that a quite valuable cluster consisting of similar higher-ranked and lower-ranked pages can be actually extracted as a pseudo-clique in G.

One might claim that a naive method would be sufficient for extracting such a cluster. That is, for a web page with a higher rank, we can gather lower-ranked pages which are similar to the higher-ranked one. As well as this kind of clusters, our method can extract other various kinds of clusters simultaneously by changing the weighting of web pages in our graph construction process. Under some weighting, for example, a cluster consisting of several similar pages which are moderately ranked might be obtained as in the top N. In this sense, our method includes such a naive method.

A meaningful cluster should have a clear explanation why the pages in the cluster are grouped together or what the common features in the cluster are. Our method described just above, unfortunately, does not have any mechanism to provide it clearly. If such an explanation mechanism is integrated, our clustering method would be more convincing. We also discuss in this paper an idea for improvement on this point. We try to realize it with the help of *Formal Concept Analysis* [8]. A formal concept explicitly gives its conceptual meaning, *intent* and *extent*. By extracting only clusters (cliques) corresponding to formal concepts, each cluster can be provided with some clear conceptual meaning. We call this kind of cluster an *FC-based cluster*. It is also noted that since cliques to be extracted are restricted further, another pruning mechanism is available in our FC-based cluster search. Our preliminary experimental results show some interesting characteristics of FC-based clusters.

Our pinpoint clustering method by clique search is a general framework. The literature [9, 12] has investigated methods for finding appropriate *data abstractions* (groupings) of attribute values for classification problems, where each abstraction is extracted as a weighted exact clique. A gene expression data has been also processed in [10]. A cluster consisting of genes which behave similarly is extracted as an exact clique. The pinpoint clustering of web pages has originated in [11] and has been then extended in order to address a problem of overlapping clusters (cliques) [13]. This paper presents our current method of web page clustering and discuss further improvement in meaningfulness of clusters from the viewpoint of Formal Concept Analysis.

The remainder of this paper is organized as follows. In the next section, we introduce some basic terminologies used throughout this paper. In Section 3, we discuss semantic similarities among web pages. Section 4 formalizes our pinpoint clustering as a Top-N weighted pseudo-clique problem. Our experimental results are presented in Section 5. Section 6 presents an idea by which our cluster can be provided with a conceptual meaning with the help of Formal Concept Analysis. Characteristics of FC-based clusters are also discussed. In the final section, we conclude this paper with a summary.

2   Preliminaries

A *simple graph* is denoted by $G = (V, E)$, where V is a set of vertices and $E \subseteq V \times V$ a set of (undirected) edges, that is, any edge $(v, v') \in E$ is identified with (v', v). For any vertices $v, v' \in V$, if $(v, v') \in E$, v is said to be *adjacent* to v'. If any pair of vertices $v, v' \in V$ $(v \neq v')$ are adjacent each other, then G is said to be *complete*. For a vertex $v \in V$, the set of vertices adjacent to v is denoted by $N_G(v)$, that is, $N_G(v) = \{v' \mid v' \in V \wedge (v, v') \in E\}$. The size of $N_G(v)$, $|N_G(v)|$, is called the *degree* of v in G. It is often referred to as $degree_G(v)$. If it is clear from the context, they are simply denoted by $N(v)$ and $degree(v)$, respectively. If each vertex $v \in V$ is assigned a positive weight, the graph is called a *weighted graph*. The weight of v is referred to as $w(v)$. For a vertex set $V' \subseteq V$, the weight of V', denoted by $w(V')$, is simply defined as the sum of individual weights, that is, $w(V') = \sum_{v \in V'} w(v)$. In this paper, we are concerned with a weighted graph unless stated otherwise.

For a graph $G = (V, E)$, let V' be a subset of V. A *subgraph of G induced by V'*, denoted by $G(V')$, is defined by $G(V') = (V', E \cap V' \times V')$. A complete subgraph is called a *clique* in G. We simply refer a clique as the set of vertices by which it is induced. For cliques C and D in G, if $C \subset D$, then D is said to be an *extension* of C. Moreover, if there exists no clique D' such that $C \subset D' \subset D$, D is called an *immediate extension* of C. For a clique C in G, if there exists no extension of C, then C is said to be *maximal*. A maximal clique with the largest size is especially called a *maximum clique*. It should be noted here that in general a maximum clique is not uniquely found in G.

3   Semantic Similarity Among Web Pages

In order to find clusters of web pages, we have to measure similarities among web pages. For the task, we adopt technique in *Information Retrieval* (IR) [4].

3.1 Term-Document Matrix

Let $\mathcal{D}$ be a set of documents and $\mathcal{T}$ the set of terms appeared in $\mathcal{D}$. Note here that in order to obtain such terms from documents without spaces among words (like Japanese documents), we need to apply *Morphological Analysis* to $\mathcal{D}$. We first remove too frequent and too infrequent terms from $\mathcal{T}$. The set of remaining terms, called *feature terms*, is denoted by $\mathcal{T}^*$. Supposing $|\mathcal{T}^*| = n$, each document $d_i \in \mathcal{D}$ can be represented as an n-dimensional document vector

$$d_i = (tf_{i1}, \ldots, tf_{in})^T,$$

where tf_{ij} is the frequency of the term $t_j \in \mathcal{T}^*$ in the document d_i. Thus, the set of documents $\mathcal{D}$ can be translated into a *term-document matrix*

$$(d_1, \ldots, d_{|\mathcal{D}|}).$$

3.2 Extracting Semantic Similarity with SVD

For the term-document matrix, we apply *Singular Value Decomposition*(SVD) in order to extract correlations among feature terms [4].

An $m \times n$ matrix A can be decomposed by applying SVD as

$$A = U \Sigma V^T,$$

where U and V are $m \times m$ and $n \times n$ orthogonal matrices, respectively. Each column vector in U is called a left singular vector and one in V right singular vector. Σ is an $m \times n$ matrix of the form

$$
\Sigma =
\left[
\begin{array}{ccc|c}
\sigma_1 & & O & \\
 & \ddots & & O_{r \times (n-r)} \\
O & & \sigma_r & \\
\hline
\multicolumn{3}{c|}{O_{(m-r) \times r}} & O_{(m-r) \times (n-r)}
\end{array}
\right],
$$

where $rank(A) = r$ $(r \leq \min\{m, n\})$ and $\sigma_1 > \cdots > \sigma_r > 0$. Each σ_i is called a *singular value*. First r left singular vectors $u_1, \ldots, u_r$ correspond to a orthonormal basis and define a new subspace of the original one in which column vectors of A exist. The $m \times r$ matrix $(u_1, \ldots, u_r)$ is denoted by U_r.

Let us assume the matrix A is a term-document matrix obtained from a set of documents. Intuitively speaking, by applying SVD to A, we can capture *potential but not presently evident* correlations among the feature terms. Highly semantically correlated terms give a base vector u_i and define a dimension corresponding to a compound term. Such new base vectors define a new subspace based on compound terms. For documents d_1 and d_2 not in A, therefore, if they are projected on the subspace, we can find similarity between them based on the semantic correlations among feature terms captured from the original documents in A.

In order to take such semantic similarities of web pages into account, we prepare a *corpus* of documents written about some specific topic. Then by applying SVD to the term-document matrix generated from the corpus, we obtain a subspace reflecting semantic correlations among feature terms in the corpus. Let U_r be the orthonormal basis defining the subspace. It should be noted here that in an actual Information Retrieval, we do not always use r left singular vectors. A part of them, that is, $U_k = (u_1, \ldots, u_k)$ $(k < r)$ is usually used for *approximation*. Such an approximation technique with U_k is known as *Latent Semantic Indexing* (LSI) [4].

Besides the corpus, with some keywords related to the corpus topic, we retrieve a set of web pages $\mathcal{P}$ from which we try to obtain clusters. Using the same feature terms for the corpus, each document $p_i \in \mathcal{P}$ is represented as a vector

$$p_i = (tf_{i1}, \ldots, tf_{in})^T,$$

where tf_{ij} is the frequency of the feature term t_j in p_i. Then each web page p_i is projected on the subspace as

$$p_i^r = U_r^T p_i.$$

A *similarity* between web pages p_i and p_j, denoted by $sim(p_i, p_j)$, is defined based on the standard *cosine measure*, that is,

$$sim(p_i, p_j) = \frac{p_i^r \cdot p_j^r}{\| p_i^r \| \times \| p_j^r \|}.$$

4 Pinpoint Clustering of Significant Web Pages

We usually try to find significant web pages according to their ranks assigned by an IR system. In many cases, we browse higher-ranked pages and often realize that some of them are actually significant. On the other hand, we will usually discard lower-ranked pages without browsing, since they appear in the lower part of a large ranking list. However, if such lower-ranked pages have contents similar to significant pages with higher-ranks, they will be surely valuable for us. In this sense, they can be considered *implicitly significant pages*. From this point of view, it would be worth finding clusters each of which consists of

- significant (probably higher-ranked) pages and
- other pages with contents similar to the significant ones.

We present here our pinpoint clustering method for finding this kind of valuable clusters of web pages. Especially, we try to extract such clusters whose evaluation values are in the Top-N.

4.1 Clusters as Weighted Maximal Cliques

Our web page clusters are extracted as *Pseudo-Cliques*, an approximation of exact cliques. In order to find this kind of cliques, a set of web pages to be clustered is represented as a weighted undirected graph.

Let $\mathcal{P}$ be a set of web pages retrieved by an IR system with some keywords. We try to obtain clusters from the web pages. It is assumed that each page $p \in \mathcal{P}$ is assigned its rank by the system, denoted by $rank(p)$. The pages to be clustered are represented as a weighted (undirected) graph G.

Let δ be a minimum threshold for similarities among web pages. Our graph G is defined by $G = (\mathcal{P}, E_\delta)$, where for any $p_i, p_j \in \mathcal{P}$ $(i \neq j)$, $(p_i, p_j) \in E_\delta$ if and only if $sim(p_i, p_j) \geq \delta$. That is, we regard any pair of pages with similarity greater than or equal to δ as similar ones. Moreover, each vertex p is weighted so that the higher the rank of page, the higher its weight.

It is clear from the graph construction process that a cluster consisting of web pages which are similar each other can be extracted by finding a maximal clique in G. Since there are in general many maximal cliques, it would be reasonable to extract *only* preferable ones. From this viewpoint, as in [9, 12, 10, 11], we can pay our attention to maximal cliques whose evaluation values are in the Top-N, where each clique is evaluated by its weight. Intuitively speaking, since web pages with higher ranks are assigned higher weights in the graph, a cluster (clique) containing higher-ranked pages tends to be preferable. Moreover, a cluster consisting of many pages might be also preferred.

Such a tendency is highly dependent on how each page is actually weighted in the graph. For example, the weight of a page p is defined in *inverse proportion* to its rank, that is, $w(p) = 1/rank(p)$. As another one, p might be weighted *linearly* as $w(p) = |\mathcal{P}| - rank(p) + 1$. Roughly speaking, by the former weighting, a cluster containing higher-ranked pages is preferred even if its size is not so large. By the latter, on the other hand, we can make a point of cluster size. That is, larger clusters are basically preferred under the weighting. Thus, we can control our preference in clusters by providing various weighting functions for the pages.

4.2   Finding Clusters by Top-N Pseudo-Clique Search

As has been just described, we can extract preferable clusters as Top-N weighted maximal cliques. However, we sometime encounter a case where each maximal clique in the top N shares most of the vertices with others. In order to address such an issue, we introduce a notion of *Pseudo-Cliques*. Then we try to extract maximal pseudo-cliques whose weights (evaluation values) are in the top N.

Top-N Weighted Pseudo-Clique Problem

We formally discuss here the notion of pseudo-cliques and define our problem of finding Top-N weighted pseudo-cliques in a given graph. A pseudo-clique is constructed from a class of maximal cliques sharing some vertices. Before giving the formal definition, we first define a *degree of overlap* for a class of maximal cliques.

Definition 1. (Degree of Overlap for Maximal Clique Class)

Let G be a graph and $\mathcal{C} = \{C_1, \ldots, C_m\}$ a class of maximal cliques in G. The *degree of overlap* for $\mathcal{C}$, denoted by $overlap(\mathcal{C})$, is defined as $overlap(\mathcal{C}) = \min_{C_i \in \mathcal{C}} \left\{ \left| \cap_{C_j \in \mathcal{C}} C_j \right| / |C_i| \right\}$.   ∎

Using the notion of overlap degree, our pseudo-cliques is defined as follows.

Definition 2. (Pseudo-Clique)

Let G be a graph and $\mathcal{C} = \{C_1, \ldots, C_m\}$ a class of maximal cliques in G. $pseudo(\mathcal{C}) = \cup_{C_i \in \mathcal{C}} C_i$ is called a *pseudo-cliques* with the overlap degree $overlap(\mathcal{C})$. Its *size* and *weight* are given by $|pseudo(\mathcal{C})|$ and $w(pseudo(\mathcal{C})) = \Sigma_{v \in pseudo(\mathcal{C})} w(v)$, respectively. Moreover, the shared vertices, $\cap_{C_i \in \mathcal{C}} C_i$, is called the *core* and the other vertices, $pseudo(\mathcal{C}) - \cap_{C_i \in \mathcal{C}} C_i$, *surroundings* of the pseudo-clique. ∎

It is noted here that we do not assume the weight of pseudo-clique should be defined as the sum of vertex weights. Technically speaking, any monotone weight under the set inclusion can be accepted in the following discussion.

From Definition 2, we have to accept any pseudo-clique that has little shared vertices as its core. However, such a pseudo-clique would not be so meaningful, since it is not convincing to combine cliques with a low commonality into a group. We consider a pseudo-clique with a certain degree of core to be valid.

Definition 3. (τ-Validness of Pseudo-Clique)

Let $\tilde{C}$ be a pseudo-clique constructed from a class of maximal cliques and τ an admissible threshold for overlap degree. If the overlap degree of $\tilde{C}$ is greater than or equal to τ, $\tilde{C}$ is said to be τ-*valid*. ∎

We can now formally define our problem of finding Top-N weighted pseudo-cliques.

Definition 4. (Top-N Weighted Maximal Pseudo-Clique Problem)

Let G be a graph and τ an admissible threshold for overlap degree. The *Top-N Weighted Maximal Pseudo-Clique Problem* is to find any τ-valid maximal pseudo-clique in G such that its weight is in the top N in descending order. ∎

Algorithm for Finding Top-N Weighted Pseudo-Cliques

Given a graph $G = (V, E)$, an admissible threshold τ for overlap degree, we find Top-N weighted maximal pseudo-cliques which are τ-valid. Before presenting our algorithm for extracting them, we give some basic theoretical properties of τ-valid pseudo-cliques.

For a clique Q in G, we try to find a τ-valid pseudo-clique $\tilde{C}$ whose core is Q. In order to precisely discuss how it can be found, we introduce a notion of *extensible candidates* for a given clique.

Definition 5. (Extensible Candidates for Clique)

Let $G = (V, E)$ be a graph and Q a clique in G. A vertex $v \in V$ adjacent to any vertex in Q is called an *extensible candidate* for Q. The set of extensible candidates is denoted by $cand(Q)$. ∎

Note that for any vertex $v \in cand(Q)$, $Q \cup \{v\}$ is still a clique in G.

From the definition, we can easily observe the followings.

Observation 1

Let Q and Q' be cliques in G such that $Q \subseteq Q'$. Then, $cand(Q) \supseteq cand(Q')$ and $w(Q) + w(cand(Q)) \geq w(Q') + w(cand(Q'))$ hold. ∎

For a clique Q, any maximal clique C_{max} in G such that $Q \subseteq C_{max}$ can be obtained by expanding Q with some vertices in $cand(Q)$. This implies that the weight of a pseudo-clique with the core Q is *at most* $w(Q) + w(cand(Q))$. Based on this fact and Observation 1, therefore, a simple property can be derived.

Observation 2

Let Q be a clique. Assume we already have *tentative* Top-N weighted maximal pseudo-cliques and the minimum weight of them is w_{min}. If $w(Q)+w(cand(Q)) < w_{min}$ holds, then for any extension Q' of Q, there exists no pseudo-clique with the core Q' whose weight is finally in the top N.   ∎

Let Q be a clique in G and τ an admissible threshold for overlap degree. Assume that a τ-valid pseudo-clique $\tilde{C}$ contains Q as its core. $\tilde{C}$ can be obtained as the union of any maximal clique C in G such that $Q \subseteq C$ and $|Q|/|C| \geq \tau$. It should be noted here that for such a clique C, there exists a maximal clique D in $G(cand(Q))$ such that $Q \cup D = C$. That is, finding any maximal clique D in $G(cand(Q))$ such that $|Q|/(|Q|+|D|) \geq \tau$ is sufficient to obtain the pseudo-clique $\tilde{C}$, where vertices in D are surroundings of $\tilde{C}$.

Thus, in order to extract $\tilde{C}$, we need to find any maximal clique in $G(cand(Q))$ satisfying a certain condition. One might claim that such a task is quite expensive from the computational point of view. However, the authors expect that it would not be so costly because of the following reasons:

- For a smaller core Q, we need to find only maximal cliques in $G(cand(Q))$ whose sizes are less than or equal to a relatively small value defined by τ and $|Q|$. Since small maximal cliques can be found efficiently, the task would be performed with reasonable cost.
- For a larger core Q, on the other hand, we have to extract larger maximal cliques from $G(cand(Q))$. In general, however, the larger Q becomes, the smaller $G(cand(Q))$ gets. The task of finding maximal cliques in a small graph would not be so difficult.

The former argument is supported by the fact that we can apply the following simple pruning rule in our maximal clique search, that is, surroundings search.

Observation 3

For a clique Q in G, let us assume that we try to find a τ-valid pseudo-clique $\tilde{C}$ whose core is Q. For a clique D in $G(cand(Q))$, if $|D| > (\frac{1}{\tau} - 1) \cdot |Q|$, then any extension of D is useless for obtaining $\tilde{C}$.   ∎

As has been just discussed, in order to extract a pseudo-clique with the core Q, we are in general required to extract maximal cliques from $G(cand(Q))$ to identify its surroundings. In a certain case, however, we can immediately obtain such a pseudo-clique without maximal clique search.

Observation 4

Let Q be a clique in G and τ an admissible threshold for overlap degree. If the following conditions hold, then $Q \cup cand(Q)$ is a τ-valid maximal pseudo-clique with the core Q.

- $(\frac{1}{\tau}-1)\cdot|Q| \geq k$ holds, where k is an upper bound for the size of the maximum clique in $G(cand(Q))$.
- For any $v \in cand(Q)$, $degree_{G(cand(Q))}(v) < |cand(Q)| - 1$ holds.   ∎

The former condition is sufficient to show that $Q \cup cand(Q)$ is a τ-valid maximal pseudo-clique. In that case, however, its core is not always Q The core might be an extension of Q. The latter condition ensures that the pseudo-clique exactly contains Q as the core.

Upper bounds for the maximum clique size have been widely utilized in efficient branch-and-bound algorithms for finding maximum cliques [5, 6, 12]. The literature [6] has summarized several classes of upper bounds. Any upper bound including them can be also adopted in our pseudo-clique search. According to the argument in [6], the *(vertex) chromatic number* χ can be tightest among well-known upper bounds. It is, however, identifying χ is an NP-complete problem. Therefore, approximations of χ have been utilized in algorithms previously proposed [5, 6, 12]. In our system, a sequential approximate coloring in [5] is currently adopted.

```
procedure main() :
    V ← the set of vertices in a graph ;
    E ← the set of edges in the graph ;
    N ← an integer for Top-N ;
    τ ← a threshold for overlap degree ;
    PC ← φ;
    weight_num ← 0 ;
    min_weight ← 0 ;
    FindPseudoCliques(φ, V ) ;
    return PC ;
```

```
procedure FindPseudoCliques(Q, R) :
    if weight_num = N and w(Q) + w(R) < min_weight then
        return ;    /* Based on Observation 2 */
    endif
    for each v ∈ R in predetermined order
        begin
            MC ← φ ;
            α ← (1/τ − 1) · (|Q| + 1) ;
            k ← an upper bound of the maximum clique in R ∩ N(v) ;
            if k ≤ α then
                if ∀w ∈ R ∩ N(v), degree_{G(R∩N(v))}(w) < |R ∩ N(v)| − 1 then
                    MC ← {R ∩ N(v), φ} ;    /* Based on Observation 4 */
                else
                    FindMaxCliques(φ, R ∩ N(v)) ; /* Surroundings Search */
                endif
            else
                FindMaxCliques(φ, R ∩ N(v)) ; /* Surroundings Search */
            endif
            if ∩_{C_i∈MC} C_i = φ then
                if weight_num < N or w(∪_{C_i∈MC} C_i ∪ Q ∪ {v}) ≥ min_weight then
                    PC ← PC ∪ {∪_{C_i∈MC} C_i ∪ Q ∪ {v}} ;
                    weight_num ← |{w(PC) | PC ∈ PC}| ;
                    min_weight ← min{w(PC) | PC ∈ PC} ;
                endif
            endif
            FindPseudoCliques(Q ∪ {v}, R ∩ N(v)) ;
        end
```

```
procedure FindMaxCliques(Q, R) :
    if |Q| > α then
        return ; /* Based on Observation 3 */
    endif
    if R = φ then
        MC ← MC ∪ {Q} ;
        return ;
    endif
    for each v ∈ R in predetermined order
        FindMaxCliques(Q ∪ {v}, R ∩ N(v)) ;
```

Fig. 1. Algorithm for finding Top-N weighted τ-valid pseudo-cliques

From the above theoretical properties, Top-N τ-valid weighted pseudo-cliques can be extracted by a depth-first branch-and-bound algorithm similar to ones in [5, 7]. Our pseudo-clique search is a *hybrid of core search and surroundings search*. The former generates a candidate of core to be examined. For the core candidate, the latter tries to find its surroundings. This procedure is iterated until no core candidate is generated.

More concretely speaking, for a clique Q in G, we try to find a τ-valid pseudo-clique $\tilde{C}$ with the core Q by extracting maximal cliques (surroundings) in $G(cand(Q))$. If $w(\tilde{C})$ is greater than or equal to the minimum weight in a tentative Top-N list, then $\tilde{C}$ is temporarily registered in the list. After that, for an immediate extension of Q, Q', we apply the same procedure to extract a τ-valid weighted pseudo-clique with the core Q'. From Observation 2, if $w(Q) + w(cand(Q))$ is smaller than the minimum weight in the tentative list, we do not have to examine any extension of Q. Starting with the initial Q of the empty set, the above procedure is iterated in depth-first manner until no Q remains to be examined. A precise description of our algorithm is shown in Figure 1[1].

5   Experimental Results

In this section, we present our experimental results[2]. The main purpose of this experimentation is to confirm that we can actually obtain a useful cluster of web pages consisting of higher-ranked pages and any other similar (or related) pages with lower ranks.

In order to capture semantic correlations among terms, we have prepared a Japanese corpus constructed from 100 web pages written about "Hokkaido". These pages have been manually selected and only visible texts on them have been manually gathered[3]. After an application of Morphological Analysis, we have obtained 2224 nouns appeared in the corpus. Nouns with frequencies more than 1000 and less than 2 were removed from them. The remaining 211 nouns were regarded as feature terms. Applying SVD to our term-document matrix constructed from the corpus, we have obtained a new 98-dimensional subspace.

Besides the corpus, we have retrieved 829 (Japanese) web pages by Google with the keywords "Hokkaido" and "Sightseeing". We have tried to extract significant clusters from these pages.

Each web page has been first represented as a document vector w.r.t. the original feature terms and then projected on the 98-dimensional subspace in order to capture potential similarities among pages. For any pair of pages, then, we have evaluated the similarity between them based on the cosine measure. Under the setting of $\delta = 0.95$, we have constructed a weighted graph G from the pages. That is, if the angle between two pages is less than or equal to about

---

[1] An unweighted version is found in [14].

[2] Our system has been implemented in C language and run on a PC with Xeon-2.40 GHz CPU and 512MB memory.

[3] That is, they are subjective, not objective in a strict sense.

18.2 degree, then they are connected by an edge. The numbers of vertices and edges are 829 and 798, respectively. Each page (vertex) d has been assigned a weight defined as $w(d) = 1/rank(d)^2$. As has been stated in the previous section, although we can define various weights according to ranks of pages, we have currently adopted the reciprocal of the rank squared. The reason why we prefer this measure is as follows:

- It is sensitive to difference of ranks in higher range.
- On the other hand, in lower range, page weights are hardly affected by difference of ranks.

From the characteristics, a clique containing higher-ranked pages is likely to be extracted even if its size is relatively small. Since we can often expect higher-ranked pages are significant, such a phenomenon would be desirable. On the other hand, we are usually careless of lower-ranked pages. In other words, difference of weights among lower-ranked pages would be unimportant for us. In this sense, a likelihood of extracting pseudo-cliques should not be sensitively affected by weights of pages with lower ranks. The above measure would be reasonable from this viewpoint as well.

We have tried to extract Top-15 weighted 0.8-pseudo cliques in the graph.

Example of Extracted Interesting Cluster

Among the extracted clusters (pseudo-cliques), the authors especially consider that the 11th cluster was quite interesting.

The cluster consists of 6 web pages. Table 1 shows their ranks assigned by Google and subjects. In the authors' opinion, their contents are considered to be very similar in the sense that all of them give us some information about accommodations in Hokkaido, especially information about hotels and foods. The 11th and 328th pages are index pages for travel information and we can make reservations for many hotels via the pages. The 416th page is an article in a private BBS site for travels. The article reports on a private travel in Hokkaido and provides an actual and valuable information about a hotel and enjoyable foods in "Furano". The 797th and 798th personal pages give us the names of two hotels serving smorgasbords in Hokkaido. The 826th page tells us several hotels which were the most popular or were most frequently reserved in 2004.

Table 1. The 11th significant cluster

Page Rank	Subject
11th	Index page for travel information maintained by a local travel agency in Hokkaido (especially, for travels in Hokkaido)
381st	Index page for travel information maintained by a famous newspaper company (for domestic and overseas travels)
416th	An article on a private BBS for travels
797th	Information about smorgasbords enjoyable at a hotel in Hokkaido
798th	Information about smorgasbords enjoyable at another hotel in Hokkaido
826th	Page for hotel awards in a famous travel site

Thus, the pages in the 11th cluster are closely related each other and give us quite valuable information. When we try to make travel plans for sightseeing in Hokkaido, we would often care about hotels and foods as important factors. In such a case, the cluster will be surely helpful for us.

Effectiveness of Pseudo-Cliques

Similar to the literature [9, 12, 10, 11], we can find clusters of web pages by *exact* clique search. In that case, however, the above 11th cluster can never be obtained. The cluster (that is, a pseudo-clique) consists of two exact maximal cliques: $\{11^{th}, 382^{nd}, 797^{th}, 798^{th}, 826^{th}\}$ and $\{382^{nd}, 416^{th}, 797^{th}, 798^{th}, 826^{th}\}$. In the exact case, the former can be ranked as 11th, whereas the latter cluster as 343rd. It should be noted that the 416th page will be invisible unless we specify a large N for Top-N. However, it would be impractical to specify such a large N because many clusters are undesirably extracted. Although 416th page has valuable contents as mentioned above, we will lose a chance to browse it.

In case of pseudo-clique search, the 343rd exact cluster can be absorbed into the 11th cluster to form a pseudo-clique. In other word, the 343rd cluster can be drastically raised its rank. As the result, 416th page can become visible by just specifying a reasonable N.

Thus, our chance to get significant lower-ranked pages can be enhanced with the help of pseudo-cliques. This is a remarkable advantage brought by pseudo-cliques.

Effectiveness of SVD

As has been explained above, each web page is represented as a vector w.r.t. 211 feature terms. Then it is projected on the 98-dimensional subspace obtained with the help of SVD. The similarity between any pair of pages is evaluated in the subspace to capture some potential similarity among pages. For the web pages in the 11th cluster, Table 2 shows the relationship between similarities evaluated in the original space and in the subspace (that is, before the projection and after the projection). The former similarities are presented in the right upper triangular part (denoted by "Before") and the latter in the left lower part (denoted by "After") of the table.

Before the projection, any pair of pages in the cluster was dissimilar. After the projection, any similarity value has been increased. As has been mentioned above, we can actually recognize some similarity among the pages in the cluster. Although our retrieved 829 web pages contain several personal articles such as

Table 2. Similarities in the original space and in the subspace

After\Before	11th	382nd	416th	797th	798th	826th
11th	–	0.015792	0.385671	0.645488	0.778707	0.73269
382nd	0.966010	–	0	0	0	0
416th	0.939910	0.977438	–	0.167191	0.222574	0.308913
797th	0.958302	0.963385	0.950516	–	0.890177	0.733688
798th	0.963662	0.964356	0.950265	0.996706	–	0.818672
826th	0.970196	0.977112	0.962140	0.955964	0.960545	–

416th page (e.g. articles on Blogs), they did not belong to the 11th cluster. In fact, such articles are not concerned with hotels and foods. For example, a Blog article of the rank 337th presents some winter festivals in Hokkaido. In the 684th page, a domestic tour conductor personally talks about actual job in ski tours in Hokkaido. Thus, it would be difficult to find some similarity among these pages and ones in the 11th cluster. From this fact, we consider that potential similarities among web pages can be successfully captured with the help of SVD.

Statistics of Pseudo-Clique Search

Our experimental result also shows that the pruning rules presented in the previous section are very effective. The number of cores actually examined was 69981 and our pruning based on the tentative minimum weight were invoked at 40801 nodes of them. Moreover, the maximal clique searches were skipped at 31 nodes. Thus, the pruning rules can be applied very frequently in our search. As the result, the total computation time was just 0.847 second.

As we have experienced, an IR system often retrieves over hundreds of thousands of web pages. Therefore our graph constructed from gathered web pages would have a large number of vertices in more practical situation. In general, however, our graph tends to be quite sparse. Therefore, it is expected that our algorithm can still work well even in such a practical case.

From the experimental result, the authors consider that our pseudo-clique search would be a promising approach to finding significant clusters of web pages.

6   Discussion on Meaningfulness of Clusters Based on Formal Concept Analysis

As has been shown in the previous section, our clusters seem to provide valuable information for us. Critically speaking, however, our method has weakness in *meanings of clusters*. A cluster should have an explicit basis to show its meaningfulness. For example, a meaningful cluster is desired to have a clear explanation why the individuals (web pages, in our case) of the cluster are grouped together. Unfortunately, one may consider that our current clusters cannot satisfactorily provide such a clear reason.

In order to overcome the weakness, we try to improve our method with *Formal Concept Analysis* [8]. Formal Concept Analysis is a theory of data analysis which identifies conceptual structures among objects (individuals).

6.1   Formal Concept Analysis

Let $\mathcal{O}$ be a set of objects and $\mathcal{F}$ a set of features (attributes). An object is represented as the set of all features in $\mathcal{F}$ which the object has.

For a set of objects $O \subseteq \mathcal{O}$ and a set of features $F \subseteq \mathcal{F}$, we define two mappings $\varphi : 2^{\mathcal{O}} \to 2^{\mathcal{F}}$ and $\psi : 2^{\mathcal{F}} \to 2^{\mathcal{O}}$, respectively, as follows.

$$\varphi(O) = \{f \in \mathcal{F} \mid \forall o \in O, f \in o\} = \bigcap_{o \in O} o \quad \text{and} \quad \psi(F) = \{o \in \mathcal{O} \mid F \subseteq o\}.$$

The former computes the feature set shared by every object in O. The latter, on the other hand, returns the set of objects with F.

Based on the mappings, a *Formal Concept* (FC) is defined as a pair of object and feature sets, (O, F), where $O \subseteq \mathcal{O}$, $F \subseteq \mathcal{F}$, $\varphi(O) = F$ and $\psi(F) = O$. Especially, O and F are called the *extent* and *intent* of the formal concept, respectively. From the definition, it is obvious that $\psi(\varphi(O)) = O$ and $\varphi(\psi(F)) = F$. That is, a formal concept is defined as a pair of *closed* sets under the mappings.

For a formal concept $FC = (O, F)$, by regarding the extent O as a cluster of objects, we can obtain a clear reason why these objects are grouped together. The objects can form the cluster because all of them share the features F and any other object never has F. In this sense, the cluster O can be considered meaningful. We try to take this kind of meaningfulness into account in our clustering method.

6.2   Web Page Clusters as Formal Concepts

Representing a web page as a document vector, the similarity among pages (documents) in our method is evaluated by the cosine measure. Then documents which are similar each other are grouped into a cluster. In this sense, our current clusters are based on *distance* among documents. In order to give a convincing basis for such a distance-based cluster, we have to make interpretation of the distance clear. However, we would not be able to easily provide a good interpretation.

On the other hand, we can also consider another similarity based on *common feature terms*. That is, if for a set of documents, some feature terms are appeared in each of the documents, they can be considered similar each other and can form a cluster. Such a cluster will be meaningful in the sense that the documents in the cluster explicitly share some feature terms. Thus, it has a quite simple and clear basis. This kind of clusters based on common feature terms can be precisely defined with the notion of Formal Concepts.

Let $\mathcal{P}$ be the set of web pages to be clustered. As has been described, each web page document $d_i \in \mathcal{P}$ can be represented as a document vector

$$\boldsymbol{d}_i = (tf_{i1}, \ldots, tf_{i|\mathcal{T}|})^T,$$

where $\mathcal{T}$ is the set of feature terms and tf_{ij} is the frequency of the term $t_j \in \mathcal{T}$ in the document d_i.

Remark

In our current method, in order to capture semantic similarities among web pages, each document vector is then projected on a new subspace obtained by applying SVD to the term-document matrix for the corpus. After the projection, however, the document vector is represented as a new vector for which each dimension corresponds to a compound term defined by the original feature terms. Since it is difficult to adequately interpret the meaning of such a compound term, we continue here our discussion without the projection process for simplicity.   ∎

For each document d_i, the set of feature terms appeared in d_i is denoted by $terms(d_i)$, that is,

$$terms(d_i) = \{t_j \mid t_j \in \mathcal{T} \text{ such that } tf_{ij} \geq 1\}.$$

Let $\mathcal{P}' = \{terms(d) \mid d \in \mathcal{P}\}$ be a set of objects and $\mathcal{T}$ a set of features in Formal Concept Analysis. A formal concept $FC = (P, T)$ such that $P \subseteq \mathcal{P}'$ and $T \subseteq \mathcal{T}$ corresponds to a cluster of web pages with the common feature terms T. Thus, by restricting our clusters to being formal concepts, we can explicitly consider their meanings based on the intents. We call this kind of clusters *Formal Concept-based clusters* (FC-based clusters in short).

The meaningfulness of FC-based cluster will be affected by both of its intent and extent. A cluster with smaller intent might be unconvincing because the evidence for the grouping seems to be weak, though its extent tends to be larger. Conversely, although a cluster with larger intent might have more convincing evidence, its extent tends to be smaller. From these observations, we formalize FC-based clusters to be found as follows:

Constraint on Intents
   An FC-based cluster to be found should satisfy a constraint on intents. As such a constraint, we will give a threshold for evaluation value of intent.
Preference in Extents
   Among the FC-based clusters satisfying the above constraint, we prefer ones with higher evaluation values of their extents. Especially, we try to extract clusters whose extents have Top-N evaluation values.

In the evaluation of intents and extents, one might simply take their *size* into account. As another candidate, an intent T might be evaluated by the sum of *weights* of the feature terms in T. An evaluation function for extents can be defined based on their ranks assigned by an IR system, as has been described previously.

Thus, intents and extents of formal concepts can be evaluated from several viewpoints. We can actually define various evaluation functions for them. From the computational point of view, however, a function which behaves *monotonically* according to expansion of intents (extents) is strongly preferred. More concretely speaking, we prefer an evaluation function f such that for any set S and its superset S', $f(S) \leq f(S')$ holds. It is obvious that the above evaluation functions based on size and based on the sum of weights behave monotonically. The reason why such a function is preferable will become clear shortly.

6.3   Finding FC-Based Clusters by Clique Search

Top-N FC-based clusters can be also extracted by clique search.

Graph Construction: The undirected graph to be explored, G, is defined as $G = (\mathcal{P}, E)$, where $\mathcal{P}$ is a set of web pages to be clustered and

$$E = \{(d_i, d_j) \mid d_i, d_j \in \mathcal{P}(i \neq j) \wedge terms(d_i) \cap terms(d_j) \neq \phi\}.$$

Moreover, for each page $p \in \mathcal{P}$, the weight $w(p)$ is assigned according to its rank, as in the previous section. Thus, if a pair of pages share at least one feature term, then they are connected by an edge. From the definition, any formal concept can be extracted as an exact clique in G which satisfies closedness under the mapping φ and ψ. It should be noted that a maximal clique in G is not always a formal concept.

Search Strategy

Let γ be a threshold for evaluation values of intents. From the graph G, we try to extract formal concepts whose intents satisfy the constraint based on γ and whose extents have Top-N evaluation values. As long as we use monotonic evaluation functions for intents and extents, we can find our Top-N formal concepts with almost the same strategy adopted in our Top-N clique search. The pruning based on tentative Top-N clusters is still available. Furthermore, we can enjoy a new pruning rule by which we can exclude examining cliques which never become Top-N formal concepts.

Briefly speaking, a clique (a candidate of extent) is expanded step by step in depth-first manner. For each clique C, the set of common feature terms $\varphi(C)$ is computed. If the evaluation value of $\varphi(C)$ is lower than γ, then any extension of C can never become a formal concept satisfying the constraint on intents. Therefore, we can immediately stop expanding C and then backtrack. If a clique C is a formal concept satisfying the constraint on intents, then the tentative Top-N list of formal concepts is adequately updated.

6.4   FC-Based Clusters vs. Distance-Based Clusters

We have conducted a preliminary experimentation to observe characteristics of FC-based clusters.

A set of web pages $\mathcal{P}$ to be clustered has been retrieved by using *Google Web API*[4] with keywords "Presidential" and "Election". The number of retrieved pages is 968. For each page, its *summary* and *snippet* extracted by Google Web API are actually gathered as a document. After the stemming process, we have obtained 3600-terms in the pages (documents) and extracted 947 of them as feature terms[5]. Therefore, each page is represented as a 947-dimensional document vector.

From the web pages, we have extracted Top-25 distance-based clusters and Top-10 FC-based clusters for comparison. For the former, a graph G_D to be explored has been constructed under the the similarity threshold $\delta = 0.7$. For the latter, according to the above graph construction process, a graph G_{FC} has been constructed. In each graph, a page p is assigned its weight $w(p) = |\mathcal{P}| - rank(p) + 1$. Furthermore, each cluster (extent) is evaluated by the sum of the page weights.

The evaluation values for an intent T, $E_I(T)$, is defined as

$$E_I(T) = \sum_{t \in T} log(|\mathcal{P}|/df(t)),$$

---

[4] http://www.google.com/apis/

[5] All terms with the frequencies above 100 and below 3 have been removed.

Table 3. FC-Based Clusters

Cluster ID.	Extent (Page IDs)	Intent
F1	194 203 205 210	Adam Archiv Back Carr39; Nation Psepho Top middot summari
F2	20 21 66 709	Administr Bush COVERAGE Coverag Elector FULL Full New RELATED Reform Yahoo amp
F3	246 280 405 600 608	05 Lanka Sri Tamil TamilNet accur concern featur focus inform issu new peopl provid reliabl servic
F4	176 205 444	2001 Adam Archiv Carr39; Nation Psepho provinc summari
F5	70 326 479	Ukrainian alleg controversi exampl fraud includ irregular massiv

where $df(t)$ is the number of pages in $\mathcal{P}$ containing the term t. The value $log(|\mathcal{P}|/df(t))$ is called the *inverted document frequency of t* and reflects ability of t for discriminating documents. The threshold γ for required intent value has been set to 33.0.

Some of the obtained FC-based clusters are shown in Table 3. By referring to the intent, we can easily understand the reason why the cluster formed. Thus, meanings of FC-based clusters are more comprehensible than Distance-based ones.

Although various clusters have been extracted by each method, the authors emphasize that some of them especially show the following interesting characteristics.

FC-Based Cluster as Refinement of Distance-Based Cluster

As one of the top-25 Distance-based clusters, we can obtain a cluster $D1$ consisting of the pages with their IDs, $176, 191, 193, 194, 203, 204, 205, 210$ and 465. FC-based cluster $F1$ is a subset of $D1$. Since any similar pages in the distance-based clustering share some feature terms, they are always connected in the FC-based graph G_{FC}. Therefore, $D1$ should be a clique in G_{FC}. However, since $D1$ does not satisfy the constraint on required intent value, it cannot be extracted as a formal concept. In other word, $D1$ is too large and no longer has any convincing basis (intent) of the grouping. In this sense, FC-based cluster $F1$ can be viewed as a meaningful *refinement* of the Distance-based cluster $D1$.

One might be able to obtain $F1$ even by Distance-based approach, if an adequate distance (similarity) threshold δ can be provided. However, it is well-known as a very difficult task. Although FC-based clustering also needs a threshold γ for required intent value, γ is more intuitively understandable than δ because the meaning of our intent value is quite clear. Thus, we can extract meaningful clusters by FC-based approach without suffering from difficult parameter setting required in the Distance-based approach.

FC-Based Cluster as Hidden Connection Between Distance-Based Clusters

Addition to $D1$, we can obtain the 21st Distance-based cluster $D2$ consisting of the pages with their IDs $187, 192$ and 444. Since $D1$ and $D2$ share no page, they seem to be quite different clusters. It is, therefore, difficult to find explicit connection between them. On the other hand, FC-based cluster $F4$ shows a certain evidence of the similarity among pages 176, 205 and 444, where both of 176 and 205 belong to $D1$ and 444 to $D2$. Based on the existence of $F4$, the authors expectantly consider that Distance-based clusters $D1$ and $D2$ are *potentially* related to each other. Although the claim would not be certain, we expect that such a FC-cluster would work as a trigger for *discovering* a hidden interesting relationship between clusters.

7   Conclusion

In this paper, we presented a method for pinpoint clustering of web pages. Our cluster can consist of similar higher-ranked and lower-ranked pages. Although we are usually careless of pages with lower ranks, they can be *explicitly* extracted together with significant higher-ranked pages. As the result, our clusters can provide new valuable information for users.

In order to obtain such clusters, we first extract semantic correlations among feature terms by applying SVD to the term-document matrix generated from a corpus w.r.t. a specific topic. Based on the correlations of terms, we can evaluate potential similarities among web pages to be clustered. The set of web pages is then represented as a weighted graph G based on the similarities and their ranks. Our clusters can be found as pseudo-cliques in G. We designed an algorithm for finding Top-N weighted pseudo-cliques. In our experimentation, we confirmed that a quite valuable cluster can be actually extracted according to our method.

In order to improve our method so that our clusters can be explicitly provided with more convincing meanings, we discussed an idea with the help of Formal Concept Analysis. By restricting our clusters (cliques) to formal concepts, we can consider their clear conceptual meanings as their intents. In our preliminary experimentation, we observed some characteristics of FC-based clusters. From the observation, we expect that our extended method based on Formal Concept Analysis would be a promising approach to finding meaningful clusters.

Needless to say, the extended method is not only for web page clustering. We can apply the method to any case in which each object to be clustered can be represented as a set of attributes. Applying the method to other practical data will be an interesting work.

References

1. L. Page, S. Brin, R. Motwani and T. Winograd, "The PageRank Citation Ranking: Bringing Order to the Web", http://dbpubs.stanford.edu/pub/1999-66, 1999.
2. A. Vakali, J. Pokorný and T. Dalamagas, "An Overview of Web Data Clustering Practices", Proceedings of the 9th International Conference on Extending Database Technology - EDBT'04, Springer-LNCS 3268, pp. 597 - 606, 2004.
3. G. Strang, "Introduction to Linear Algebra", 3rd Edition, Wellesley-Cambridge Press, 2003.
4. K. Kita, K. Tsuda and M. Shishibori, "Information Retrieval Algorithms", Kyoritsu Shuppan, 2002 (in Japanese).
5. E. Tomita and T. Seki, "An Efficient Branch-and-Bound Algorithm for Finding a Maximum Clique", Proceedings of the 4th International Conference on Discrete Mathematics and Theoretical Computer Science - DMTCS'03, Springer-LNCS 2731, pp. 278 - 289, 2003.

6. T. Fahle, "Simple and Fast: Improving a Branch-and-Bound Algorithm for Maximum Clique", Proceedings of the 10th European Symposium on Algorithms - ESA'02, Springer-LNCS 2461, pp. 485 - 498, 2002.

7. R. Carraghan and P. M. Pardalos, "An Exact Algorithm for the Maximum Clique Problem", Operations Research Letters, vol. 9, pp. 375 - 382, 1990.

8. B. Ganter and R. Wille, "Formal Concept Analysis: Mathematical Foundations", Springer, 1999.

9. K. Satoh, "A Method for Generating Data Abstraction Based on Optimal Clique Search", Master's Thesis, Graduate School of Eng., Hokkaido Univ., March, 2003. (in Japanese)

10. S. Masuda, "Analysis of Ascidian Gene Expression Data by Clique Search", Master's Thesis, Graduate School of Eng., Hokkaido Univ., March, 2005. (in Japanese)

11. B. Shi, "Top-N Clique Search of Web Pages", Master's Thesis, Graduate School of Eng., Hokkaido Univ., March, 2005. (in Japanese)

12. Y. Okubo and M. Haraguchi, "Creating Abstract Concepts for Classification by Finding Top-N Maximal Weighted Cliques", Proceedings of the 6th International Conference on Discovery Science - DS'03, Springer-LNAI 2843, pp. 418 - 425, 2003.

13. Y. Okubo, M. Haraguchi and B. Shi, "Finding Significant Web Pages with Lower Ranks by Pseudo-Clique Search", Proceedings of the 8th Internatinal Conference on Discovery Science - DS'05, Springer-LNAI 3735, pp. 345 - 352, 2005. (in press)

14. Y. Okubo and M. Haraguchi, "Finding Top-N Pseudo-Cliques in Simple Graph", Proceedings of the 9th World Multiconference on Systemics, Cybernetics and Informatics - WMSCI'05, Vol. III, pp. 215 - 220, 2005.

Specific-Purpose Web Searches on the Basis of Structure and Contents

Mineichi Kudo and Atsuyoshi Nakamura

Graduate School of Information Science and Technology, Hokkaido University,
Kita 14, Nishi 9, Kita-ku, Sapporo, 060-0814, Japan
{mine, atsu}@main.ist.hokudai.ac.jp

Abstract. We introduce methods for two specific-purpose Web searches. One is a search for *Web communities* related to given keywords, and the other is a search for texts having a certain relation to given keywords. Our methods are based on both structure and contents of WWW. Our method of Web community search uses global structure of WWW to discover communities, and uses content information to label found communities, where global structure means Web graph composed of Web pages and hyperlinks between them. On the other hand, our method of related text search uses local structure of WWW to extract candidate texts, and uses content information to filter out wrongly extracted ones, where local structure means DOM-tree structure of each page. We report the latest results on these Web search methods.

1 Introduction

Motivation. The World Wide Web is now a rich resource for obtaining valuable information. The problem to be solved is how to choose important information only for a specific user or a specific demand. One solution for this problem is to make a search engine for a specific purpose. By using a specific-purpose search engine, we can enjoy high-performance search results for the purpose though available cases of the engine are limited.

Usefulness of a specific-purpose search engine is determined by how popular and important the purpose is.

One important purpose is knowledge discovery, or data mining. In this purpose, search results are not mere a set of pages satisfying a certain conditions but higher-level knowledge. One such knowledge is that members in a certain set of sites share the same topic, which indicates that a kind of *community* is composed of corresponding organizations or persons. One subject of this paper is automatic discovery and labeling of Web communities related to given keywords.

Another important purpose is to gather information supporting user's decisions. Much of such information appears in the form of texts that describe people's experiences, opinions and feelings. The other subject of this paper is automatic extraction of texts having a specific relation with given keywords. Extracting people's review texts for a certain kind of restaurants, books and music CDs is an example of such specific relations.

K.P. Jantke et al. (Eds.): Federation over the Web, LNAI 3847, pp. 79–96, 2006.
© Springer-Verlag Berlin Heidelberg 2006

Key Concepts. Since most informations important for human being are written in natural language, we cannot expect high-performance search results without using content information of Web pages. Several sophisticated text search techniques have been already developed in the area of information retrieval [3], and we can obtain search results of some performance level by applying such techniques to the Web search. Different from a mere set of plain texts, Web has explicit structures both globally and locally. Here, the global structure is a graph structure in which each Web page is regarded as a vertex and each hyperlink between Web pages is regarded as an edge. The local structure is the DOM(Document Object Model)-tree structure in a page. Performance of Web search depends on how effectively these structural information is used in addition to content information.

In order to automatically discover and label Web communities, our approach makes use of information of the global structure. A densely connected subgraph of Web graph is a set of pages that might be created by people or organizations having an interest in the same topic. Such sets of pages are called *Web communities* in a narrow sense, and many researchers are studying how to discover Web communities [5, 7, 13]. In our approach, focusing on graph structure, Web communities that strictly satisfy the conditions defined by us are extracted first. Then, focusing on content similarity of member pages in each extracted Web community, they are labeled using frequency mining techniques [1], namely, labeled by frequent *index-term* sets.

In order to automatically extract texts having a specific relation with given keywords, our approach uses information of the local structure. Several methods of information extraction using DOM-tree structure have been already developed [16, 4, 10, 18]. However, those previous methods are only applicable to extraction from specific sites. In our approach, content information is also used in addition to information of DOM-tree structure, which enable texts related with given keywords to be extracted from search results by general search engine. First, candidate texts are selected using DOM-tree patterns, which are extracted from training data by frequency mining technique. Then, inappropriate texts are filtered out by text classifier, which is also created from training data.

Main Results. On the subject of automatic discovery and labeling Web communities, we recently proposed stricter community definition [11], which reduces boundary ambiguity of communities defined by Flake, Lawrence and Giles [5]. Though finding all communities of our definition is known to be a computationally hard problem [6, 17], we also proposed efficient algorithm with constructing a Gomory-Hu tree that possibly finds many communities. Actually, in our previous experiments, more than 100 communities were found for a graph of about 3000 vertices [11]. However, many similar communities containing almost all vertices in the same connected component were included in the set of those found communities. In many cases, intersection of those communities also satisfies our community definition, and partitioning by all communities does not change even if all those communities are replaced with one intersection community. Even in the case that intersection of communities does not satisfy our community definition, the maximum community included in the intersection can be found [11], and such maximum community may make the partition finer. In this paper, we propose a modified method using above replacement and addition of communities to obtain a community set composed of more essentially-distinct ones. We also propose a labeling method of found communities by frequent *index-term* [3] sets, which can be obtained by an algorithm [21] for frequent item sets. According to our preliminary experiments, our modified method replaced most of uninformative large communities with several smaller ones and added more than 100 communities that make the partitioning finer. As for labeling by frequent index-term sets, some appropriate keywords such as page-owner's company's or organization's names and summary keywords such as "racing" and "game" were included in created index term sets. Labeling by not mere index-term list but a list of index-term sets sometimes gave us hints on the contexts in which the words were used.

On the subject of automatic extraction of texts having a specific relation with given keywords, we developed a method using structure matching and text classification [9, 8]. Patterns we use in structure matching consist of a root node and two paths leading to leaf nodes, a *keyword* node and a *target* node. Structure matching to a pattern set is conducted for DOM-trees converted from retrieved HTML pages. In this matching, a text node containing given keywords is matched to a keyword node of a pattern, and nodes matching to its target node are extracted, and all the texts included in the subtrees rooted by the extracted nodes are candidate texts. Matching used here is elastic like the ones used in [22, 18], namely, only subsequence of nodes in a path has to be matched to a sequence of nodes in a path of a pattern. This flexibility allows many texts having target relation with given keywords to be extracted using small number of patterns. On the other hand, many non-target texts are also extracted, but those are filtered out by text classification. Patterns used in this structure matching are learned from training data using algorithm [2] for frequent sequence mining. The text classifier is also learned automatically using given positive instances and *generated* negative instances, which are texts wrongly extracted from training data using learned patterns. According to our experiment of extracting people's reviews for given restaurants, which are categorized into Ramen, Sushi, curry in Sapporo and Sushi in New York, precision of our method is at least 70% and its recall is at least 40% for all the categories except Sushi in New York.

Relation to the topic "Federation over the Web". One subject of this paper is automatic discovery and labeling of Web communities. For knowledge federation, we first have to select pieces of knowledge to federate. An extracted Web community may be used as a set of such pieces to federate. Automatic extraction of texts having a specific relation with given keywords, for example, extracting people's reviews for a given restaurant from search results of a general Web search engine, is the other subject of this paper. Restaurants nearby depend on people's current place, and we can obtain various information by federating Web pages related to those nearby restaurants. Extracted reviews of those restaurants are a kind of such information.

Paper Organization. This paper is organized as follows. Section 2 is devoted to our method of automatic discovery and labeling of Web communities. In that section, after our previous method is described, we propose a modified method and reports the results of experiments for examining effectiveness of the modification. Section 3 is devoted to our method of automatic extraction of texts having a specific relation with given keywords. We mention our text extraction method using patterns and a text classifier, and our learning method of the patterns and the classifier. Recent experimental results are also shown in this section. Related work is described in Section 4, and this paper is concluded by Section 5.

2 Automatic Discovery and Labeling of Web Communities

In this section, we deal with the problem of automatic discovery and labeling of Web communities.

We divide the problem into two subproblems, community discovery and labeling. In our method, Web communities are discovered first by using structural information, and then each community is labeled automatically using content information.

2.1 Community Discovery Using Structural Information

As a method of community discovery, we use a method of finding communities that we have developed recently [11]. We defined communities by stricter conditions than Flake, Lawrence and Giles did, and proposed a method finding such communities efficiently by constructing a Gomory-Hu tree. In the followings, we first mention our community definition and community-finding method we proposed previously, then propose a modified method.

Base Method. A Web graph we consider here is an undirected graph $G = (V, E)$ that is composed of a vertex set V representing the set of Web pages, and an edge set E representing the set of links connecting between two distinct pages. For a vertex u and a vertex set $C(\not\ni u)$, let $\#(u, C)$ denote the number of edges between u and any $v \in C$. The community definition we proposed in [11] is as follows.

Definition 1. *A community is a vertex subset $C \subset V$ that satisfies the following two conditions.*

1. $\#(u, C - \{u\}) > \#(u, V - C)$ for all $u \in C$.
2. $\#(u, C) \leq \#(u, V - C - \{u\})$ for all $u \in V - C$.

The first condition in Definition 1 says that each member vertex has more edges connecting to member vertices than it does to non-member vertices. Note that the original definition by Flake, Lawrence and Giles is the same as this

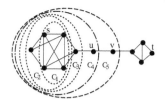

Fig. 1. Example of Communities $C_1, C_2, ..., C_5$

first condition except it allows the case with $\#(u, C - \{u\}) = \#(u, V - C)$. The second condition says that each non-member vertex has at least as many edges connecting to non-member vertices as it does to member vertices. One merit of our definition is reduction of community-boundary ambiguity. For example, sets $C_1, C_2, ..., C_5$ in Fig. 1 are all communities by the definition of Flake, Lawrence and Giles, but those are essentially the same densely connected part. In this case, only C_3 satisfies our community definition.

Finding communities defined by Definition 1 looks computationally difficult, because the problem of deciding whether a community exists or not in a given weighted graph is known to be NP-complete[1] [6]. Even for non-weighted graphs, graphs in which weights for all edges are 1, NP-completeness was also proved for the problem of deciding whether a community that includes s and excludes t for given vertices s and t exists or not [17].

However, for given vertices s and t, the smallest set C for which $(C, V - C)$ is a *minimum cut* [19] dividing s and t satisfies our community conditions except for vertices s and t [11]. Thus, it is very easy to decide whether such a set C is community or not. By using Gomory-Hu tree construction method, $n - 1$ such minimum cuts can be found efficiently, where n is the number of vertices. By checking our community condition for two vertices of each minimum cut, many communities are possibly obtained. Actually, more than 100 communities were found from graphs with about 3000 vertices in our previous experiments.

Modified Method. Our previous method has the following two problems. First, minimum cuts represented by a Gomory-Hu tree are ones that divide two distinct vertices. So, community C_7 in Fig. 2, which divides vertex s and vertex-set $\{t_1, t_2\}$, cannot be found by the method. Community C_{14} in Fig. 2 cannot be found by the same reason. Furthermore, three communities C_{11}, C_{12} and C_{13} are found by th method, but those communities are essentially the same community having C_4 as its core. This means that the problem of boundary ambiguity still exists, which is the second problem.

To cope with these problems, we consider the following two operations for any two communities C_1 and C_2 in set $\mathcal{C}$ of found communities such that $C_1 \cap C_2$, $C_1 \setminus C_2$ and $C_2 \setminus C1$ are all non-empty.

---

[1] In this paper, communities are defined only for non-weighted graphs, but it is easy to extend our community definition for weighted graphs. See [11].

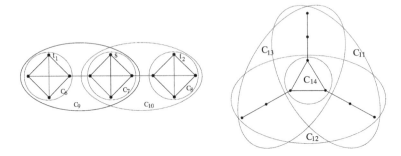

Fig. 2. Problem cases of our previous method

Operation 1. Add $C_1 \cap C_2$ if $C_1 \cap C_2$ is a community, and the partitioning by all communities, a set of connected components cut by boundaries of communities, is not changed by adding $C_1 \cap C_2$ and removing at least one of two communities C_1 and C_2. Remove all such C_i for $i = 1, 2$.

Operation 2. Add the maximum community contained in $C_1 \cap C_2$ if $C_1 \cap C_2$ is not a community.

Note that, for any pair of communities, there is the maximum community contained in their intersection by Proposition 4(2) in [11]. Community C_7 in Fig. 2 is added, and two communities C_9 and C_{10} are removed by Operation 1. Similarly, C_{14} is added, and three communities C_{11}, C_{12} and C_{13} are removed. Thus, the two problems above are solved in the cases shown in Fig. 2.

Note that the number of communities increases by Operation 2 but does not increase or even decreases by Operation 1. Applying these procedure for all pair of found communities has high computational cost if many communities are found. Thus, we first apply Operation 1 to all pairs of found communities including newly found ones by this operation to reduce the number of communities. Then, apply Operation 2 to all pairs of the communities. After that, repeat these two procedures in this order until no change occurs by the procedures.

2.2 Labeling Using Content Information

As to labeling found communities, we apply frequent item set mining method to this problem. A frequent item set is a set that is included in more than σ percentage of transactions for a given transaction database, where σ is a given minimum support value. By regarding each Web page as a transaction that composed of *index terms* [3] appeared in the page, frequent index-term set can be obtained by efficient algorithm for frequent item sets [21]. Then, a community can be labeled by maximal frequent index-term sets.

When the minimum support σ is fixed, no frequent index-term set exists for some communities, which is not appropriate for labeling. Therefore, we propose the labeling method that always uses the most frequent N index-terms in a community, where frequency is counted by the number of pages contains the index-term. Let the number of pages in a community be m and let the frequency of the Nth frequent index-term be n. Then, σ is set to n/m. In this case, all the frequent index-term sets must be subsets of the most frequent N index-terms. So, calculation has to be done only for index-term sets restricted to the most frequent N index-terms.

2.3 Preliminary Experiment

For keyword "jaguar", we construct a subgraph by using the *Subgraph* procedure proposed by Kleinberg [12], which retrieves t pages by using a search engine and adds all pages that are linked from or linking to at least one of them, though the number of pages linking to is restricted within d pages. In our experiment, we used search engine Google (www.google.co.jp), and set t and d to 845 and 100, respectively[2]. Note that we removed all *intrinsic* links [12], namely, links to pages of the same domain, as Kleinberg did.

We judged that two domains $d1$ and $d2$ are the same as follows. Let components of a domain mean strings separated by periods '.'. Assume that the number of components for $d1$ is at most that for $d2$. Then,

1. if $d1$ is composed of more than two components, $d1$ and $d2$ are judged as the same if and only if the $d1$'s suffix beginning with the second component is a $d2$'s suffix. For example, 'ccc.bbb.aaa' and 'ddd.bbb.aaa' are the same domain, and 'eee.ccc.bbb.aaa' and 'fff.ddd.bbb.aaa' are different domains.
2. If $d1$ is composed of at most two components, $d1$ and $d2$ are judged as the same if and only if $d1$ is a suffix of $d2$. For example, 'bbb.aaa.' and 'ccc.bbb.aaa' are the same domain but 'bbb.aaa' and 'eee.ddd.aaa' are different domains.

The summary of our data is shown in Table 1. Note that the number of connected components is counted by excluding isolated vertices.

First, we examined effectiveness of our modified method for finding communities. The result is shown in Table 2. The number of found communities are reduced from 478 to 160 using Operation 1 only. This means that, for many pairs $\{C_1, C_2\}$ of communities found by our previous method, two communities C_1 and C_2 can be replaced with one community $C_1 \cap C_2$ without changing the partitioning by all communities. Most of such deleted communities are large ones that contain almost all vertices of one connected component, and those are not interesting. Using Operation 1 repeatedly, many such large communities are replaced with a few smaller communities that are intersections of subsets of those communities. (See Fig. 3.) Thus, the average size of communities are dramatically decreased by Operation 1. Using Operation 2 in addition to Operation 1, new communities that change the partitioning by all communities are found. This increases the number of communities from 160 to 307 though this also increases the average size of communities. Our modified method seems effective from the fact that new communities are found and many unimportant communities are removed.

---

[2] Precisely speaking, 845 is the number of pages retrieved by Google with keyword "jaguar" using the mode of excluding similar pages.

Table 1. Data summary

Number of vertices	11888
Number of edges	76922
Number of isolated vertices	2740
Number of connected components	135

Table 2. Found communities

Method	Previous	+Operation 1	+Operations 1 and 2
Number of communities	478	160	307
Average community size	5770	551	2697
Standard deviation of community size	6934	2017	4002

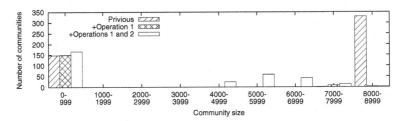

Fig. 3. Size distribution of found communities

Next, we examined effectiveness of our labeling method. From the 307 communities found by our modified method, we selected communities that are not supersets of other communities containing at least 15 pages. There were 14 such communities of English pages, which are listed in Table 3. In the table, communities are sorted by the number of member pages that contain word "jaguar". We applied our labeling method to these 14 communities. As inputs to our method, only pages containing "jaguar" are used because we want to analyze communities in context of "jaguar". Index terms we used in our experiment are standard forms of nouns, verbs and adjectives though the following two types of words are excluded: (1) the most frequent 500 words [15], (2) popular words used in footer of Web pages ("copyright", "right", "reserve", "privacy", "policy", "site", "map", "contact", "web", "search", "links", "link", "home" and "page"). In the experiment, we used the most frequent 4 index-terms except "jaguar" for labeling.

Now, let us see the labels generated by our labeling method, which are shown for each community in Table 3. First, let check whether selected index-term sets contain keywords appropriate for each community. For more than half of communities, those contain page-owner's company's or organization's names: "Jaglovers"(1), "Justia"(2), "Wikipedia"(3), "HighBeam" " research"(6), "Roadfly"(9), "eBay"(11), "PRIMEDIA"(12) and "IGN"(13), where the number n in the parenthesis means that the word appears in the label of the nth community.

Table 3. Found communities that do not contain any other communities with size ≥ 15 (A: Number of pages containing "jaguar", B: Number of pages, C: Number of distinct sites)

[Id] A/B (C)	Maximal frequent index-term sets: [words, frequency] Most popular 2 pages: #incoming links title (url)
[1] 127/133 (14)	[Jag-lovers,121],[Internet, image,120],[original,120],[post,120],[XK,120],[August,120],[forum,120],[support,120] 155 A1 JagWeb - Jaguar restoration, trimming, bodywork, panels, performance, parts & spares (www.jagweb.com) 127 JagXCHANGE from Jag-lovers (jagads.jag-lovers.org)
[2] 99/120 (16)	[personal, recall,98],[learn, recall,98],[sport, recall, service, design, SEO, Justia, firm, contract, legal, law, auto, Blog, RSS,98] 97 Auto Recalls - JAGUAR − Justia (auto-recalls.justia.com/JAGUAR.html) 2 Free Recall Warnings and Alerts, Consumer Product Recalls, Baby Product Recalls, Food Recalls, Car and Auto Recalls, Drug Recalls, Tire Recalls (www.recall-warnings.com)
[3] 62/91 (18)	[license, free, gnu,45],[Wikipedia,44] 24 Jaguar - Wikipedia, the free encyclopedia (en.wikipedia.org/wiki/Jaguar) 5 Category:Jaguar vehicles - Wikimedia Commons (commons.wikimedia.org/wiki/Category:Jaguar_vehicles)
[4] 47/238 (67)	[news, feature,42],[announce,42],[buy, feature,42],[plan,42],[picture, feature,42],[market, feature,42],[design,42],[Maybach,42],[available, share, resource,42] 198 Autoblog - www.autoblog.com _ (www.autoblog.com) 196 HD Beat (www.hdbeat.com)
[5] 37/50 (45)	[racing,26],[Jordan,24],[Ferrari,23],[Minardi,22] 86 Jaguar UK - R is for Racing (www.jaguar.co.uk/uk/en/vehicles/r-performance/overview/r_racing.htm) 0 Sports Links (homepage.eircom.net/ nworc/sports_links.htm)
[6] 29/37 (2)	[term, source, HighBeam, research, date, reference, free,29] 1 HighBeam Research: Library Search: Results (www.highbeam.com/library/search.asp) 0 jaguar on Encyclopedia.com (www.encyclopedia.com/html/j1/jaguar.asp)
[7] 29/29 (5)	[Infiniti, Geo, Mitsubishi, BMW, Audi, Kia, factory, jeep, stereo, Audio, Volkswagen, Mazda, Daewoo, repair, Isuzu, ford, Nissan, Benz, Volvo, shipping, Honda, rover, Mercedes, Hyundai, Toyota,29] 37 Factory Car Audio Repair For All Makes and Models - Jaguar Car Stereo Removal - BOSE Car Stereo, Speaker /Amplifier Repair (www.carstereohelp.com/strjaguar.htm) 1 Car Stereo Removal and Installation For Jaguar, Car Audio Installation, Car Stereo Front Speaker Removeing Guide (www.carstereoremoval.com/htm/stereoremovalJaguar93-94P.htm)
[8] 23/31 (30)	[Honda, ford,13],[Peugeot, Mazda, Vauxhall, rover, ford, Renault,13],[seat, rover, Renault,13] 40 Jaguar UK - Jaguar Cars (www.jaguar.co.uk/uk/en/home.htm) 0 Links to Major Car Manufacturers (www.psychovinyl.co.uk/Links/Carmanufacturers.htm)
[9] 17/21 (2)	[register, Roadfly, check, photo, forum, gallery, feature, index, Login, review, message, Email, account, view, magazine,16],[advertise, Roadfly, service, term, webmaster@roadfly.com, email, jump, medium, please, comment,16] 16 Jaguar message board forums at Roadfly (www.roadfly.com/jaguar/forums)
[10] 16/19 (4)	[service,7],[sorry, doesn't, support, browser, frame,7],[XJ, S-TYPE, aluminium, X-TYPE, XK,7] 27 Jaguar INT - Jaguar Cars (www.jaguar.com/int/en/home.htm) 1 Jaguar Cars gt (www.jaguarcars.com/global/index.cgi)
[11] 16/34 (4)	[respective, price, brand, pay, property, owner, user, list, item, agreement, in/out, sign, motor, eBay, service, view,16] 2 eBay Stores - Jaguar, Passenger Vehicles, eBay Motors items on eBay.com (motors.stores.ebay.com/Passenger-Vehicles-Jaguar-W0QQcatZ6272QQtZlw) 1 eBay - 2005, 2005 Jaguar, XK8, S-Type - buy and sell on eBay Motors (motors.search.ebay.com/2005_Jaguar_W0QQfclZ3QQfsooZ2QQfsopZ2QQsacatZ6272QQssPageNameZWLRS)
[12] 15/50 (10)	[vehicle, PRIMEDIA, lease, truck, price, free,14],[motor, PRIMEDIA,14] 16 Motor Trend en Espanol - Pruebas de carretera, articulos, exposiciones automotrices con sedans, cupes, camionetas, y vehiculos del futuro (www.motortrendenespanol.com) 12 Used Car Truck SUV Research by Make Model Price - IntelliChoice (www.intellichoice.com/search/used)
[13] 14/140 (55)	[arcade, IGN, game, vault, planet, Gamers, GameSpy,13] 110 GameStats: Cheats, Movies, Screenshots, Previews and Reviews (www.gamestats.com) 14 IGN Cheats, Codes and Game Cheats (cheats.ign.com)
[14] 10/21 (10)	[term, reference, news, tool,10] 1 jaguar (www.infoplease.com/ce6/sci/A0825869.html) 1 Automotive News: Sports cars and opulent sedans, Jaguar is all things to lovers of luxury.(The 100-Year Almanac and 1996 Market Data Book)@ HighBeam Research (www.highbeam.com/library/doc0.asp)

These keywords are considered to be one of appropriate keywords though communities labeled index-term sets containing such keywords are possibly composed of one company's sites. Next, let see whether keywords that summarize each community are selected. For some communities, their labels contain such important keywords: "forum"(1,9), "recall"(2), "racing"(5), "Audio" "repair" (7), "price"(11,12), "vehicle"(12) and "game"(13). These keywords help up know what communities they are. Proper nouns like product names are sometimes included, and those words also help us guess what communities they are.

As sets of index-terms, sets of words appeared in the fixed part of pages in the same owner's sites were selected. For example, the footer of Wikipedia's pages always contains a note "Gnu Free Documentation License" which caused the word set { "license", "free", "gnu"} to be generated. One merit of labeling by frequent *sets* is that you can guess in what context the set of words are used in many cases. However, fixed headers or footers do not always represent contents of pages appropriately. The fact that words appeared in such fixed part are frequent for a community, also indicates that the community is mainly composed of the same owner's sites.

Interesting communities are considered to be ones composed of many different owner's pages. To investigate that such interesting communities are extracted, we calculated the number of distinct domains for each community. For a given set D of domains, the number of distinct domains is the minimum size of its subset S such that for any $d \in D$ there exists $s \in S$ which is the same with d. Note that the definition of the same domains here is before mentioned one. The number of distinct communities are shown in the parenthesis of the first column of Table 3. In context of "jaguar", interesting communities are the 5th and 8th communities because most member pages are distinct and word "jaguar" appears in more than half member pages. The 5th community is a community of jaguar car racing, and the 8th community is a community composed of major manufacturer home pages containing the *jaguar* home page and *hub pages* linking to them.

3   Automatic Extraction of Texts Having a Specific Relation with Given Keywords

Town information magazines are useful for finding restaurants suited for your taste. However, depending too much on such information is not recommended because the restaurants might pay some money for the articles and the reporter's taste might be different from your taste. Your decision should be made based on restaurant reviews by several people, which are obtainable through the WWW.

We are now developing a search engine for extracting restaurant reviews from the WWW. For a given restaurant name, the engine collects information of the restaurant using a conventional search engine, and displays its review texts only by extracting from collected Web pages. The problem is how to extract only review texts of a given restaurant name from collected Web pages. We assume that every page contains some information of a target restaurant, which

```
<html>
 <head><title> Hokudai Sushi: the best Sushi restaurant </title></head>
 <body bgcolor="yellow">
  <big><strong> Hokudai Sushi </strong></big><br>
  <small>tel: 000-000-0000, fax: 111-111-1111</small><br><br>
  <font color="blue">The best Sushi restaurant I've ever been to.</font><br>
 </body>
</html>
```

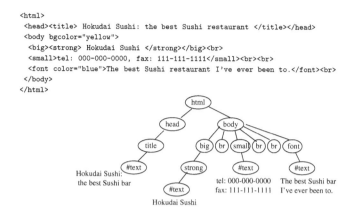

Fig. 4. Example of an HTML document and its DOM-tree representation

is possible if we give its telephone number or address to a conventional search engine in addition to its name.

The difficulty of the above problem exists in the following points.

1. There are pages which do not contain reviews.
2. Some pages contain reviews of more than one restaurants.
3. Various information other than reviews might be contained.
4. Various page layouts exist.

Here, target reputation texts are ones structurally separated from other texts. So, reputations that are appeared in BBS (Bulletin Board System) conversation or someone's diary are not targeted.

Our search engine for extracting restaurant reviews uses both structural and content information. Structural information is used to narrow candidates by structural relation between a reputation candidate text and a text containing a given restaurant name. Content information is used to judge whether each candidate is a reputation or not by classifying texts into two categories, review texts and other texts.

3.1   Structure-Based Filtering Phase

Structure we consider here is a (simplified) DOM-tree, a representation of an HTML document in *document object model*. A simplified DOM-tree is an ordered tree in which each node has two attributes, *tag* and *text*. A value of the tag attribute is '#text' for text nodes and a HTML tag otherwise. A value of the text attribute is a text for text nodes and *null* otherwise. Fig. 4 is an example of an HTML document and its DOM-tree representation. In our problem setting, text "The best Sushi restaurant I've ever been to." must be extracted from this example page when restaurant name 'Hokudai Sushi' is given.

Candidates are narrowed to texts below the nodes matched to certain structural patterns, which are learned from training data. A pattern (P, r) is com-

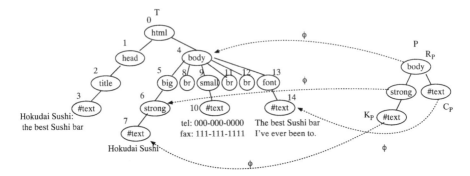

Fig. 5. Example of a pattern tree P. The structural relation of the node 14 to keyword "Hokudai Sushi" matches the pattern (P, r) when $r \geq 7$. In this case, that of the node 10 to the keyword also matches (P, r).

posed of a pattern tree P and integer r. A pattern tree P is a special DOM-tree without the text attribute. It is composed of a root node R_P, two leaf nodes K_P and C_P, and paths from the root node to leaf nodes. An example pattern tree P is shown in Fig. 5. A node C_T in a DOM-tree T is said to be matched to a pattern (P, r) for a given restaurant name W if P is embeddable in T by one-to-one mapping ϕ that satisfies the following conditions. Note that node ids are their positions in the preorder traversal.

1. **Target matching:** $C_T = \phi(C_P)$
2. **Keyword matching:** $\phi(K_P)$ is a text node of which text contains W.
3. **LCA matching:** The least common ancestor of nodes $\phi(K_P)$ and $\phi(C_P)$ is $\phi(R_P)$.
4. **Label preserving:** The tag attribute value of N_P coincides with that of $\phi(N_P)$ for all nodes N_P in P.
5. **Ancestor-descendant relation preserving:** If node $N_{P,1}$ is a child of node $N_{P,2}$ in P, node $\phi(N_{P,1})$ is a descendant of node $\phi(N_{P,2})$ in T.
6. **Sibling relation preserving:** The left-right relation of K_P and C_P is preserved by ϕ, that is, the id of $\phi(K_P)$ is smaller than the id of $\phi(C_P)$.
7. **Acceptable distance:** Absolute difference between ids of $\phi(K_P)$ and $\phi(C_P)$ is at most r.

An example embedding mapping ϕ is shown in Fig. 4. Note that our pattern matching allows elastic matching, which makes a pattern more general. Candidates narrowed by pattern matching are all nodes that are matched to one of pattern (P, r) in a pattern set $\mathcal{P}$. Elastic matching enable us to extract reputation texts embedded in various structures by a small number of patterns.

3.2   Content-Based Filtering Phase

In order to judge whether each candidate is a reputation or not, we use a text classifier of which input is an *index term vector* [3] that is created from all the texts of the descendant text nodes of the candidate node. An index term vector is a collection of weights associated with each representative keyword called *index term*. Its weights can be binary, normalized term frequencies or *tf-idf*s. The text classifier can be any one that inputs a real valued vector.

If all the candidate nodes in a Web page are judged not to be reputations, no text is output. If more than one candidate nodes in a Web page are judged to be reputations, a node $\phi(C_P)$ with the smallest id difference from $\phi(K_P)$ is selected, and all the texts of its descendant nodes are output.

3.3   Learning Patterns and a Text Classifier

Our method explained in the previous subsection needs a pattern set $\mathcal{P}$ and a text classifier, which can be learned from training data. In this subsection, we mention how to learn them.

A training data set $\mathcal{D}$ is a set of triples (W, T, N_T^*), where W is a restaurant name, T is a DOM-tree that has text nodes containing W, and N_T^* is the least common ancestor of all the text nodes which contain review texts for W. N_T^* is *null* when there is no such text node in T. To create each triple (W, T, N_T^*), we have to specify where the review texts for W are written. However, this task is easy because we do not have to specify the place of W and we may neglect all other review texts for other restaurants.

For each training data (W, T, N_T^*) with $N_T^* \neq$ null, and for the last text node K_T that contains W and appears before N_T^*, the minimum connected subgraph S containing K_T and N_T^* is extracted from T.

For example, when $W =$ 'Hokudai Sushi', T is the tree shown in Fig. 4 and N_T^* is node 14 in T, tree S_1 shown in Fig. 6 is extracted from T. Let S denote a

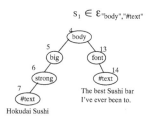

Fig. 6. Minimum connected subgraphs S_1 containing nodes 7 and 14 extracted from tree T shown in Fig. 5

set of such trees extracted from trees in training data. S is partitioned into $\{\mathcal{E}_{l,t}\}$ by values l and t of tag attribute for a root node and a target node, respectively. For example, S_1 in Fig. 4 belongs to partition $\mathcal{E}_{\text{"body","#text"}}$. Members of a pattern set $\mathcal{P}$ are created by extracting maximal common patterns (P, r) from each partition $\mathcal{E}_{l,t}$. Pattern (P, r) is said to be a *maximal common pattern* of partition $\mathcal{E}_{l,t}$ when the following conditions are satisfied.

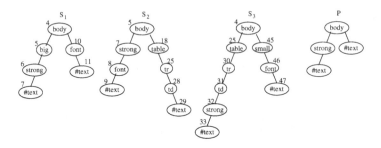

Fig. 7. A maximal common pattern of $\{S_1, S_2, S_3\}$ is $(P, 20)$

1. Tree P is a maximal tree that is embeddable in all trees belonging to $\mathcal{E}_{l,t}$.
2. Integer r is the maximum difference between two leaf node ids of trees in $\mathcal{E}_{l,t}$.

For example, in Fig. 7, $(P, 20)$ is a maximal common pattern of $\{S_1, S_2, S_3\}$.

A maximal common embeddable tree can be obtained by using TreeMiner algorithm [22] with minimum support 1.0. However, the computational time of the algorithm is exponential with respect to the size of a found maximal common tree. We can reduce the computational time by dividing the problem into two problems that finds a maximal common sequence of tag sequences from a root node to one leaf node, which can be obtained by AprioriAll [2]. The computational time of AprioriAll is still exponential with respect to the size of a found maximal common sequence, but its size is smaller than the size of a maximal common tree.

For learning a text classifier, all we have to do is generation of its training data set. Then, we can create one of conventional text classifiers by using any existing learning method for the classifier. One problem is that a training data set for a text classifier cannot be obtained directly from a given training set $\mathcal{D}$. For data (W, T, N_T^*) with $N_T^* \neq$ null, a positive training text is a concatenated text of all the texts contained in the subtree rooted by the target node N_T^*. However, it is not trivial how to extract negative training texts.

In our method, negative training texts are generated from each training data (W, T, N_T^*) using pattern set $\mathcal{P}$ that have already been learned, namely, a negative training text is a concatenated text of all the texts contained in the subtree rooted by non-target node C_T that is matched to one pattern in $\mathcal{P}$ for keyword W. In order to prevent reputations of other restaurants from being included in negative training texts, node N_T with a larger id than the id of N_T^* is not considered as above C_T.

3.4   Experiments

We conducted experiments for performance evaluation of our methods using real data. We created four data sets, Ramen (lamian, Chinese noodles in Soup),

Sushi, curry, in Sapporo and Sushi in New York. All the data sets but Sushi in New York are composed of Web pages written in Japanese. Sushi in New York is composed of Web pages written in English. Each data set is composed of Web pages collected by Google using restaurant name and its telephone number as keywords. For each data set, we collected pages for 10 restaurants that are ranked top in lists provided by some information sources[3] and that also have at least 15 retrieved Web pages. For each page retrieved by keyword W, we created a training data (W, T, N_T^*) by specifying the position of the reputation texts for W and using a HTML parser.

Table 4. Experimental data

Category	Ramen	Sushi	Curry	Sushi (NY)
#HTML	301	285	414	331
#REVIEW	189	127	265	125

In Table 4, the number of HTML pages and the number of review texts for a target restaurant in our data sets are shown. For each data set, we conducted cross validation by using data of 9 restaurants as training data and data of rest one restaurant as test data.

Table 5. Extraction performance

Category	Ramen	Sushi	Curry	Sushi (NY)
Precision (%)	73	76	70	82
Recall (%)	52	41	43	18

Extraction performance for four data sets are shown in Table 5. Note that, in our calculation of precision and recall, extracted texts are regarded as correct ones even if those are only parts of target texts. Precision for the four data sets is ranged from 70 ∼ 82%, which looks low a little. For practical use, it should be at least 90%. So, some improvements are necessary. Recall is ranged from 41 ∼ 52% except Sushi (NY). These values also look low a little because recall should be more than 50% for miner restaurants to obtain enough information. As for Sushi (NY), it suffers very low recall (18%). This is because words used in reviews depend on restaurant categories, and variance of words used in a page is large for Sushi (NY) compared to other categories.

Example of extracted texts for a Sushi restaurant in New York is shown in Table 6. In this example, only one text, which is a review for another restaurant, was wrongly extracted.

---

[3] [Ramen]: Hokkaido Walker 2002 No.3, [Sushi, curry]: Yellow Page's Palette Search (www.ypp.co.jp/search/), [Sushi (NY)]: New York metro.com (www.newyorkmetro.com/restaurants/)

Table 6. Extracted texts for a Sushi restaurant in New York (○:Correctly extracted, ×:Wrongly extracted, ******: Restaurant names)

○ A dependable choice for fresh, inexpensive Japanese food with typical sushi and sashimi options such as the hamachi yellowtail. The menu offers some surprises: for example, a not-so-typical sauted scallops with jalapeno sauce. The shitake string bean sesame is a safe bet. Recommended Dishes: Sauted Scallops with Jalapeno Sauce, $9.50; Shitake String Bean Sesame, $6.75

○ I did the Omakase and let the chef decide...with a budget of $60. I ordered (outside of the $60) the Sushi Pizza, which was fantastic. As for the sushi and sashimi, it was good, but not great. I've had better quality and creativity at ****** and ******. I only received about 8 pieces, which left me very hungry. Definitely not worth $60 plus the cost of the sushi pizza and beverages.

○ The New York Times named ****** a top pick for Sushi, calling it an "affordable neighborhood place several cuts above the ordinary". The owner brings his innovative style to this new location, which has been open for the better part of two years. ****** is proud to offer both authentic and modern dishes...

× Where else can you find modestly-priced, first-rate Thai, Vietnamese, Malaysian & Japanese (sushi bar) under one roof? You love the exotic Asian decor including the unique tables. This place has it all: variety, great prices, handsome surroundings, delicious food, and attentive service! L & D!. All cards. 242 W. 56th St. (Bdway-8th Ave.), 212-265-8588...

---

4   Related Work

There are mainly two approaches to find Web communities, densely connected subgraphs of Web graph. One is an approach of finding *cores* of communities, the most densely connected parts inside them, and the other is an approach of finding *boundaries* of communities, sparse connections between their insides and outsides. Method of finding complete bipartite subgraphs proposed by Kumar et al. [13] belongs to the former approach. Methods belonging to the latter approach are a method based on *edge betweenness* proposed by Girvan and Newman [7], and a method using *maximum flow algorithm* proposed by Flake, Lawrence, Giles [5]. Our method also belongs to the latter one, especially, based on the method using maximum flow algorithm. One merit of boundary approach is clarity of page's membership to found communities. Besides, meaning of boundaries is also clear for the method using maximum flow algorithm.

As for extraction of texts related to given keywords, there are also mainly two approaches, wrapper induction approach and natural language processing approach. The former approach uses only structure of HTML documents such as a DOM-tree [16, 4, 10, 18] and a mere character or token sequence [14, 10]. The latter approach uses information of natural language such as structure of sentences and language expressions useful to extract target information [20]. One shortcoming of wrapper induction approach is that it is basically applicable only to pages in a specific site. The natural language processing approach is mainly used to extract texts sentence by sentence, and sometimes needs to manually make language expressions used for extraction. In addition to wrapper induction approach, our method uses text information, but only information of what words appear, which is a low-level information in the area of natural language processing. Extraction unit of our method is not a sentence but a block of texts, which is also different from the method proposed by Tateishi, Ishiguro and Fukushima [20].

5 Concluding Remarks

In this paper, we introduced our methods for two specific-purpose Web searches, search for Web communities related to given keywords and search for texts having a specific relation with given keywords. The key of high performance Web search methods is how efficiently structural information is used in addition to content information. Our methods use both informations but separately. In Web community search, structural information is used to find communities and content information is used to label them. In related text search, structural information is used to find candidates and content information is used to filter out non-target texts. However, to achieve further performance improvements, hybrid methods that use both informations simultaneously should be developed, which is our future work.

Acknowledgments

We would like to thank Yoji Shidara and Hiroyuki Hasegawa for helping us to conduct experiments.

References

1. R. Agrawal and R. Srikant. First algorithms for mining association rules. In *Proc. 20th Int'l Conf. on VLDB*, pages 487–499, 1994.
2. R. Agrawal and R. Srikant. Mining sequential patterns. In *Proc. 11th Int'l Conf. on Data Eng.*, pages 3–14, 1995.
3. R. Baeza-Yates and B. Ribriro-Neto. *Modern Information Retrieval.* ACM Press, New York, NY, 1999.
4. W. W. Cohen, M. Hurst, and L. S. Jensen. A flexible learning system for wrapping tables and lists in html documents. In *Proc. of 11th Int'l World Wide Web Conf.*, pages 232–241, 2002.
5. G. Flake, S. Lawrence, and C.Giles. Efficient identification of web communities. In *Proceedings of the 6th ACM SIGKDD International Conference on Knowledge Discovery and Data Mining*, pages 150–160, 2000.
6. G. Flake, R. Tarjan, and K. Tsioutsiouliklis. Graph clustering and mining cut trees. *Internet Mathematics*, 1(3):355–378, 2004.
7. M. Girvan and M. Newman. Community structure in social and biological networks. *Proc. Natl. Acad. Sci. USA*, 99:7821–7826, 2002.
8. H. Hasagawa, M. Kudo, and A. Nakamura. Empirical study on usefulness of algorithm sacwrapper for reputation extraction from the www. In *Proceedings of the 9th International Conference on Knowledge-Based & Intelligent Information & Engineering Systems*, 2005. To appear.

9. H. Hasagawa, M. Kudo, and A. Nakamura. Reputation extraction using both structural and content information. Technical Report TCS-TR-A-05-2, Division of Computer Science, Hokkaido university, 2005. http://www-alg.ist.hokudai.ac.jp/tra.html.

10. D. Ikeda, Y. Yamada, and S. Hirokawa. Expressive power of tree and string based wrappers. In *Proc. of IJCAI-03 Workshop on Information Integration on the Web (IIWeb-03)*, pages 21–26, 2003.

11. H. Ino, M. Kudo, and A. Nakamura. Partitioning of web graphs by community topology. In *Proceedings of WWW2005*, pages 661–669, 2005.

12. J. Kleinberg. Authoritative sources in a hyperlinked environment. *Journal of the ACM*, 46(5):604–632, 1999.

13. R. Kumar, P. Raghavan, S. Rajagopalan, and A. Tomkins. Trawling the web for emerging cyber-communities. *Computer Networks*, 31(11-16):1481–1493, 1999.

14. N. Kushmerick. Wrapper induction:efficiency and expressiveness. *Artificial Intelligence*, 118:15–68, 2000.

15. R. Mitton. A description of a computer-usable dictionary file based on the oxford advanced learner's dictionary of current english, June 1992. Downloaded from ftp://sable.ox.ac.uk/pub/ota/public/dicts/710/.

16. Y. Murakami, H. Sakamoto, H. Arimura, and S. Arikawa. Extracting text data from html documents. *The Information Processing Society of Japan (IPSJ) Transactions on Mathematical Modeling and its Applications (TOM)*, 42(SIG 14(TOM 5)):39–49, 2001. In Japanese.

17. A. Nakamura, T. Shigezumi, and M. Yamamoto. On nk-community problem. In *Proceedings of the Winter LA Symposium*, pages 12.1–12.8, 2005.

18. T. Sugibuchi and Y. Tanaka. Interactive web-wrapper construction for extracting relational information from web documents. In *Proceedings of WWW2005*, pages 968–969, 2005.

19. R. Tarjan. *Data Structure and Network Algorithm*. Society for Industrial and Applied Mathematics, 1983.

20. K. Tateishi, Y. Ishiguro, and T. Fukushima. A reputation search engine that collects people's opinions by information extraction technology. *The Information Processing Society of Japan (IPSJ) Transactions on Databases (TOD)*, 45(SIG 07), 2004. In Japanese.

21. T. Uno, T. Asai, Y. Uchida, and H. Arimura. Efficient mining algorithms for frequent/closed/maximal itemsets. In *Proceedings of FIMI04*, 2004.

22. M. J. Zaki. Efficiently mining frequent trees in a forest. In *Proc. SIGKDD'02*, pages 71–80, 2002.

Graph Clustering Based on Structural Similarity of Fragments

Tetsuya Yoshida[1], Ryosuke Shoda[2], and Hiroshi Motoda[2]

[1] Graduate School of Information Science and Technology,
Hokkaido University,
N-14 W-9, Sapporo 060-0814, Japan
`yoshida@meme.hokudai.ac.jp`
[2] Institute of Scientific and Industrial Research, Osaka University,
8-1 Mihogaoka, Ibaraki, Osaka 567-0047, Japan
{`shoda, motoda`}`@ar.sanken.osaka-u.ac.jp`

Abstract. Resources available over the Web are often used in combination to meet a specific need of a user. Since resource combinations can be represented as graphs in terms of the relations among the resources, locating desirable resource combinations can be formulated as locating the corresponding graph. This paper describes a graph clustering method based on structural similarity of fragments (currently, connected subgraphs are considered) in graph-structured data. A fragment is characterized based on the connectivity (degree) of a node in the fragment. A fragment spectrum of a graph is created based on the frequency distribution of fragments. Thus, the representation of a graph is transformed into a fragment spectrum in terms of the properties of fragments in the graph. Graphs are then clustered with respect to the transformed spectra by applying a standard clustering method. We also devise a criterion to determine the number of clusters by defining a pseudo-entropy for clusters. Preliminary experiments with synthesized data were conducted and the results are reported.

1 Introduction

1.1 Motivation

A huge number of (computing) resources are now available over the Web. Users may select some of these resources by exploiting relations among them. For example, URLs represent resources available over the Web, connected to each other by hyperlinks as shown on the left-hand side of Fig. 1 (hyperlinks, depicted as dotted lines, are directed edges). Suppose that the pattern comprising URLs {K, M, A, B} is frequently observed in a log file of Web browsing. When a user follows or selects URLs {K, M, A}, it is likely that he/she may select URL B. Thus, by discovering the pattern shown on the right in Fig. 1, it will be possible to help users to select or locate further resources by recommending other resources that appear in the pattern. As another example, Web citation analysis is reported and compared with bibliographical citation analysis in [12].

K.P. Jantke et al. (Eds.): Federation over the Web, LNAI 3847, pp. 97–114, 2006.

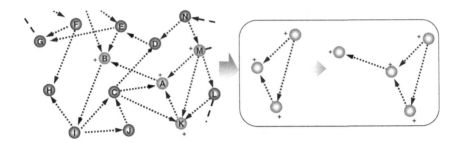

Fig. 1. Example of resource selection (web browsing pattern)

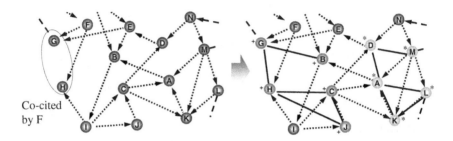

Fig. 2. Example of co-citation graph

Although URLs G and H are not connected to each other directly, they are both pointed to (cited) by F. Thus, G and H are co-cited by F, as shown on the left-hand side of Fig. 2. In terms of this kind of co-citation relation, URLs are (implicitly) connected to each other as shown on the right in Fig. 2 (co-citation relations, depicted as thick lines, are undirected edges). Once co-citation graphs are constructed, various analyses can be conducted on the graphs. For instance, URLs H and A might be interesting because they each have a large number of co-citation relations.

As illustrated in the above examples, since resource combinations can be represented as graphs in terms of the relations among the resources, locating desirable resource combinations can be formulated as locating the corresponding graph. In our approach it is assumed that relations among resources are specified externally, such as hyperlinks or co-citation relations; how to define relations among resources to construct appropriate graph-structured data is beyond the scope of this research. When a user tries to locate desirable resource combinations, the ultimate goal of this research is to support the selection of resource combinations in terms of graph structures over the resources.

1.2   Mining Graph-Structured Data

Various research efforts have addressed the extraction of knowledge from the vast body of unstructured Web data [2]. The majority of widely used data mining methods are for data that does not have structure, and is represented by attribute-value pairs. Decision trees [14, 15] and induction rules [10, 3] relate attribute values to target classes. Association rules often used in data mining also utilize this attribute-value pair representation. However, the attribute-value pair representation is not suitable for representing a more general data structure, and there are problems that need a more powerful representation. The most powerful representation, capable of handling relations and therefore structure, would be inductive logic programming (ILP) [11] based on first-order predicate logic. It can represent general relationships embedded in data, and has the merit that domain knowledge and acquired knowledge can be utilized as background knowledge. However, in exchange for its rich expressibility it has problems of time complexity [5].

On the other hand, any structure that can be represented as a relation can be considered as a graph. Therefore, knowledge discovery from such structures can be addressed as a case of discovery from graph-structured data. Various research approaches such as AGM [6], FSG [7], Subdue [4] have been pursued for mining from graph-structured data. Some applications of graph mining are the finding of typical Web browsing patterns, identifying typical substructures of chemical compounds, finding typical subsequences of DNA, and discovering diagnostic rules from patient-history records.

We have applied our graph mining method called GBI [8] to extract typical patterns from the hepatitis dataset provided by Chiba University Hospital in the Active Mining project [9, 20]. GBI extracts connected subgraphs from graph-structured data by conducting greedy search without backtrack. Because of its greedy search, it can handle large-scale graph-structured data. One drawback of its search strategy is that search is incomplete in the sense that not all the subgraphs are enumerated. One of the problems we encountered in the project is that a huge number of patterns (connected subgraphs, in our approach) can be extracted from large-scale graph-structured data by applying our method. The number of extracted subgraphs will be even greater, and the problem more severe, if one applies methods that conduct complete search for subgraphs. Thus, although patterns can be extracted from graph-structured data by applying graph mining methods, it becomes very difficult to evaluate all the extracted patterns.

1.3   Clustering Graph-Structured Data

Although the number of graphs to be considered can be huge, some components of graphs share structural properties. For example, chemical compounds that include a benzene ring (aromatic compounds) have similar chemical properties because they share the benzene ring. This motivates a research branch of computational chemistry called (quantitative) structure activity relationships. In QSAR, the relationship between the property or activity of chemical compounds and their structure has been studied. As another example, starting from the pioneering work in [19], much research has been carried out showing that many graphs or networks can be categorized as so-called "small world" networks in terms of their structure [1]. Small-world networks share the properties that, although nodes are densely connected locally with their neighbors, the overall average path length between two nodes in the network is relatively short due to the existence of some edges connecting distant nodes.

By assuming that graphs with similar structure share some properties, in this research we aim at clustering graph-structured data based on their structural similarity. When graphs are categorized into clusters, a small number of graphs can be selected from each cluster as representatives. As in the research on small-world networks, we consider the structural properties of a graph in terms of connectivity (degree) of nodes in the graph, and transform the graph representation graph into a corresponding spectrum. This transformation into a spectrum acts as a kind of hash function. Thus, if a user can specify the desirable resource combinations as a graph, our method can be utilized to discriminate the graphs of resource combinations into similar and dissimilar ones in terms of their corresponding spectra. Graphs are then clustered with respect to the transformed spectra by applying a standard clustering method. We also propose a method, based on our notion of pseudo-entropy of a cluster, to determine the appropriate number of clusters to create. Preliminary experiments on synthetic data were conducted; the results are reported in this paper.

As described in Sect. 1.2, this research is motivated by the application of GBI, which can handle general graph data with both directed and undirected edges. However, as a first step, only undirected graphs are considered in this paper, and labels of nodes and edges are not dealt with yet. The graph structure currently handled corresponds to the example in Fig. 2. Since labels are not yet dealt with, the two co-citation graphs on the right of Fig. 2 are considered as isomorphic, and are categorized into the same cluster. Thus the work reported here is preliminary in nature, since we do not yet deal with resources' content (e.g., the text within a Web page). However, filtering out graphs with respect to structure can be utilized as preprocessing for more fine-grained and detailed analysis of contents.

Various existing research has addressed similarity measures and clustering methods for graph-structured data. Related work includes Topological Fragment Spectra (TFS) [17] which characterizes the properties of chemical compounds in terms of fragments (subgraphs) within the compounds. ANF [13] is an approach to the fast calculation of similarity for large-scale graph-structured data. Our method is motivated by TFS, but differs in two respects: 1) calculation of fragment spectra, and 2) extension to clustering of spectra.

Organization. This paper is organized as follows: Section 2 describes a method for representing the properties of a graph as a spectrum of fragments (subgraphs). Experiments on the calibration of the proposed fragment spectrum are also reported. Section 3 describes the clustering of fragment spectra and a method for determining the number of clusters. Preliminary experiments with synthetic data are reported in Section 4. Brief concluding remarks and future directions are given in Section 5.

2   Fragment Spectrum of a Graph

2.1   Preliminaries

A simple graph is denoted by $G = (V, E)$ where V is a set of vertices and $E \subseteq V \times V$ a set of (undirected) edges in G. For any vertices v, $v' \in V$, if $(v, v') \in E$, v is said to be adjacent to v'. Let $G = (V, E)$ be a graph. For a vertex $v \in V$, the set of vertices adjacent to v is denoted by $N_G(v)$. $|N_G(v)|$, the size of $N_G(v)$, is called the degree of v with respect to G. $|N_G(v)|$ is also referred to as $degree_G(v)$. Let $G = (V, E)$ and $G' = (V', E')$ be two graphs. G is called a subgraph of G' when $V \subseteq V'$ and $E \subseteq E'$, and is denoted as $G \subseteq G'$.

2.2   Fragment Spectrum

Similarity measures for graphs can be categorized into two approaches: the direct-comparison approach and the fingerprint-based approach [16]. In the former approach, the similarity between two graphs is measured either using their maximum common subgraphs or the maximum common edge subgraphs. The maximum common subgraphs are identified in the two graphs, and the sizes (either the number of nodes or of edges) of these subgraphs are used to measure the similarity. Although the similarity can be measured directly on the graphs, exact identification of the maximum common subgraphs can be very expensive in practice. On the other hand, in the latter approach, a graph is represented as a bit string, each bit indicating the presence or absence of a predefined substructure (which acts as a key descriptor). The similarity between two graphs is measured by comparing their corresponding bit strings. Although the fingerprint-based approach requires selection of the key descriptor, we take this approach since it is simple, and is easy to put into practice.

We aim to capture structural properties of a graph based on the fragments within the graph, and represent it as a fragment spectrum[1]. Currently a fragment of a graph is defined as a connected subgraph in the graph. Hereafter, we consider only connected subgraphs. Figure 3 shows an example of the construction of a fragment spectrum using our approach. The score of a fragment in a graph G is calculated by a function FScore, which is explained in Sect. 2.3. The graph in Fig. 3 has one fragment with score 1, three fragments with score 5, three fragments with score 6, etc. Based on the frequency of fragments with the same score, the fragment spectrum for the graph is represented as a vector $fs = (0, 0, 1, 4, 3, \ldots)$, where $fs[i]$ represents the frequency (count) of fragments with score i. Pseudo-code for constructing a fragment spectrum is shown in Fig. 4.

2.3   FScore Function

A fragment F in a graph G is characterized as a score by a function called FScore, based on the fragment's connectivity. Each node v in a fragment F is scored based on its degree, and the score of F is calculated from the scores of its nodes. We consider the following two measures of 'degree' for a node $v \in F$:

---

[1] The name "fragment spectrum" follows the work on Topological Fragment Spectra (TFS) [17].

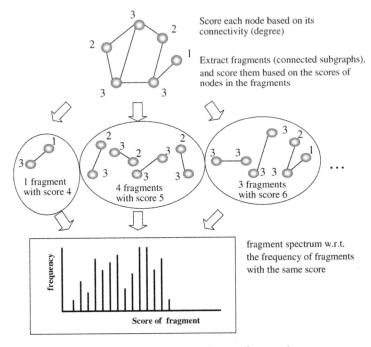

Fig. 3. Fragment spectrum of a graph

fragment_spectrum(graph G)
  fs: fragment spectrum of G
  initialize fs to **0**
  forall fragment (connected subgraph) $F \in G$
    $fs[\mathbf{FScore}(F, G)] := fs[\mathbf{FScore}(F, G)] + 1$
  return fs

Fig. 4. Fragment spectrum construction

– degree solely within the fragment
– degree within the original graph

The former follows the standard definition of degree in a graph, and focuses on the connectivity solely in the fragment. However, the degree in a fragment is invariant with respect to the graph containing that fragment. To reflect differences between the original graphs, the latter measure considers the degree within the original graph, in the expectation that that the relationship of F to the remaining part of G works as a sort of context of F within G.

In addition, the difference between the scores of nodes can be magnified using polynomials of the score. The score of a fragment is calculated based on the scores of the fragment's nodes, using one of the following methods:

– sum of the scores of nodes
– square sum of the scores of nodes

Table 1. FScore function

	degree of node	
	original graph	fragment
sum	FScore1	–
square sum	FScore3	FScore2

FScore functions to calculate the score of a fragment are summarized in Table 1. With the combination of "sum" and "fragment", the fragments with the same number of nodes and edges have the same score regardless of their structure or connectivity. Thus, since it does not reflect structural properties of the graph, it is not considered and thus is left blank (–) in the table.

The number of fragments in a graph G increases exponentially with respect to its size (the number of nodes and edges). Thus, it becomes difficult to compare spectra of graphs with different size since the overall shape of the spectra can be very different. To make it easy to compare fragment spectra of graphs with different size, a normalized fragment spectrum is defined by dividing each value (frequency of fragments) in the fragment spectrum by the total number of fragments in the graph. Note that currently normalization is considered only for the frequency of fragments. Normalization of scores is not yet considered.

In summary, six FScore functions (three variations in Table 1, and their corresponding normalizations NFScore1, NFScore2, NFScore3) are currently used.

2.4   Calibration of Fragment Spectrum

This section reports the experiments on the calibration of the proposed fragment spectrum, to verify that graphs with different structure can be differentiated with respect to the corresponding fragment spectra. Four types of graph structure are considered: line, ring, ring lattice and star. Graphs with these structures are prepared such that the average path length between two nodes, which corresponds to the characteristic path length in small-world networks [19], decreases in the order of line, ring, ring lattice and star structure. To simplify the calibration, relatively small graphs of these types were prepared, as shown in Figs. 5, 6, 7 and 8.

For graphs with the same number of nodes, a graph with line structure and one with ring structure differ only by a single edge. Thus these two structures can be considered as being very similar. The ring lattice structure in Fig.7 corresponds to the β model in [18]. It is similar to the ring structure, but each node is connected to k neighbors (here, k was set to 4). On the other hand, a star structure is different from these in terms of connectivity, since a graph with star structure has one "central" node which is connected to all the other nodes. When each node corresponds to a scientific paper, and the relations among nodes are defined as co-citation relations (similar to the example in Fig. 2), a node that appears at the center of a star may represent a seminal paper.

Examples of fragment spectra for these graphs are shown in the appendix. For instance, using the NFScore3 function described above, spectra of graphs with star structure in Fig. 8 have peak band elements (normalized frequencies)

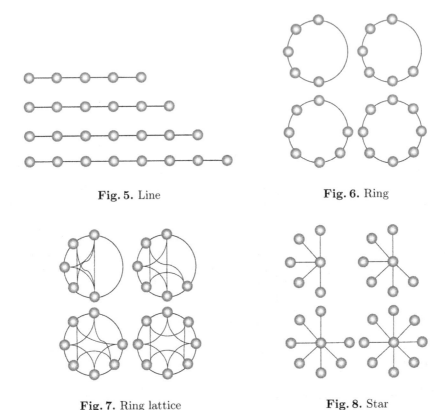

Fig. 5. Line   **Fig. 6.** Ring

Fig. 7. Ring lattice   **Fig. 8.** Star

at the tail of the spectra[2], as shown in Fig. 21. Thus, if the maximal value of score is known for each graph, or the spectrum is normalized with respect to the score, a high-pass filter for fragment spectra might be useful for extracting from a collection of graphs those that have star structure.

Spectra for the 8-node graphs in Figs. 5, 6, 7 and 8 are compared in Fig. 9. Fragment spectra were created using NFScore3 (a normalized score function was used to reveal the overall shape of spectra). The graph with ring structure has an almost flat spectrum (upper right in Fig. 9), because the frequency of fragments for each score is almost the same. The graphs with line structure and ring structure are quite similar in terms of the number of nodes or common subgraphs. The spectrum of the former also has flat components, but it includes additional components with decreasing relative frequency. Using NFScore3, the graph with ring-lattice structure (lower left) has just a few elements with growing frequencies. The graph with star structure (lower right) has a peak band, which arises because the central node has a large score (degree) compared to the other nodes; since the scores of fragments in a star graph differ only with respect to the number of non-central nodes, they tend to be very similar.

---

[2] As described in the appendix, horizontal axes (score of fragment) are aligned to the maximal score in the rightmost graph in each figure.

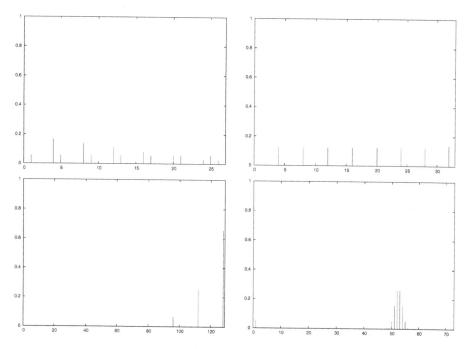

Fig. 9. Fragment spectra of graphs with eight nodes using NFScore3 (upper left: line (Fig. 5), upper right: ring (Fig. 6), lower left: ring lattice (Fig. 7) lower right: star (Fig. 8))

From this result, it can be said that fragment spectra of graphs with different structure also tend to have rather different shape or pattern. Thus, the score functions can be used as a kind of hash function to discriminate graphs with different structure. However, graphs with different spectra can be considered as different, but different graphs may come to the same spectrum when a hash collision occurs, as in many hash functions. Thus, we do not claim that fragment spectra alone are enough to differentiate graphs with different structures.

3   Clustering Fragment Spectra

After transforming the representation of graphs into the corresponding fragment spectra by the method in Sect. 2, graphs are clustered with respect to the transformed spectra by applying a standard clustering method. Among various clustering methods, we simply utilize the K-means method with respect to the similarity of fragment spectra. Our main contribution for clustering is to devise a criterion to determine the number of clusters, since the number of clusters must be specified beforehand in many clustering methods. Inspired by the divide-and-conquer strategy in decision tree construction algorithms [14, 15], we view clustering of data as the division of the whole data into the specified number of clusters. By defining a pseudo-entropy for a cluster, the quality of clustering is measured as the information gain ratio [15] in the clustered data relative to its unclustered state.

3.1   Similarity of Fragment Spectra

A spectrum is conceived as a vector in a multi-dimensional space, where each dimension corresponds to a fragment score and the value represents the frequency or normalized frequency of fragments with that score. When comparing two fragment spectra of different dimensions (scores), the one with smaller dimension is padded with zeroes for the larger dimensions. By regarding the spectra as vectors, it might be possible to utilize similarity measures for vectors such as cosine similarity. However, toward incorporating nominal attributes such as labels of nodes and edges in future work, currently similarity is measured for each dimension separately and averaged. Similarity in one dimension is calculated by projecting the vector onto the corresponding dimension, and measured as the relative range of the projection, as shown in Fig. 10. Our similarity measure of graphs G_i and G_j in terms of their spectra is defined as:

$$S_{ij} = \frac{1}{M} \sum_{m=1}^{M} (1 - \frac{|\boldsymbol{fs}_{im} - \boldsymbol{fs}_{jm}|}{\max \boldsymbol{fs}_m - \min \boldsymbol{fs}_m}) \tag{1}$$

$\boldsymbol{fs}_{im}$: mth coordinate value of $\boldsymbol{fs}_i$ for graph G_i
$\max \boldsymbol{fs}_m$: maximal value for the mth coordinate for all spectra
$\min \boldsymbol{fs}_m$: minimal value for the mth coordinate for all spectra
M: maximal dimension for all the spectra

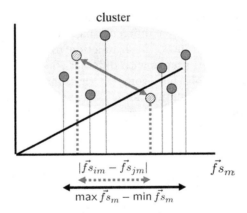

Fig. 10. Similarity of spectra

3.2   Pseudo-Entropy of a Cluster

A machine learning method C4.5 [15], which constructs a decision tree, selects an attribute to divide the data based on the entropy of data before and after the division. We apply this approach to determine the number of clusters by defining a pseudo-entropy of data in clustering. Figure 11 illustrates our notion of pseudo-entropy of a cluster. In the standard concept of entropy, concentrated data has low entropy while scattered data has high entropy. However, we regard a cluster with concentrated data as good, since it certainly forms a cluster of data, but we also regard a cluster with scattered data as good, since it is difficult to further divide them into (meaningful) sub-clusters. Thus, we would like to give low pseudo-entropy to these clusters. On the other hand, if the data inside a cluster is rather separated, as shown on the right in Fig. 11, we regard it as bad since it is possible to further divide the cluster. Thus, we would like to give high pseudo-entropy to this kind of cluster.

We define a pseudo-entropy of cluster C_k as $PEnt(C_k)$ such that it has low value either when data is evenly distributed in a cluster or when all the data concentrate on a small portion in a cluster, as follows:

$$PEnt(C_k) = -\frac{1}{\mid C_k \mid^2} \sum_{i=1}^{|C_k|} \sum_{j=1}^{|C_k|} (S_{ij} \log_2 S_{ij} + (1 - S_{ij}) \log_2 (1 - S_{ij})) \quad (2)$$

$PEnt(C_k)$: pseudo-entropy of cluster C_k
$|C_k|$:   size (number) of data in cluster C_k
$S_{ij} \in [0,1]$:   similarity of fragment spectrum $\boldsymbol{fs_i}$ and $\boldsymbol{fs_j}$

$PEnt(C_k)$ is calculated based on the pair-wise comparison of data within the cluster. $S_{ij} \in [0,1]$ corresponds to the similarity of two data (spectra of graphs G_i and G_j) within the cluster, and $D_{ij} = 1 - S_{ij}$ corresponds to the dissimilarity.

Intuitively, when comparing two graphs G_i and G_j, let's consider an event I where G_i and G_j are isomorphic. Also, let's consider an event N where G_i and G_j are not isomorphic. These two events are mutually exclusive. Since $S_{ij} \in [0,1]$, $D_{ij} \in [0,1]$, and $S_{ij} + D_{ij} = 1$, we treat S_{ij} as the probability of the event I and $D_{ij} = 1 - S_{ij}$ as the probability of the event N. The value $-(S_{ij} \log_2 S_{ij} + (1 - S_{ij}) \log_2 (1 - S_{ij})) = -(S_{ij} \log_2 S_{ij} + D_{ij} \log_2 D_{ij})$ corresponds to the binary entropy function for a binary random variable, whose value is I with probability S_{ij} and N with probability D_{ij}. The average of this value for all pair-wise comparisons of data in a cluster is calculated in (2).

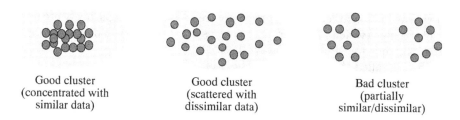

Good cluster
(concentrated with
similar data)

Good cluster
(scattered with
dissimilar data)

Bad cluster
(partially
similar/dissimilar)

Fig. 11. Pseudo-entropy of cluster

When all the data in a cluster are the same, and concentrated on a single point in multi-dimensional space, $S_{ij} = 1$ for all pairs of data in the cluster, so the numerator of (2) becomes 0 and the pseudo-entropy is minimized. Likewise, when all the data in a cluster are completely dissimilar ($S_{ij} = 0$) and scattered within the cluster, the numerator also becomes 0. On the other hand, when the data are partially similar and dissimilar to each other ($S_{ij} = 0.5$), the numerator is maximized.

3.3   Information Gain Ratio for Cluster

Based on the difference of pseudo-entropy of cluster in (2) before (i.e., the whole unclustered data) and after clustering, we define an information gain ratio of cluster (IGRC) for the situation where the data are assigned to K clusters as:

$$IGRC = \frac{PEnt(C) - \sum_{k=1}^{K} \frac{|C_k|}{|C|} PEnt(C_k)}{-\sum_{k=1}^{K} \frac{|C_k|}{|C|} \log_2 \frac{|C_k|}{|C|}} \tag{3}$$

$PEnt(C_k)$: pseudo-entropy of cluster C_k
$PEnt(C)$: pseudo-entropy of the whole unclustered data

Note that when each data item is assigned to a cluster containing only that item, the numerator of (3) is maximized since the entropy of each cluster is 0. Thus, to penalize such an over-clustered situation, the difference is divided by the split gain of clustering as in C4.5 [15].

Our criterion for the number of clusters is to select the number of clusters which maximizes the value of IGRC. This criterion is used in the experiments reported in the following section.

4   Preliminary Experiment

Preliminary experiments were conducted to evaluate the proposed method over synthetic data. This section explains experimental settings and reports the results.

4.1   Synthetic Data

In experiments, synthetic data (graphs) were created by preparing a predefined set of graphs (which we refer to below as base graphs) and appending the subgraphs shown in Fig. 12. The synthesized graphs are called derived graphs. The base graphs are prepared with respect to 1) the number of nodes and edges, and 2) configuration. The following two experiments were conducted:

Fig. 12. Appended subgraphs

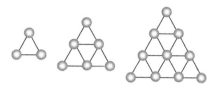

Fig. 13. Example of graphs in Exp.1

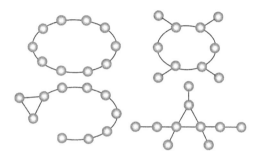

Fig. 14. Examples of graphs in Exp.2

Exp.1. number of nodes and edges: graphs with different numbers of nodes and edges but similar configuration

Exp.2. configuration: graphs with dissimilar configurations but the same number of nodes and edges

Base graphs used in Exp.1 and Exp.2 are shown in Figs. 13 and 14, respectively. The number of graphs (with the base graphs and derived graphs) was 18 in Exp.1 and 61 in Exp.2. One drawback in the above setting is that, despite much research, it is not yet known what constitutes the "correct" measure of similarity/dissimilarity of graph configurations. Thus, when preparing graphs in Exp.2, similarity is based on our subjective assessment.

4.2   Results

Six functions from Sect. 2 were used to create fragment spectra for the graphs in Exp.1 and Exp.2. The spectra were then clustered by K-means by setting K so as to obtain the maximal value of IGRC. If the structural properties of graphs are to be reflected on the number of nodes/edges and the configuration, we hypothesized that graphs should be categorized into clusters such that each cluster includes only the graphs that share the same base graph. Thus, the desirable value of K would be 3 for Exp.1 and 4 for Exp.2. The number of clusters K with the maximal value of IGRC in the experiments is summarized in Table 2. Changes of IGRC with NFScore1 for Exp.1 and Exp.2 are shown in Figs. 15 and 16 respectively.

In Exp.1, the desired value of K (K=3) was obtained with NFScore1 and NFScore3. In addition, the graphs were clustered as intended, in the sense that

Table 2. k with maximal IGRC

FScore function	k with maximal IGRC	
	Exp.1	Exp.2
FScore1	9	2
FScore2	2,3	2
FScore3	8	17
NFScore1	3	2
NFScore2	2	2
NFScore3	3	2

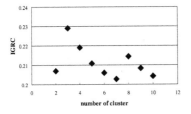
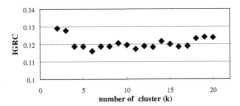

Fig. 15. IGRC in Exp.1 (with NFScore1) **Fig. 16.** IGRC in Exp.2 (with NFScore1)

all the graphs with the same base graph were categorized into the same cluster. On the other hand, except for FScore3, K=2 gave the maximal value of IGRC in Exp.2, and the hypothesized value (K=4) was not attained.

4.3   Discussion

From Table 2, it can be said that normalized score functions gave better clustering. The number of subgraphs in a graph G increases exponentially with respect to its size (the number of nodes and edges). Thus, as the size of graph increases, the similarity of graphs that share some base graph tends to decrease since the difference in the frequency of fragments with the same score gets larger in (1). This results in categorizing the graphs into different clusters. Normalization contributed to reducing this effect. On the other hand, with FScore2 and NFScore2, which use the degree of a node within the (extracted) fragment, the maximal value of IGRC was obtained at K=2 for both Exp.1 and Exp.2. Thus, these functions were not effective for clustering graphs with respect to configuration. This indicated that considering the degree of each node in the context of the original graph may be effective in reflecting structural properties of fragments.

As described above, the value of IGRC was maximized at K=2 except for FScore3 in Exp.2. Figure 17 illustrates the clustered graphs with NFScore1. As shown in that figure, all the graphs that share the same base graph were assigned into the same cluster, not split between clusters. However, our criterion (maximization of IGRC) could not divide the clusters into smaller ones.

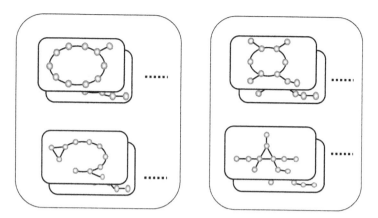

Fig. 17. Clustered graphs in Exp.2

The two graphs on the left in Fig. 14 were categorized into the same cluster. One possible conjecture is that a graph with ring structure can be rewritten into the other graph just by removing one edge and adding it as another edge. If these graphs are considered as similar in terms of rewriting operations for graphs[3], the desirable number of clusters may be considered as 3. In the previous result, the value at K=3 is similar to the value at K=2 with NFScore1, albeit that it was not the maximal. Still, the results of Exp.2 indicate that much work needs to be done to improve our clustering method with respect to configuration.

5 Concluding Remarks

This paper has described a graph clustering method based on structural similarity of fragments (currently, connected subgraphs are considered) in graph-structured data. The representation of a graph is transformed into a fragment spectrum which represents the frequency distribution of fragments, in terms of the connectivity of a node within the fragment. The graphs are then clustered by applying a standard clustering method (K-means) with respect to the transformed fragment spectra. The quality of clustering is estimated based on a pseudo-entropy for a cluster, in order to determine the number of clusters. Preliminary experiments with synthesized graphs were conducted and the results reported. The results indicate that our method can cluster graph-structured data with respect to the number of nodes and edges, but much further work is needed with respect to the configuration. Especially, the number of clusters tends to be under-estimated by our criterion. Currently our method only deals with superficial similarities in structure; we would like to extend the method to incorporate node and edge labels, so that resource combinations over the Web can be considered in terms of their contents.

---

[3] A kind of edit-distance measure is used in Subdue [4] for inexact graph matching.

Acknowledgments

The authors are grateful to the editors for fruitful discussions to refine this paper. They also gratefully acknowledge the enormous help by Takashi Matsuda for his advice on the implementation and experiments. This work was partially supported by grants-in-aid for scientific research (No. 60002309, No. 13131206) funded by the Japanese Ministry of Education, Culture, Sport, Science and Technology.

References

1. L.A.N. Amaral, A. Scala, M. Barthélémy, and H. E. Stanley. Classes of small-world networks. *Proceedings of the National Academy of Sciences*, 97(21):11149–11152, 2000.
2. S. Chakrabarti. *Mining the Web: Discovering Knowledge from Hypertext Data*. Morgan Kaufmann, 2002.
3. P. Clark and Niblett T. The cn2 induction algorithm. *Machine Learning*, 3:261–283, 1989.
4. D. J. Cook and L. B. Holder. Graph-based data mining. *IEEE Intelligent Systems*, 15(2):32–41, 2000.
5. L. Dehaspe, H. Toivonen, and R. D. King. Finding frequent substructures in chemical compound. In *Proc. the 4th International conference on Knowledge Discovery and Data Mining*, pages 30–36, 1998.
6. A. Inokuchi, T. Washio, and H. Motoda. Complete mining of frequent patterns from graphs: Mining graph data. *Machine Learning*, 50(3):321–354, 2003.
7. M. Kuramochi and G.Karypis. Frequent subgraph discovery. In *Proc. of the 1st IEEE ICDM*, pages 313–320, 2001.
8. T. Matsuda, H. Motoda, T. Yoshida, and T. Washio. Mining patterns from structured data by beam-wise graph-based induction. In *Proc. of The Fifth International Conference on Discovery Science*, pages 422–429, 2002.
9. T. Matsuda, T. Yoshida, H. Motoda, and T. Washio. Beam-wise graph-based induction for structured data mining. In *International Workshop on Active Mining (AM-2002): working notes*, pages 23–30, 2002.
10. R. S. Michalski. Learning flexible concepts: Fundamental ideas and a method based on two-tiered representaion. *Machine Learning: An Artificial Intelligence Approach*, 3:63–102, 1990.
11. S. Muggleton and L. de Raedt. Inductive logic programming: Theory and methods. *Journal of Logic Programming*, 19(20):629–679, 1994.
12. S. Nomura, T. Miki, and T. Ishida. Comparative Study of Web Citation Analysis and Bibliographical Citation Analysis in Community Mining. *IEICE Transaction*, J87-D-I(3):382–389, 2004. (in Japanese).
13. C.R. Palmer, P.B. Gibbons, and C. Faloutsos. ANF: A fast and scalable tool for data mining in massive graphs. In *Proc. of the KDD-2002*, 2002.
14. J. R. Quinlan. Induction of decision trees. *Machine Learning*, 1:81–106, 1986.
15. J. R. Quinlan. *C4.5:Programs For Machine Learning*. Morgan Kaufmann Publishers, 1993.
16. J.W. Raymond, C.J. Blankley, and P. Willett. Comparison of chemical clustering methods using graph- and fingerprint-based similarity measures. *Molecular Graphics and Modelling*, 21(5):421–433, 2003.

17. Y. Takahashi, H. Ohoka, and Y. Ishiyama. Structural similarity analysis based on topological fragement spectra. *Adavances in Molecular Similarity*, 2:93–104, 1998.

18. D.J. Watts. *Small Worlds: The Dynamics of Networks Between Order and Randomness*. Princeton University Press, 2004.

19. D.J. Watts and S. H. Strogatz. Collective dynamics of 'small-world' networks. *Nature*, 393:440–442, 1998.

20. T. Yoshida, G. Warodom, A. Mogi, K. Ohara, H. Motoda, T. Washio, H. Yokoi, and K. Takabayashi. Preliminary analysis of interferon therapy by graph-based induction. In *Working note of International Workshop on Active Mining (AM-2004)*, pages 31–40, 2004.

Appendix: Examples of Fragment Spectrum

Fragment spectra of graphs shown in Figs. 5, 6, 7 and 8 are shown in Figs. 18, 19, 20 and 21, respectively. For each type of graph, the horizontal axes (fragment score) are aligned to the maximal score in the rightmost graph in each figure. To see the overall shape of spectra, normalized score functions are used to create fragment spectra and thus the maximal value of vertical axis is set to 1.0. Since the normalized frequency in NFScore1 is the same as that in NFScore3 (except that the x-axis is rather stretched out since the score of each node is square summed), NFScore2 and NFScore3 are used to create the spectra. Figs. 18,

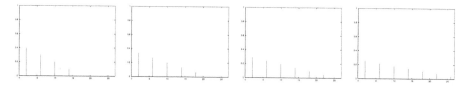

Fig. 18. Spectra for graphs with line structure (with NFScore2)

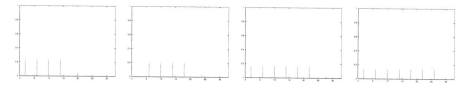

Fig. 19. Spectra for graphs with ring structure (with NFScore2)

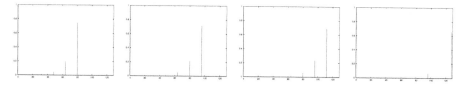

Fig. 20. Spectra for graphs with ring lattice structure (with NFScore3)

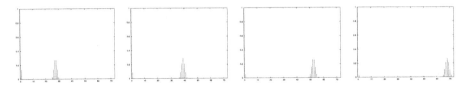

Fig. 21. Spectra for graphs with star structure (with NFScore3)

19, 20 and 21 indicate that fragment spectra of graphs with the same structure have similar shape or pattern, and that fragment spectra of graphs with different structure also tend to have rather different patterns in terms of the corresponding spectra.

Connecting Keywords Through Pointer Paths over the Web

Mina Akaishi[1], Nicolas Spyratos[2], Koichi Hori[1], and Yuzuru Tanaka[3]

[1] Rcast, University of Tokyo,
4-6-1 Komaba Meguro-ku Tokyo 153-8904, Japan
{akaishi, hori}@ai.rcast.u-tokyo.ac.jp
[2] Laboratoire de Recherche en Informatique, Université de Paris-Sud,
LRI-Bât 490, 91405 Orsay Cedex, France
spyratos@lri.fr
[3] Meme Media Laboratory, Hokkaido University, Japan
tanaka@meme.hokudai.ac.jp

Abstract. We propose a framework for discovering connections from a source keyword to a target keyword through the Web pages containing them. We are interested in connections provided by pointer paths leading from a source page to a target page (a source page being a page containing the source keyword, and a target page being a page containing the target keyword). Each such path provides an "explanation" of the connection, and the set of all such paths is considered as the "semantics" of the connection.

When one talks about federation in the context of the Web, one usually means connecting a number of Web resources to cooperate towards a common goal. A complementary though less known aspect is that of *discovering* federations of Web resources by interpreting the pointer paths connecting them. The work presented in this paper is a step in that direction, introducing concepts and tools for discovering federations over the Web.

1 Introduction and Basic Definitions

The rapid proliferation of information sources in recent years and the advent of the Internet have created a world-wide web of interconnected information resources. Today, the Web represents the largest collection of information resources to which individuals have ever had access — and it continues to grow at an accelerated pace.

Search engines of the Web allow users to access indexed resources using a very simple search mechanism, namely keywords. When a keyword is submitted to a search engine such as Google, the result is a ranked list of URLs of pages, each of which contains the keyword. Similarly, when two or more keywords are submitted the result is a ranked list of URLs of pages, each of which contains *all* the keywords. In this context, co-occurrence of keywords in a page is one way of relating keywords.

In this paper, we are interested in a different kind of relationship between keywords that can be seen as complementary to the co-occurrence relationship.

K.P. Jantke et al. (Eds.): Federation over the Web, LNAI 3847, pp. 115–129, 2006.

More precisely, we consider a source keyword and a target keyword, and we are interested in connections provided by pointer paths leading from a source page to a target page. Here, a *source page* is defined to be any page containing the source keyword, and a *target page* is defined to be a page containing the target keyword.

Such pointer paths may reveal unexpected ways in which the source keyword is connected to the target keyword. For example, if the name of a Japanese professor (the source keyword) has often been cited in connection with the Computer Science Institute of Crete (the target keyword), one may wonder how such a connection might have been created.

One way to go about it is to start with the set of all source pages, and then follow all pointer paths leading to target pages. Each such path is called a *connection path*, and the pages and pointers that constitute the path provide incremental knowledge that describes one connection from the source keyword to the target keyword. Therefore a connection path is defined to be a sequence of pairs of the form

$$\langle url_0, anchor_1 \rangle, \langle url_1, anchor_2 \rangle, ..., \langle url_n, anchor_n \rangle$$

Here, url_0 is the URL of a page containing the source keyword and an anchor ($anchor_1$) pointing to a page whose URL is url_1; the page whose URL is url_1 contains an anchor ($anchor_2$) pointing to the page whose URL is url_2; and so on, until $anchor_n$ points to a page whose URL is url_n and contains the target keyword. This definition of connection path is shown schematically in Fig. 1.

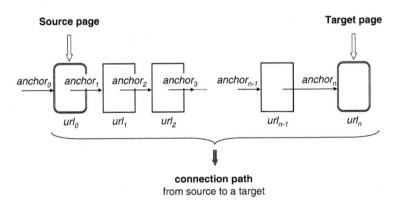

Fig. 1. A connection-path

A connection path can serve as the basis for an "explanation" of the connection between the source keyword and the target keyword. This explanation is formed based on some or all of the following information items that are available in each node of the path:

- the anchor (if it is meaningful);
- the paragraph of text in which the anchor is embedded;
- the URL of the page.

In as much as names carry semantics, the above information items can help explain the connection from the source keyword to the target keyword along the path in question.

The main motivation of this work is to provide the possibility of "explaining", online, the connections between a pair of keywords (a source and a target), by returning a set of paths connecting them, in much the same way as a search engine "explains" a set of keywords by returning the set of pages that each contain all the keywords. In this sense, our proposal complements the functionality of keyword queries supported by search engines.

What we call a *connection query* is a pair of keywords (s, t), s being the source keyword and t being the target keyword. The answer to a connection query is defined to be the set of all connection paths from s to t. Connection queries are the basic means that we use for discovering federations over the Web, and the goal of this paper is to propose a software tool for evaluating connection queries and visualizing their results.

The remainder of the paper is organized as follows. In Section 2, we discuss the size of answers to connection queries, and propose ways of restricting that size to manageable proportions. In Section 3, we present a mechanism for finding connection paths and a system architecture, together with some examples. Finally, in Section 4 we offer some concluding remarks and outline perspectives.

2   The Semantics of Connections over the WWW

When one needs to access information, one often does not know exactly what one is searching for. Most of the existing systems — knowledge bases, databases, and Web applications — only work when requirements are articulated in advance; for example, one cannot search for information using Web search engines unless one can describe the information in terms of keywords [1]. In general, only those users who know what they are looking for can describe their request in the form of a query. In a sense, they are looking for already known information, which means that they have already accessed the target information in the past, or that they are somehow convinced of its existence. However, for persons who do not know what information they actually need, it is difficult to describe it in the form of a query. By suggesting possible paths from a source page to a target page, connection queries assist the user in discovering information of interest.

The key concept here is that of a (directed) relationship between two keywords, a source and a target. As we explained in the introduction, connection queries capture precisely the semantics of that relationship, by providing as an answer the set of all pointer paths from the source page to the target page. Each of these paths provides an explanation of the relationship between source and target in the way described earlier. Clearly, in general, the set of such paths is huge; therefore one has to settle for "partial semantics", that is, considering only reasonable-sized subsets of the set of all paths. In order to define such subsets, we propose to restrict the set of paths in three ways:

− restricting the set of source pages;
− restricting the set of target pages;
− restricting the length of paths.

As a consequence, in the remainder of the paper, we shall consider connection queries of a restricted form (that we shall still call connection queries). The connection queries that we consider are specified by giving the following five parameters:

− the source keyword
− the target keyword
− a set of source pages
− a set of target pages
− a maximal length of connection path

The answer to such a query is the set of all connection paths from a source page (in the specified set of source pages) to a target page (in the specified set of target pages) whose length is less than or equal to the specified maximal length. We call this a connection-path graph.

It is important to note that co-occurrence of two keywords in a page cannot be considered as a special case of connection between the two keywords, in the sense explained above. Indeed, two keywords may co-occur in each of two pages without being connected, while they can be connected without co-occurring in any page. As mentioned earlier, search engines are mainly geared to co-occurrence of keywords, while our proposal is mainly concerned with connectivity of keywords. Therefore connectivity of keywords can be considered as an additional functionality that complements that of co-occurrence.

We consider that knowledge is not a static entity but a dynamically evolving entity that depends on context [1]. The descriptors of HTML documents are given by other HTML documents. Even the creator of a page is not aware what descriptors are given to his page. Descriptors involve a brief introduction of the content, the role of a page or the purpose of its existence. Since anyone can attach any descriptor as an anchor text to a Web page, a large knowledge pool is dynamically formed.

In our framework, paths from a source page to a set of target pages are dynamically extracted from the current collection of Web pages. Each path describes a different context in which some desired information may be embedded, helping users select the correct ways to reach the needed information. Paths also suggest new contexts for the needed information, of which users may not have been aware. Therefore, we contend that paths from a specified page to a set of target pages lead users to desirable information. In addition, a path suggests unknown narrative relations between a source and a target page.

3   A Framework for Connection Search

The main contribution of this paper is to propose a software tool for evaluating connection queries and visualizing their results. We call this tool the *Connection*

Search System (or CSS for short). The present system relies on the help of a search engine, and works as follows:

- *Query Formulation*
  The user specifies the five parameters defining the connection query, by submitting to the system the source and target keywords, as well as an integer l specifying the desired maximal length for connection paths. As for the sets of source and target pages to be considered in the query, they are defined as follows: the user is asked to submit an integer k; the source keyword is submitted to a search engine, and the top k pages returned (as ranked by the search engine) are taken to be the set of source pages for the query. Similarly, the user is asked to submit an integer m; the target keyword is submitted to a search engine, and the top m among the pages returned are taken to be the set of target pages for the query. Clearly, other methods for specifying the sets of source and target pages can be considered.
- *Query Answering*
  The system returns the number of paths in the answer (or an estimate thereof). If the user agrees then the system returns the actual set of paths; otherwise the user can modify the parameters in the query so as to obtain a result of reasonable size.
- *Visualization of Results*
  The interface allows the user to explore each path in the answer as follows: In each node of the path, the user can visualize the URL, the anchor and the text in which the anchor is embedded, by clicking on appropriate buttons.

Figure 2 shows the architecture of the Connection Search System. The user specifies the five parameters of the connection query, i.e., the source keyword, the target keyword and the three integer bounds k, m and l restricting the set of source pages, the set of target pages and the length of connection paths,

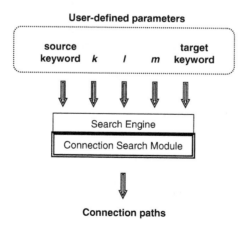

Fig. 2. Architecture of the Connection Search System

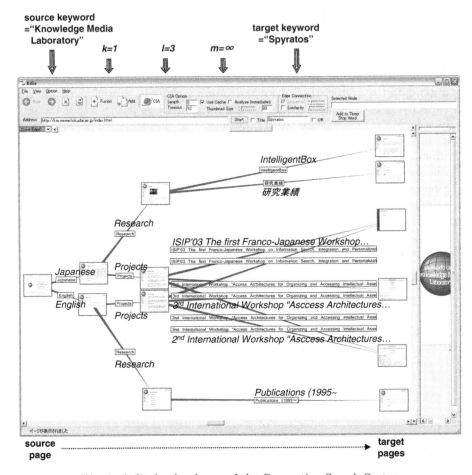

Fig. 3. A display hardcopy of the Connection Search System

respectively. The system then returns the set of connection paths satisfying the query, in the form of a graph as shown in Figure 3.

The design of our connection search system uses two basic concepts, those being the concept of context [2, 3, 4, 5, 6] and that of scope of a context. In the following subsections, we introduce these two concepts and describe the implementation details of the system.

3.1 The Notion of Context

In this paper we introduce the notion of context as proposed by Theokorakis et al [2, 3, 4, 5, 6] as a conceptual modeling mechanism for organizing and managing very large information bases. In computer science, some notion of context has appeared in several areas, such as artificial intelligence [7, 8], software development [9, 10, 11, 12], databases [13, 14, 15, 16], machine learning [17], and knowledge representation [18, 19, 20]. All these notions are very diverse and serve different purposes.

A context is a set of objects of interest, in which each object is associated with a set of descriptors, and possibly with a reference to some other context. A context is regarded as a modular representation of information, whose objective is to model an object under different perspectives. Moreover, contextualization can be used orthogonally to usual abstraction mechanisms such as instantiation, attribution or class inheritance [2, 3, 4, 5, 6].

In some application environments the object descriptors are just keywords, and such keywords may come from a controlled vocabulary. Furthermore, such a vocabulary may be structured by a subsumption relation. For example, if the objects are the books of a computer science library then their descriptors most likely will be keywords from the ACM Computing Classification System (ACM, 1999, http://www.acm.org/class/). However, for the purposes of this paper, it is immaterial whether descriptor definitions follow given rules or not.

What is important to keep in mind is that descriptors and references are context dependent: an object can belong to different contexts and may have different descriptors and/or different references in each context. This feature is useful when we want to view an object from several perspectives.

3.2 Descriptors of Objects in the WWW

We treat a large collection of Web pages as a massive information base. Each Web page is regarded as an object whose (location) identifier is given by a URL. Each Web page is connected to other Web pages by hyper links, which on the WWW are tagged by text or images in HTML documents. Users can browse pages by following the hyper links embedded in each page. When a hyper link is represented by text, the text is regarded as a descriptor of an object indicated by the associated URL. We interpret this "anchor text" as a descriptor of the linked document.

According to this interpretation, a *Connection Search Module* extracts descriptors from Web pages as follows: In HTML documents, an anchor is a piece of text or some other object (for example, an image) that marks the beginning and/or the end of a hypertext link. The <A> element marks that piece of text (or inline image) and gives its hypertextual relationship to other documents. The text between the opening and closing tags, <A attributes > ...text... </A> is the start or destination (or both) of a link. The text written between the start/end tags of an anchor is regarded as the descriptor of the object.

For example, let us examine the top page at the site of the Knowledge Media Laboratory at Hokkaido University (url_0 at top left in Figure 4). Two text anchors are embedded in this page:

1. *"Japanese"*, linked to a page url_1
2. *"English"*, linked to a page url_2

Consequently, in the context of page url_0, *"Japanese"* is the descriptor of page url_1 and *"English"* is the descriptor of page url_2.

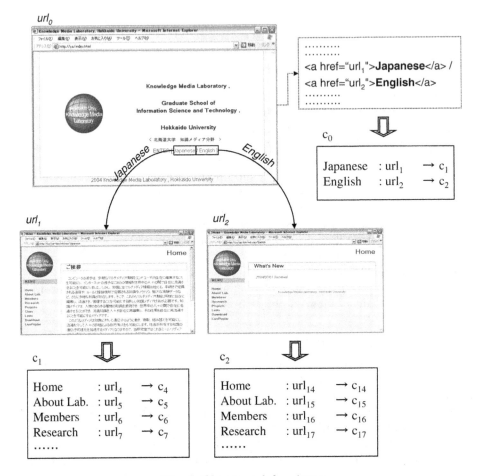

Fig. 4. Objects and descriptors

3.3   Scope of a Context

Contexts are identified by context identifiers and objects by object identifiers, but to keep the presentation simple we refer to these identifiers as contexts and objects respectively. We use $\mathrm{obj}(c)$ to denote the set of objects of a context c, $\mathrm{dscr}(o, c)$ for the set of descriptors of object o in context c, and $\mathrm{ref}(o, c)$ for the reference of object o in context c. We recall that the reference of an object is another context, and that an object might have no reference at all (in which case $\mathrm{ref}(o, c)$ is considered to be undefined).

We call *successor* of a context c any context c' referenced by an object of c, and we use $\mathrm{succ}(c)$ to denote the set of all successors of c. More formally we have:

$$\mathrm{succ}(c) = \{\mathrm{ref}(o) | o \text{ in } \mathrm{obj}(c) \text{ and } \mathrm{ref}(o, c) \text{ is defined}\}$$

We call *descendant* of c any context c' such that either c' is a successor of c or there is a sequence of contexts $c_1, c_2, \cdots, c_n$ such that c_1 is successor of c, c' is successor of c_n, and c_i is a successor of c_{i-1} for $i=2, \cdots, n$.

We call *scope* of c, denoted by scope(c), the set of contexts consisting of c together with all successors of c. For two contexts c_1 and c_2 in the scope of c, we use the symbol $c_1 \rightarrow c_2$ to denote that c_2 is a successor of c_1. In this way, scope(c) is turned into a graph, also denoted by scope(c). Clearly, this graph can be infinite and/or cyclic. However, for the purposes of this paper, we shall make the following basic assumption:

Assumption: The scope of any context c is a finite, acyclic graph.

Obviously, the scope of c has c as its only root, and every leaf of the scope is a context whose objects have no references. The longest path from the root c to a leaf of the scope of c is what we shall call the depth of c, denoted by depth(c). Figure 5 shows an example of the graph scope(c_0).

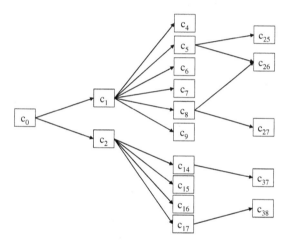

Fig. 5. An example of the graph scope(c_0)

The graph scope(c) shows all possible nodes that a user can reach from the context c along reference links.

To find the relationships between a source and a target, we define the graph connection-path(s_kw, k, l, m, t_kw). This is a subgraph of scope(c), where s_kw is a source keyword, t_kw is a target keyword and three integer bounds k, m, and l restrict, respectively, the sets of source and target pages and the length of paths. A connection-path graph has the following features.

1. the root c is a context whose content includes keyword s_kw,
2. each leaf c' is a context whose content includes keyword t_kw.

Figure 6 shows a connection-path graph, where c_{25}, c_7, c_{15} and c_{38} correspond to the target pages.

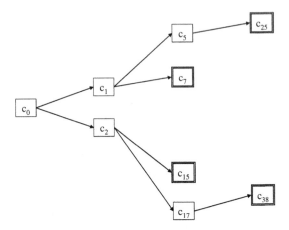

Fig. 6. An example connection-path graph

3.4   Connection Search System: Examples

Let us examine some examples of connection path search. The connection-path graph is constructed dynamically based on the dynamics of the Web resources. Roughly speaking, a descriptor d is a keyword that briefly introduces the content, the role of an object and the purpose of using an object that a user has in mind. The connection-path graph gives not only the content information that includes the keyword but also the path to reach the desired information.

First, let us see the connection-path graph from the context c_0 in Fig. 4 to the keyword *"IntelligentPad"*. Figure 7 shows the connection-path graph providing different perspectives that lead to pages about the *"IntelligentPad"* system. IntelligentPad is a meme media system developed at Hokkaido University in Japan. The graph shows four paths, reaching the following kinds of page:

1. a Japanese page for downloading the software,
2. a Japanese page of introduction to research concerning IntelligentPad,
3. an English software downloading page and
4. an English page of introduction to IntelligentPad.

Without actually seeing the contents of pages, the user can guess the content because the path to each page gives such information.

Second, let us assume that we want to know the role of a person named *"Ken Satoh"* at the *"Knowledge Media Laboratory at Hokkaido University."* Figure 8 shows the connection-path graph as a graph of thumbnail icons of the object pages on the paths.

We input *"Knowledge Media Laboratory..."* as a source keyword and *"Ken Satoh"* as a target keyword in Japanese, then the Connection Search Module gives a connection-path graph. A descriptor of each page is defined by a referral page. In Figure 8, the descriptors are shown along the links. The meanings of descriptors are the following.

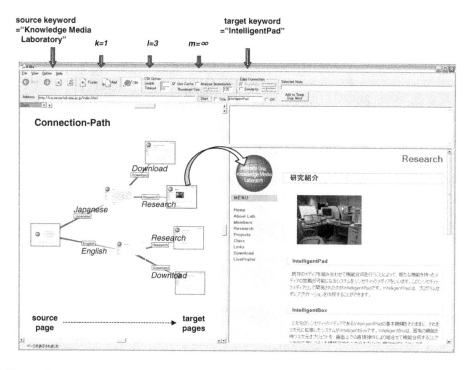

Fig. 7. Connection-paths from *"Knowledge Media Laboratory at Hokkaido University"* to *"IntelligentPad"*

d_0: *Knowledge Media Laboratory at Hokkaido University*
d_1: *Japanese*
d_2: *Project*
d_3: *Intuitive Human Interface for Organizing and Accessing Intellectual Assets* (Japanese)
d_4: *Project contents* (Japanese)
d_5: *Theoretical approach and simulation of Intuitive Human Interface for Accessing* (Japanese)
d_6: *English*
d_7: *Project*
d_8: *Intuitive HumanInterface forOrganizing andAccessing Intellectual Assets*

The paths from a source to target objects denote the relations between *"Knowledge Media Laboratory at Hokkaido University"* and *"Ken Satoh."*

1. The path $d_1.d_2.d_3.d_4$ is *"Knowledge Media Laboratory at Hokkaido University"*. *"Japanese"*. *"Project"*. *"(J) Intuitive Human Interface for Organizing and Accessing Intellectual Assets"*. *"contents of the project"*. It exists because *"Ken Satoh"* is a member of that project at the Knowledge Media Laboratory.

2. Another path, $d_1.d_2.d_3.d_5$, shows more details about the research subject for which he is responsible.

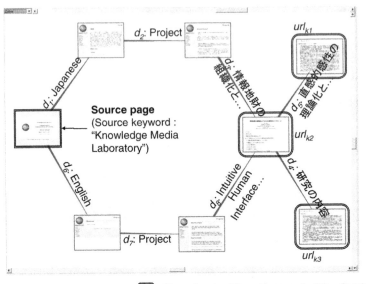

Fig. 8. Connection-paths from *"Knowledge Media Laboratory at Hokkaido University"* to *"Ken Satoh"*

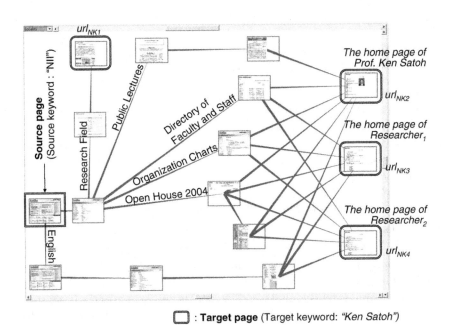

Fig. 9. Connection-paths from *"NII"* to *"Ken Satoh"*

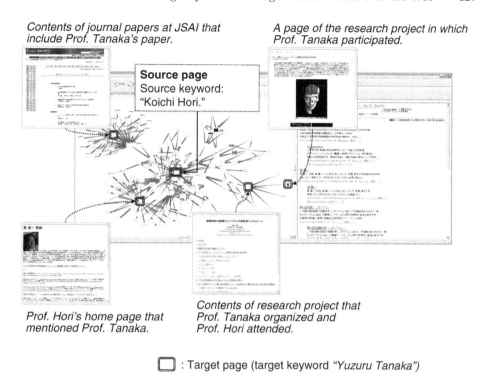

Contents of journal papers at JSAI that include Prof. Tanaka's paper.

Source page Source keyword: "Koichi Hori."

A page of the research project in which Prof. Tanaka participated.

Prof. Hori's home page that mentioned Prof. Tanaka.

Contents of research project that Prof. Tanaka organized and Prof. Hori attended.

☐ : Target page (target keyword *"Yuzuru Tanaka"*)

Fig. 10. Connection-paths from *"Koichi Hori"* to *"Yuzuru Tanaka"*

These paths show some aspects of *"Ken Satoh"* under the viewpoint of *"Knowledge Media Laboratory."*

The next example is shown in Figure 9. In this case, we see the position of *"Ken Satoh"* in *"National Institute of Informatics" (NII)* and his activities. The system finds the profile page of Prof. *"Ken Satoh"* from the *NII* top page through the path *"NII"*.*"Research Organization"*.*"Ken Satoh"*. The last page gives information about his position at *NII*. Moreover, the system returns other paths from *NII* to researchers in *NII* whose publication lists include the name *Ken Satoh* as a coauthor. It shows collaboration works among researchers around Prof. *Ken Satoh.*

A final example is finding paths between *"Koichi Hori"* and *"Yuzuru Tanaka"* to discover the relationships between the two authors of this paper.

When a user does not know the exact page for the source page, or he has only a limited knowledge about it, finding the source page is difficult. In this case one can use a search engine to find possible candidates as source pages. In the example of Fig. 10, the integer bound $k = 100$ was used to restrict the set of source pages. The connection-path graph is shown in Fig. 10, and gives several connections between them. Among the source pages returned by Google, only six pages gave connections: those with rankings 1, 2, 7, 26, 73 and 96.

At the same time, the connection-path graph works as a search method to find *"Yuzuru Tanaka"* who has a connection to *"Koichi Hori."* In fact, there is another Prof. *"Yuzuru Tanaka"* without any connection to Prof. *"Koichi Hori."*

4   Conclusion

We have presented a framework for discovering narrative relationships on the WWW and discussed its implementation in the form of what we call a Connection Search System. We have also presented examples showing how our system works for discovering such narrative relationships, which might be unexpected in some cases. We believe that the development of such tools can contribute significantly in exploiting the wealth of information stored in the WWW.

One possible generalization of our framework is to consider a set of source keywords and a set of target keywords, and find that subset of target keywords to which *all* source keywords connect. These target keywords are then the common "acquaintances" of all source keywords. We are currently investigating this and other relationships among keywords, as well as their possible uses in forming collections of keywords that are similar in some respects.

One aspect of our framework that was not discussed in this paper is how to delimit a part of the Web, of manageable size, in which the search for connections is to take place. One way to go about it is to specify a set of pages of interest to a community of users. The set of pages, together with the links connecting them, will then constitute the community repository: a user scope will be formed only from pages and links within the repository. The maintenance of such a repository can be supported by a crawler whose main tasks are to discover links among the pages and to maintain the scope graphs of the users dynamically (i.e., update the links and/or nodes as they are created or destroyed).

Acknowledgments

The authors would like to thank Prof. Ken Satoh (National Institute of Informatics, Japan) and Toshiyuki Kikuchi (NorthGrid Corporation, Japan) for their constructive comments and technical support.

References

1. K. Hori: Do knowledge assets really exist in the world and can we access such knowledge? – Knowledge evolves through a cycle of knowledge liquidization and crystallization. Lecture Notes in Computer Science, Springer, pp.1-13, 2005.
2. M. Theodorakis, A. Analyti, P. Constantopoulos, N. Spyratos: Context in Information Bases. Proc. of Third IFCIS Conference on Cooperative Information Systems (CoopIS'98), pp.260-270, 1998.
3. M. Theodorakis, A. Analyti, P. Constantopoulos, N. Spyratos: Contextualization as an Abstraction Mechanism for Conceptual Modelling. Proc. of International Conference on Conceptual Modeling / the Entity Relationship Approach (ER'99), pp.475-489, 1999.

4. M. Theodorakis, A. Analyti, P. Constantopoulos, N. Spyratos: Querying Contextualized Information Bases. Proc. of 24th International Information and Communication Technologies and Programming (ICTP'99), pp.260-270, 1999.
5. M. Theodorakis, A. Analyti, P. Constantopoulos, N. Spyratos: A Theory of Contexts in Information Bases. Information Systems Journal, Vol.19, No.4, pp.1-54, 2001.
6. M. Theodorakis, A. Analyti, N. Spyratos, P. Constantopoulos: Contextualization as an Independent Abstraction Mechanism for Conceptual Modeling. Information Systems Journal. (To Appear)
7. J. McCarthy: Notes on Formalizing context. Proc. IJCAI-93, pp555-560, 1993
8. R. Guha: Contexts: A Formalization and Some Applications. PhD thesis, Stanford University, 1991
9. G. Gottlob, M. Schrefl and B. Rock: Extending Object-Oriented Systems with Roles. ACM Trans. Inf. Syst., 14(3), pp.268-296, 1996
10. Y. Shyy and S. Su.: K, A High-level Knowledge Base Programming Language for Advanced Database Applications. Proc. ACM-SIGMOD conference, pp.338-347, 1991
11. R. Katz: Towards a Unified Framework for Version modeling in engineering Databases. ACM Comput. Surv., 22(4), pp.375-408, 1990
12. G. Kotonya, I. Sommerville: Requirements Engineering with Viewpoints. Software Engineering Journal, pp.5-19, 1996
13. F. Bancilhon, N. Spyratos: Update Semantics of Relational Views. ACM Trans. Database Syst., 6(4), pp.557-575, 1981
14. S. J. Hegner: Unique complements and decompositions of database schemata. Journal of Computer and System Sciences, 48(1), pp.9-57, 1994
15. S. Abiteboul, A. Bonner: Objects and Views. Proc. ACM-SIGMOD conference, pp.238-247, 1991
16. A. Ouksel, C. Naiman: Coordinating Context Building in Heterogeneous Information Systems. Journal of Intelligent Inf. Systems, 3(2), pp.151-183, 1994
17. S. Matwin, M. Kubat: The role of Context in Concept Learning. Proc. ICML-96, Workshop on Learning in Context-Sensitive Domains, pp.1-5, 1996
18. J. Mylopoulos, R. Motschnig-Pitrik: Partitioning Information Bases with Contexts. Proc. CoopISf95, pp.44-55, 1995
19. B. Czejdo, D. Embley: View Specification and Manipulation for a Semantic Data Model. IS, 16(6), pp.585-612, 1991
20. L. Campbell, T. Halping, H. Proper: Conceptual Schemas with Abstractions: Making Flat Conceptual Schemas More Comprehensible. DKE, 20(1), pp.39-85, 1996

Querying with Preferences in a Digital Library*

Nicolas Spyratos[1] and Vassilis Christophides[2]

[1] Laboratoire de Recherche en Informatique,
Université Paris Sud,
91405 Orsay Cedex, France
spyratos@lri.fr
[2] Institute of Computer Science,
Foundation for Research and Technology-Hellas,
P.O. Box 1385, 71110 Heraklio, Greece
christop@ics.forth.gr

Abstract. We consider a collection of federated sources on the Web, and a community of users who are interested in documents residing in one or more of those federated sources. The search for documents of interest is supported by a mediator that we call a digital library. The library simply indexes all documents that are made available to users by the federated sources. When a user addresses a query to the library, the library returns the URLs of documents satisfying the query. In such a context, one of the factors influencing user satisfaction is the size of the answer set, in particular when it is too small (few or no documents) or too large (several hundreds or thousands of documents). In this paper, we address the problem of answer sets that are too large, and we call *personalized query* a usual query together with (a) an upper bound on the number of documents returned, and (b) a set of preferences as to the order in which the returned documents should be presented to the user; *both* these parameters are defined by the user *online*, during query formulation. The main contribution of the paper is to propose a framework in which the problem can be stated formally, and a method for the evaluation of personalized queries.

1 Introduction

As information becomes available in increasing volumes, and to growing numbers of users, the shift towards a more user-centered access to information is becoming an important issue. As a consequence, support of personalized user interaction is an important concern in the design of advanced information systems in general and of e-services in particular [3, 4, 9].

Personalization in an interactive information system is about building a meaningful one-to-one relationship by understanding the needs of each individual user. Personalization can involve either adapting the user interface or adapting

---

* This work is partially supported by the EU Network of Excellence in Digital Libraries (Delos NoE-6038-507618).

K.P. Jantke et al. (Eds.): Federation over the Web, LNAI 3847, pp. 130–142, 2006.

the content to the needs or preferences of a specific user. Both aspects have received increasing attention during the past few years. In this paper we propose to study a specific aspect of content adaptation, namely query personalization, in the context of a digital library.

We view a digital library as a mediator over a collection of federated sources that store electronic documents of various kinds. The sources make available (i.e., accessible) some or all of their documents to a community of users (the library subscribers). Users address their queries to the library, in search of documents of interest residing in one or more federated sources. Access to documents is done transparently – that is, the users are not aware of the sources in which the documents reside. In such a context, one of the factors that influences user satisfaction is the size of the answer set, in particular when it is too small (few or no documents) or too large (several hundreds or thousands of documents).

In this paper, we address the problem of answer sets that are too large, and we call *personalized query* a usual query q together with (a) an upper bound k on the number of documents returned and (b) a set of preferences as to the order in which the returned documents should be presented; *both* these parameters are defined by the user *online*, during query formulation. In other words, the query q specifies (intentionally, as usual) a set of documents which is unordered, whereas the preferences and the bound k select an ordered subset of desired size. The main contribution of the paper is to propose a framework where the problem can be stated formally, and a method for the evaluation of personalized queries.

Regarding related work, first we note that personalization in electronic publishing mainly addresses three items:

- *Notification*: The user's need to receive timely and accurate information relevant to his interests.
- *Query personalization*: The user's need to be adequately supported during search of archive information.
- *Recommendation*: The publishers' need to proactively disseminate information only to interested users.

An essential feature of personalization techniques for information access is the capability to learn, autonomously and automatically, user interests and preferences from the observation of user's behavior. In other words, adaptability. This adaptability is based on various machine learning techniques and provides the means to unobtrusively build user profiles [5, 12]. However, profiles contain information describing *past* interests or preferences of the user. In this paper, we are interested in query personalization based on *current* interests and preferences of the user, expressed *online*, during query formulation.

The possibility for the user to express preferences online, during query formulation, is an aspect of personalization that has received increasing attention over the past few years. The main reason for this increasing attention is that traditional systems require the user to specify the information to be retrieved *exactly*, allowing no provision for "customizing" the answer set. In the area of databases, two different approaches of query personalization are currently being pursued:

qualitative [6, 7, 11, 13, 15, 17] and quantitative [1, 14, 16]. A fundamental study concerning general preference relations is presented in [2].

In the qualitative approach, the preferences among tuples in the answer to a query are specified directly, typically using so-called preference relations. These are binary relations over tuples, satisfying certain natural conditions such as transitivity and reflexivity. In the quantitative approach, preferences are specified indirectly using scoring functions that associate a numeric score with every tuple of the query answer. Once scores are assigned, a tuple t is preferred to a tuple t' if the score of t is higher than the score of t'. Very roughly, the difference between the two approaches is described by the following examples:

- Qualitative Approach: I *prefer* Comedies to Thrillers
- Quantitative Approach: I like Comedies *very much*; I like Thrillers *a little*

The qualitative approach seems to be more general than the quantitative one, since one can define preference relations in terms of scoring functions, whereas not every (intuitively plausible) preference relation can be captured by scoring functions. The approach that we propose in this paper is related to the qualitative approach, and is in fact motivated by current research in that area. It also draws on ideas and results from [19] and [20].

A notable feature of the qualitative approach is the clear separation of the formal specification of preferences from their embedding in the query language, which allows abstract properties of preferences to be studied separately from query evaluation (similarly to the separation between relational algebra and its embedding into the algebraic query language, in the relational database model).

The remainder of the paper is organized as follows. In Section 2 we define the model of digital library that we use, and recall some basic definitions from [18]. In Sections 3 and 4 we define formally a personalized query and its answer, respectively, and in Section 5 we outline an algorithm for the evaluation of personalized queries. Finally, in Section 6 we discuss ongoing research and offer some concluding remarks.

2   Digital Libraries

A *digital library* serves a network of federated sources that store electronic documents of various kinds. The sources make available (i.e., accessible) some or all of their documents to a community of users (the library subscribers). Users address their queries to the library, in search of documents of interest residing at the local repositories of one or more federated sources. The digital library acts as a mediator, supporting transparent access to all shareable documents by library users.

We emphasize the fact that the library stores no documents at its local repository: the documents stay at the sources, and the library merely acts as a mediator to access them. We note that since the documents accessible through the library reside at the local repositories of the participating sources, the local repositories can be seen collectively as a single distributed repository of documents spread over the network [18].

In order to carry out its basic function (i.e., that of a mediator), the library is required to support two basic services: *registration* of documents that the sources are willing to make available to library users, and *querying* for documents of interest by the library users. In the remainder of this section we describe these services in more detail.

2.1   Registration

When a source wishes to make a document shareable (i.e., accessible) to library users it must register the document at the library. To do so the source must provide two items to the library:

- the document identifier (indispensable for document registration)
- the document description (optional)

We assume that the document identifier is just the URL where the document can be accessed by library users. Clearly, as the document identifier is the only means for accessing the document, no document can be registered unless its identifier is provided by the source to the library. This is why providing the document identifier is indispensable for document registration. Hereafter, in our examples, for convenience of notation we use integers as document identifiers instead of URLs.

As for document description, we consider only content description and we assume that such a description is provided by the source in the form of a set D of keywords, or *terms*. For example, if $D = \{\text{QuickSort, Java}\}$ this suggests a document about the quicksort algorithm written in Java. We make no assumption as to the provenance of the terms in the description of the document. These terms may or may not be taken from a controlled vocabulary, and they may be given manually or extracted from the document content using some document mining algorithm. Moreover, some sources may simply provide the document identifier without providing any content description. It will then be the job of the library to provide such a description (manually or using some mining algorithm). Finally, it may be the case that the source does provide a content description but the library "augments" this description to provide a finer one for its users (see [18] for more details).

Therefore registration of a document at the library requires the document identifier, say i, and a set of terms D (defined as explained above). The actual registration of the document by the library is done by storing a pair $<i, t>$ in the library repository, for each term t in D. Thus if i is the document identifier, and $D = \{\text{QuickSort, Java}\}$ is the document description, then the library will store two pairs: $<i,\text{QuickSort}>$ and $<i,\text{Java}>$. The set of all such pairs $<i, t>$ for all registered documents is what we call the library directory, or simply *directory* (the well known Open Directory of the Web is an example of such a directory). Clearly the directory is a binary relation between document identifiers and terms. As such, it can also be seen as a formal context [8].

Each term in the directory has an extension, and each document identifier has a description (also called its intension, or its index). The *extension* of a term t, denoted by ext(t), is the set of all document identifiers i such that $< i, t >$ is in the directory; and the *description* of a document i, denoted descr(i), is the set of all terms t such that $< i, t >$ is in the directory. More formally, we have the following definitions:

ext(t) ::= $\{i :< i, t >$ is in the directory $\}$
descr(i) ::= $\{t :< i, t >$ is in the directory $\}$

We assume that if a term does not appear in the directory then its extension is empty. Similarly, we assume that if a document identifier does not appear in the directory then its description is empty.

We note that, from a mathematical point of view, ext and descr are set-valued functions, and that they may change over time as the directory is updated. Moreover, either of these functions is sufficient to define the directory, and conversely the directory is sufficient to define each of these functions.

2.2   Querying

Library users access the library in search of documents of interest, either to use them directly (e.g., as learning objects) or to reuse them as components in new documents that they intend to compose (see [18]). Search for documents of interest is done by issuing queries to the library, and the library uses its directory to return the identifiers (i.e., the URLs) of all documents satisfying the query.

The query language that we use is a simple language in which a query q is just a Boolean combination of terms:

$$q ::= t \mid q1 \wedge q2 \mid q1 \vee q2 \mid q1 \wedge \neg q2$$

The answer to a query q is defined recursively as follows:

```
if q is a term then ans(q):=ext(q)
else begin if q=q1 ∧ q2 then ans(q):=ans(q1)∩ans(q2);
           if q=q1∨q2 then ans(q):=ans(q1)∪ans(q2);
           if q=q1∧¬q2 then ans(q):=ans(q1)\ans(q2)
      end
```

In other words, to answer a query q, the library simply replaces each term appearing in q by its extension from the directory, and performs the set theoretic operations corresponding to the Boolean connectives.

3   Personalized Queries

In our approach, a personalized query Q consists of three parts:

- a usual query q, e.g., QuickSort $\vee$ Java,
- an integer k, expressing the maximum number of documents to be returned,
- a set of preferences, e.g., "I prefer documents about QuickSort to those about Java"

In this paper, we model the set of preferences as a *pre-order* over terms, i.e., as a binary relation over terms which is reflexive and transitive. These two properties of preferences seem to be reasonable in our context, although no strong argument can be presented in their favor; Fishburn [10], for example, considers non-transitive preferences in decision theory .

In contrast, a strong argument can be made *against* including anti-symmetry as a property of preferences. Indeed, preferring QuickSort over Java *and* Java over QuickSort doesn't make QuickSort equal to Java but simply equivalent to Java (with respect to user preferences).

In fact, in our context, equivalence of terms is a highly desirable property, as it implies the existence of one or more *alternatives*. For example, assume that QuickSort is equivalent to Java (according to the preferences declared by the user), and that documents described by one or the other term are the most preferred by the user. If no document described by QuickSort is currently available in the directory, then the system can return any document described by Java as an alternative.

Therefore, we allow the user to declare two kinds of statements over terms: alternatives and preferences. Alternatives are statements of the form $t \equiv t'$, meaning that the user is equally interested in documents described by either t or t', while preferences are statements of the form $s \leq s'$ meaning that the user prefers documents described by s (or any term equivalent to s) to documents described by s' (or any term equivalent to s'). In what follows we assume that alternatives form an equivalence relation over terms, i.e., a binary relation that is reflexive, symmetric and transitive. We note that this assumption is made here in order to simplify the presentation. However, the set of user statements declaring alternatives do not necessarily define an equivalence relation over terms. In case they do not, one has to consider the minimal equivalence relation implied by the set of user statements (and this is obtained by computing the closure of the set of user statements under reflexivity and transitivity). We also note that synonyms are alternatives as well, and are captured by the equivalence relation just defined, as long as they are declared, e.g., Databases $\equiv$ DBs. In other words, alternatives extend synonyms in the following sense: if two terms are synonyms then they are alternatives. Clearly the opposite is not true.

Now, if we consider the equivalence classes of terms formed by the alternatives, then the preference relation becomes a partial order over those equivalence classes. In what follows, in order to further simplify the presentation, we shall consider the terms of the directory up to equivalence. So when we speak of a term, we shall actually mean the equivalence class of that term (with respect to the equivalences declared by the user).

Following our discussion so far, we can define a personalized query, formally, as follows:

Definition 1. *Personalized Query*
A personalized query over the library directory is a triple $Q = (q, k, \leq)$, where q is a Boolean query, k is a positive integer, and $\leq$ is a partial order relation over terms, called the preference relation.

In the above definition, we note that the Boolean query q can be evaluated as described in the previous section, and that the evaluation returns a set of documents, which we shall call Ans(q). In a traditional system, what is returned to the user is the set Ans(q). In our approach, however, as explained in the introduction, what is returned to the user is *not* necessarily the whole set Ans(q) but a subset thereof, of size at most k; and moreover, the subset returned to the user is ordered according to the preference relation. So, in the next section, we explain how one orders the set Ans(q) based on the preference relation, and how one selects the subset of Ans(q), of size k, to be returned to the user.

We also note that the terms appearing in the preference relation may not appear in the query q. This means that it is perfectly possible to ask for all documents concerning Quicksort and Java, but preferring those concerning Theory to those concerning Applications.

4   Answering a Personalized Query

The first thing to note is that the preference relation is defined over terms, and not over documents. Therefore we use the preference relation to define a pre-order $\preceq$ over documents as follows.

Definition 2. *Ordering Documents*
Let d, d' be two documents. We define $d \preceq d'$ iff $\forall t \in \text{descr}(d) \exists t' \in \text{descr}(d') t \leq t'$

It is easy to see that $\preceq$ is reflexive and transitive but not anti-symmetric (as two documents can have the same description, while being different documents). Therefore we define two documents d, d' to be *equivalent*, denoted by $d \equiv d'$, iff $d \preceq d'$ and $d' \preceq d$. With this definition at hand, the preorder $\preceq$ becomes a partial order over equivalence classes of documents.

Proposition 1. *The relation $\preceq$ is a partial order over (equivalence classes of) documents.*

In the following we shall talk about documents up to equivalence; in other words, we shall not distinguish between documents that are equivalent. Therefore $d \preceq d'$ will mean that the equivalence class of d is less than or equal to the equivalence class of d'. With this partial order at hand, we now proceed to define the answer to a personalized query.

Let $Q = (q, k, \leq)$ be a personalized query and let Ans(q) be the answer to the (usual) query q. What we want to define as the answer to Q is a subset of the ordered set (Ans(q), $\preceq$), having k documents listed in increasing order with respect to $\preceq$ (i.e., in decreasing order of preference). This subset, denoted by *Ans(Q)*, will be returned to the user as the answer to the personalized query. To make this intuitive definition more formal, we first need to introduce some auxiliary definitions and notation.

We call a document of Ans(q) *active* if it appears in some comparison under $\preceq$, and *inactive* otherwise. Roughly speaking, active documents are those that can be ordered with respect to other documents (as they participate in at least one comparison), while inactive documents are those that cannot be ordered. As a consequence, the set $\text{Ans}(q)$ is partitioned into two sets, denoted $\text{Act}(q)$ and $\text{Inact}(q)$, of active and inactive documents respectively. Our approach to answering the personalized query Q uses only the set of active documents, so hereafter whenever we say "document" we mean "active document". In a nutshell, our approach can be described as follows:

1. Define a partition of the set $\text{Act}(q)$ into blocks, and a linear ordering of the blocks, satisfying the following properties:
   (a) Each block consists of non-comparable documents
   (b) The first block contains the most-preferred documents
   (c) For each block B other than the first, and for each document in B, there is a more preferred document in the previous block
2. Start presenting each block of documents to the user, one by one, in their linear order
3. If the number of all documents in $\text{Ans}(q)$ is less than or equal to k then show all documents, else terminate the presentation of documents after showing the k-th document (this can happen before all documents of a block have been shown to the user)

To define our approach formally we need some auxiliary definitions and notation that we adapt from [8]. First, let us call *path* from a document d to a document d' any sequence of pairs of the form $< d, d_1 >, < d_1, d_2 >, \ldots, < d_{n-1}, d_n >,$ $< d_n, d' >$ such that $d \preceq d_1, d_n \preceq d'$, and $d_{i-1} \preceq d_i$ for $i = 2, \ldots, n$. The integer $n + 1$ is called the length of the path, and it should be clear that there may be zero, one or more paths from d to d'.

Roughly speaking, the partition of the set $\text{Act}(q)$ that we define next uses the set B_0 of all documents that are minimal with respect to $\preceq$ as the basic block. The definition of each other block B_i of the partition relies on the notion of distance of a document from B_0. The *distance* of a document d' from B_0 is defined to be the length of a longest path from a document d to the document d', when d ranges over all documents of B_0; if d' belongs to B_0 then this distance is defined to be equal to 0. The block B_i is defined to be the set of all documents that are at distance i from B_0. The following theorem (which is our main theorem) states formally the definition of the partition, as well as its basic properties.

Theorem 1. *Partitioning the Set* $\text{Act}(q)$
Let B_0 be the set of all documents that are minimal with respect to $\preceq$, and let m be the length of a longest path from B_0 to a maximal document of $\text{Ans}(q)$. For $i = 1, \ldots, m$, define the set B_i as follows: d' is in B_i iff d' is at distance i from B_0. Then the following statements hold:

(a) The collection $\{B_0, B_1, \ldots, B_m\}$ is a partition of $\text{Act}(q)$.
(b) In every block B_i no two documents are comparable, $i = 0, 1, \ldots, m$.
(c) For every document d' in B_i there is a document d in B_{i-1} such that $d \preceq d'$, $i = 1, 2, \ldots, m$.

Proof.
(a) It suffices to observe that every document will belong to some B_i (because it appears in at least one comparison) and that no document can belong to two different B_is (as its distance from B_0 is unique). Therefore, the B_is are mutually disjoint and their union is $\text{Act}(q)$; in other words, the collection of all B_is is a partition of $\text{Act}(q)$.
(b) Suppose now that there are documents d, d' in B_i such that $d \preceq d'$. As the distance of d from B_0 is i, it follows that the distance of d' from B_0 is $i + 1$, a contradiction.
(c) For every document d' in B_i there is a longest path p from some document of B_0 to d'. Let d be the predecessor of d' in p. Clearly, the sub-path of p ending in d is a longest path from B_0 to d (otherwise, p is not a longest path to d', a contradiction). It follows that d is in B_{i-1} and that $d \preceq d'$.

We now define a partial order over sets of documents and show that the sequence $B_0, B_1, \ldots, B_m$ is actually a chain in that partial order. This is one of the possible orders one can define over sets of documents, which are induced by the partial order $\preceq$ over documents (see [18, 20] for more details).

Definition 3. *Ordering Sets of Documents*
Let D, D' be two sets of documents. We define $D \sqsubseteq D'$ iff $\forall d' \in D' \; \exists d \in D$ such that $d \preceq d'$

Clearly, the relation $\sqsubseteq$ is reflexive and transitive but not anti-symmetric; hence it is a pre-order over sets of documents. However, it is not difficult to see that if each set of documents consists of mutually incomparable documents, then $\sqsubseteq$ becomes anti-symmetric, and thus a partial order (see also [20]). Now, each block B_i of the partition defined earlier does have this property (see Theorem 1(b)), and thus $\sqsubseteq$ is a partial order over the partition $\{B_0, B_1, \ldots, B_m\}$. Moreover, in view of Theorem 1(c), we have $B_0 \sqsubseteq B_1 \sqsubseteq \ldots \sqsubseteq B_m$. In other words, the sequence $B_0, B_1, \ldots B_m$ is a chain in $\sqsubseteq$; hence the following proposition.

Proposition 2. *Ordering the Partition of $\text{Act}(q)$*
The relation $\sqsubseteq$ is a partial order over sets of non comparable documents, and the sequence $B_0, B_1, \ldots, B_m$ is a chain in $\sqsubseteq$, i.e., $B_0 \sqsubseteq B_1 \sqsubseteq \ldots \sqsubseteq B_m$

Thus the sequence $B_0, B_1, \ldots, B_m$ is actually the right sequence for presenting documents to the user, in the sense that each document in B_i is less preferred than some document of B_{i-1}. Of course, there may be documents in B_{i-1} that have no less-preferred documents in B_i. However, this doesn't go against the intuition "most-preferred documents first".

In the following section we present an algorithm for evaluating the answer to a personalized query Q.

5   The Evaluation Algorithm

Our algorithm constructs the blocks of the sequence $B_0, B_1, \ldots, B_m$, one by one, while keeping track of the number of documents produced. If the size of $\text{Act}(q)$

is less than or equal to k then all blocks are constructed. Otherwise computation should normally terminate when the k-th document is produced – something that could happen before all documents of the k-th document's block have been produced. However, in the following definition of answer to Q, in order to simplify matters, we include in the answer *all* documents of the block containing the k-th document. We use the notation $\text{card}(X)$ to denote the cardinality of a set X of documents.

Definition 4. *The Answer to a Personalized Query*
Let $Q = (q, k, \leq)$ be a personalized query. The answer to Q is the sequence of blocks $B_0, B_1, \ldots, B_j$, $0 \leq j \leq k$, defined as follows:
if $\text{card}(\text{Act}(q)) \leq k$ then the answer is $B_0, B_1, \ldots, B_m$
else the answer is the sequence $B_0, B_1, \ldots, B_j$ such that
$$\text{card}(B_0) + \ldots + \text{card}(B_{j-1}) \leq k \leq \text{card}(B_0) + \ldots + \text{card}(B_{j-1}) + \text{card}(B_j)$$

Our algorithm is best understood if we view the pair $G = (\text{Act}(q), \preceq)$ as a graph, defined as follows:

- the documents in $\text{Act}(q)$ are the nodes of G
- there is an arrow from document d to document d' iff $d \preceq d'$

We note that, as $\preceq$ is a partial order, this graph is acyclic.
To keep the presentation of the algorithm as simple as possible, we assume the following:

1. There is a function that takes as input the personalized query $Q = (q, k, \leq)$, computes successively $\text{Ans}(q)$, $\text{Act}(q)$, $G = (\text{Act}(q), \preceq)$ and the length m of a longest path from the set of minimal documents to a maximal document. In the presentation of the algorithm we assume that the set $\text{Act}(q)$ is not empty, i.e., the graph G has at least one edge.
2. There is a function card that takes as input a set of documents $B = \{d_1, d_2, \ldots, d_j\}$ and computes the number of documents in B, as follows:

$$\text{card}(B) = \text{card}(d_1) + \text{card}(d_2) + \ldots + \text{card}(d_j)$$

We recall that documents are considered up to equivalence, hence $\text{card}(d)$ returns the number of documents in the equivalence class of d.

```
Algorithm PERSO
Input : A personalized query Q = (q, k, ≤)
Output: The answer to Q
Method
count:=0; i:=0
repeat Bᵢ:={all roots of G}; output Bᵢ;
       count:= count + card(Bᵢ);
       remove from G all nodes of Bᵢ and all edges
       emanating from nodes of Bᵢ;
       i:=i+1
until G = ∅ or k ≤count;
```

The correctness of this algorithm follows rather easily from Theorem 1, and our preceding discussions. Complexity and performance issues, however, lie outside the scope of the present paper, and will be discussed in the full paper.

6   Concluding Remarks

We have presented an approach to defining and evaluating personalized queries in the context of digital libraries. A personalized query is defined as a usual Boolean query together with an upper bound on the number of documents returned and a set of preferences and alternatives as to the order in which the returned documents should be presented; both these parameters can be defined by the user *online*, during query formulation. We have also presented an evaluation algorithm for answering personalized queries.

However, the research reported in this paper is preliminary, and much work remains to be done in support of the proposed approach, in particular with respect to the implementation of the evaluation algorithm and its performance. Once this is done, our plan is to use the query evaluation algorithm for implementing the following two-step interactive scheme for query personalization:

Step 1
The user submits a query q and the system returns an integer, which is the size of the answer set (or an estimate thereof);

Step 2
If the user is satisfied then the system returns the actual answer set; else if the user judges the size of the answer set too large then he/she can "personalize" the query (by declaring an upper bound k plus preferences and alternatives); the system then returns the desired ordered subset of the answer set.

Concerning the implementation of the algorithm, the choice of an appropriate representation for the library directory seems to be essential. The obvious candidates are the binary relation $< doc\text{-}id, term >$ and the set-valued functions ext and int defined earlier (see Sect. 2).

The influence of structure over the set of terms may also prove significant. Indeed, although no assumption of structure was made here over the set of terms, in many applications the terms come from a controlled vocabulary, possibly structured as taxonomy according to a subsumption relation (see [18]). Structuring the set of terms will have an influence on the evaluation of a personalized query $Q = (q, k, \leq)$ at two levels. First, on the evaluation of the Boolean query q, as the extension of a term will now include the extensions of all its sub-terms; and second, on the preferences, as we may or may not have the ordering of two terms to imply a "similar" ordering on the sets of their sub-terms.

Concerning performance, a detailed complexity analysis of the evaluation algorithm is necessary. This analysis should take into consideration several factors, including the size of the set of preferences (i.e., the number of terms appearing in preferences), the size of the query q (i.e., the number of terms appearing in q), the bound k, the size of the set $\text{Ans}(q)$, and the number of active documents.

A final remark concerns the inactive documents. Indeed, the answer to a personalized query as defined here is based solely on the active documents. However, when the set of active documents turns out to be relatively small (with respect to the bound k) then one may wish to include some inactive documents in the answer as well. In this respect, inactive documents whose description contains at least one term appearing in the preference relation should naturally be preferred to the remaining inactive documents (i.e., those whose description contains no term appearing in the preference relation).

Summarizing, further research and extensive experimentation is needed to evaluate the proposed approach and query-answering algorithm, thus validating the choices made here.

References

1. R. Agrawal and E.L. Wimmers. A Framework for Expressing and Combining Preferences. In *Proceedings of the ACM-SIGMOD International Conference on Management of Data, Dallas, USA*, pages 297–306, 2000.
2. H. Andreka, M. Ryan, and P-Y. Schlobbens. Operators and Laws for Combining Preferential Relations. *Journal of Logic and Computation*, 12(1):13–53, 2002.
3. R. Brafman, J. Doyle, U. Junker, and P. Pu. Tutorial on Preference Models and Application, 2005. 19th International Joint Conference on Artificial Intelligence, IJCAI.
4. S. Braynov. Personalization and Customization Technologies, 2003. Seminar on Personalization and Customization in E-Commerce, Available at: http://www.cs.buffalo.edu/~ sbraynov/seninar2003/papers/Personalization.pdf.
5. L. Chen and P. Pu. Survey on Preference Elicitation Methods, 2004. Ecole Politechnique, Federale de Lausanne (EPFL), Switzerland.
6. J. Chomicki. Querying with Intrinsic Preferences. In *Proceedings of the 8th International Conference on EDBT, Prague, Czech Rep.*, pages 34–51, 2002.
7. J. Chomicki. Preference formulas in relational queries. *ACM Transactions on Database Systems*, 28(4):427–466, 2003.
8. B.A. Davey and H.A. Priestly. *Introduction to Lattices and Order (2nd edition)*. Cambridge Mathematical Textbooks. Cambridge University Press, 2002.
9. J. Doyle and U. Junker. Tutorial on Preferences, 2004. 19th AAAI National Conference on Artificial Intelligence.
10. P.C. Fishburn. Non-transitive Preferences on Decision Theory. *Journal of Risk and Uncertainty*, 4:113–134, 1991.
11. K. Govindarajan, B. Jayaraman, and S. Mantha. Preference Queries in Deductive Databases. *New Generation Computing*, 19(1):57–86, 2000.
12. S. Holland, M. Ester, and W. Kießling. Preference Mining: A Novel Approach on Mining User Preferences for Personalized Applications. Technical report, Institute of Computer Science, University of Augsburg, Germany, 2003.
13. S. Holland and W. Kießling. Situated Preferences and Preference Repositories for Personalized Database Applications. In *Proceedings of the 23rd International Conference on Conceptual Modeling, ER, Shanghai, China*, pages 511–523, 2004.

14. V. Hristidis, N. Koudas, and Y. Papakonstantinou. PREFER: A system for the efficient execution of multiparametric ranked queries. In *Proceedings of the ACM-SIGMOD International Conference on Management of Data, Santa Barbara, California*, page 259269, 2001.
15. W. Kießling. Foundations of Preferences in Database Systems. In *Proceedings of the 28th International Conference on Very Large Databases, Hong Kong, China*, pages 311–322, 2002.
16. G. Koutrika and Y. Ioannidis. Personalization of Queries in Database Systems. In *Proceedings of the 20th International Conference on Data Engineering, Boston, USA*, pages 597–608, 2004.
17. M. Lacroix and P. Lavency. Preferences: Putting More Knowledge Into Queries. In *Proceedings of the International Conference on Very Large Databases*, pages 217–225, 1987.
18. Ph. Rigaux and N. Spyratos. Metadata Inference for Document Retrieval in a Distributed Repository (Invited Paper). In *Proceedings of the 9th Asian Computing Science Conference (ASIAN'04) (LNCS 3321), Chiang-Mai, Thailand*, 2004.
19. N. Spyratos. A Functional Model for Dimensional Data Analysis. Course notes 2001-2004, LRI Research Report, To appear.
20. N. Spyratos. Decision Support Problems. Course notes 2001-2004, LRI Research Report, To appear.

An Enhanced Spreadsheet Supporting Calculation-Structure Variants, and Its Application to Web-Based Processing

Aran Lunzer[1] and Kasper Hornbæk[2]

[1] Meme Media Laboratory, Hokkaido University, Sapporo 060-8628, Japan
[2] Department of Computer Science (DIKU), University of Copenhagen, 2100 Copenhagen Ø, Denmark

Abstract. This paper reports our work towards an end user environment for building and experimenting with federations of Web-based processing resources. We present the key concepts and an initial interface for the RecipeSheet, a spreadsheet-like environment with explicit support for creating and comparing alternative scenarios, based on the principles of subjunctive interfaces. A key feature of the RecipeSheet is that alternative scenarios can differ in terms of the processing used to calculate cells' values; in the context of the Web, this is useful for gathering and comparing results from alternative resources that offer nominally the same processing. We show various usage cases for our prototype, including an example from Web-based bioinformatics.

1 Combining Web-Based Resources

One characteristic of what many people now refer to as 'Web 2.0' [12] is the offering of Web resources not through monolithic, one-stop sites but as fine-grained service-providing components. Components from different providers can be assembled to create applications offering useful new services. An early example was the BookBurro agent [1], that lists the prices of a given book in a number of online stores. More complex is Google Maps [4], that draws together a wide range of resources such as shop and business listings, tourism information, and driving directions.

As well as integration by professional Web-application writers to produce sophisticated, polished applications such as Google Maps, the component-based approach in theory opens the way for end users to assemble their own ad-hoc combinations of resources to serve specialised needs. But supporting non-specialist programmers in achieving this kind of programming task is still a formidable challenge.

One domain in which this challenge is reduced, both by being able to circumscribe the variety of resources to be handled and by the fact that many of the target users are already comfortable programming in languages such as Perl, is that of Scientific Workflow (recently surveyed in [18]). Scientific workflow systems allow scientists to create, run and share data-analysis and knowledge-discovery 'pipelines' serving their individual interests. However, the emphasis

K.P. Jantke et al. (Eds.): Federation over the Web, LNAI 3847, pp. 143–158, 2006.
© Springer-Verlag Berlin Heidelberg 2006

in most of these systems is on creating multi-step processes that can then be run repeatedly without the intervention of the user. Some systems have specialised facilities for computational steering, but there is little general support for interactively exploring alternative results.

Lack of support for exploring alternatives is a common characteristic of today's computer applications, to such an extent that Terry and Mynatt [15] speak of a prevalent and inconvenient 'single-state document model'. For some years we have been investigating how to improve on this situation by building interfaces that support the setup and use of alternative scenarios side by side [9, 10, 11].

We see an especially strong need to support the use of alternatives when working with Web-based resources. The Web offers multiplicity not just with respect to book stores, but for many kinds of information and processing resources. Having access to multiple resources can give various potential benefits: BookBurro illustrates the power of comparing resources against each other; resource-access redundancy can improve overall reliability of access; and complementary resources may add up to a breadth of information that is not available from any single location. In general, the Web is a domain in which users may sometimes want to make multiple requests of a single resource, and sometimes want to send the same request to alternative resources.

What kind of environment would be suitable for building custom applications within this domain? We believe that an adapted form of spreadsheet may provide the necessary support. Spreadsheets have proved popular with end users, and features such as tabular layout and the use of relative operand addressing help users to set up related calculations. The spreadsheet approach has already been applied to various specialised domains in which users want to build and manipulate processing flows side by side, such as image processing [8] and data visualisation [2, 5]. Each domain imposes requirements in terms of handling the appropriate data types and processing; the same will be true of the Web. In addition, as argued above, we believe that the adapted spreadsheet must support flexible interactive exploration of alternatives.

1.1   Data and Processing in a Web-Resource Spreadsheet

Whereas scientific workflow systems are concerned with the communication and processing of (potentially huge) files or tables of data, the bulk of day-to-day communication with Web services occurs by transferring chunks of XML. So a basic requirement is that our spreadsheet support the creation, communication and processing of XML (including XHTML, and thus Web pages). There should also be straightforward ways to extract and work with simple string and numerical values that the XML may hold. If the need does arise to process large data sets, this should be achieved by storing them in files and passing URI-style references between processing components, rather than by channelling the data through the spreadsheet itself.

The spreadsheet must offer facilities to invoke processing resources that are offered over the Web. One form of resource is a Web service, callable through an XML-based protocol such as SOAP. Another is a Web application that has been 'wrapped', meaning that facilities designed for interactive use through a Web browser can instead be used through a programmatic interface. Recent surveys of Web-application wrapping include [6, 7]; in our own work on C3W [3] we have investigated how simple applications may be wrapped interactively by end users.

The system must also let the user define how data is passed between processing resources. In the simplest case, data is just copied from from one place to another; in many of today's scientific workflow systems this is specified using a wiring diagram. However, it is not always the case that data produced by one resource is in exactly the form needed as input for another. If just a standard kind of conversion is needed, such as between number and string formats, this can be achieved with a lightweight approach such as the 'shim services' available for the Taverna workflow system [13]. More generally, a user will need to interpose some specialised 'glue code' to perform the necessary data manipulations.

Offering a suitable language for the glue code depends on what operations are needed. For simple manipulation of strings and numbers, the kind of formula language found in a standard spreadsheet may suffice. For more complex operations, such as iterative calculations or the analysis of strings, there is still no single language that clearly offers both expressibility and ease of use. Among string-processing languages, IBM's REXX remains popular for its ease of use, while Perl has superior power based on its regular-expression support. Languages such as XQuery offer the facilities needed for processing XML, but are hard to master. For the time being, it appears that our system must support several glue languages and let its users choose among them.

As noted above, in the domain of Web-based processing a user might invoke multiple resources for the same request, or might send multiple requests to a single resource. This suggests that the two situations should be supported in similar ways. But spreadsheets typically make a clear distinction between cell values and their processing; while the values may be changed easily (such as by pasting a new set of values onto a range), the processing elements – that is, the formulas – are relatively static. Part of the issue is that for reasons of space efficiency and tidiness most spreadsheet interfaces show either the cells' values or their connections, but not both. One exception in the commercial world was Spreadsheet2000 [17], where the cells and their derivation connections were all made visible. We believe that a similar approach may be appropriate for a Web-resource spreadsheet.

1.2   Interactive Exploration of Alternatives

A key property of the traditional spreadsheet is that alternative derivations, based on variation in values or in formulas, can be laid out side by side, typically in neighbouring rows or columns. This sets up a long-lived view in which alternatives can be calculated and compared. If a new set of data is loaded into the sheet, the equivalent comparisons for that data conveniently come into view.

However, neither this kind of variation built into a sheet, nor the availability of 'scenario management' facilities for evaluating and displaying a batch of alternatives, constitutes good support for exploring alternatives interactively. For exploring the effect of alternative data values, some researchers have proposed using interaction widgets such as sliders to set cells' values, letting users apply incremental, reversible adjustment [16, 14]. But in this approach the sheet's cell values are constantly being overwritten, denying the possibility of side-by-side comparison. Interactive exploration based on changing formulas, or adding even simple extra calculation steps, has received little attention in existing work.

In addition, we would like to overcome the problem that a spreadsheet's layout freezes into the sheet one particular dimension of side-by-side comparison; to explore a different dimension may require completely rebuilding the sheet. Our goal is to let users switch easily between comparisons on any of several dimensions.

We report on the design and implementation of a prototype RecipeSheet, a spreadsheet-like environment that can be used to access, combine and explore Web resources. In the next section we demonstrate the RecipeSheet's basic features, then in Sect. 3 we describe the abstraction, called a recipe, that underlies its processing. Finally, Sect. 4 includes examples of the prototype being put to use on Web-based processing.

2   A Spreadsheet with Built-In Support for Alternatives

The RecipeSheet interface is based on the principles of subjunctive interfaces [9, 10, 11], our approach to supporting users in working with alternative scenarios. We first describe these principles, then show examples of multiple scenarios in the RecipeSheet.

2.1   Principles of Subjunctive Interfaces

The purpose of a subjunctive interface is to support the user of a computer application in viewing and manipulating many alternative application scenarios in parallel. The key features of an application with a subjunctive interface are as follows:

Multiple scenarios can co-exist. At any given time the application can support multiple scenarios, which may be created at the request of a user or automatically by the application. The scenarios typically deal with mutually incompatible application states. For example, when asked to choose a single value for some application input, a user who is equally interested in several values may request the creation of a separate scenario to cater for each value.

The user can view scenarios side by side. The application displays all currently existing scenarios side by side, in a way that helps the user to compare them, or to examine each scenario individually.

The user can adjust scenarios in parallel. The user can make changes to many scenarios at the same time, for example by adjusting an input that is shared across scenarios and seeing immediately how this affects the outcome of each one.

2.2 Multiple Scenarios in a RecipeSheet

In a RecipeSheet, alternative scenarios arise from specifying variants for cell values or for the processing between cells.

Figures 1 and 2 show a simple recipe sheet with six cells, one of which is derived from the values in the other five. Figure 1 shows the user starting from a single-scenario state, where each cell contains a single value, and editing the contents of the *fontSize* cell. As well as letting the user edit the existing value, the interface allows specification of variants for that value, causing new scenarios to be created. Say that some cell holds a value v_0, currently being used in scenarios s_1 and s_2. If the user edits that value and specifies new variants, then for each variant v_i, scenarios s_1 and s_2 will be copied to create two new scenarios, each with v_i as the value for that cell. In Fig. 1 the user edits the value 14, adding values 18 and 20 that then appear in two new scenarios.

Scenarios are shown side by side using a technique that we call widget multiplexing. A widget multiplexer is a user-interface element that handles the presen-

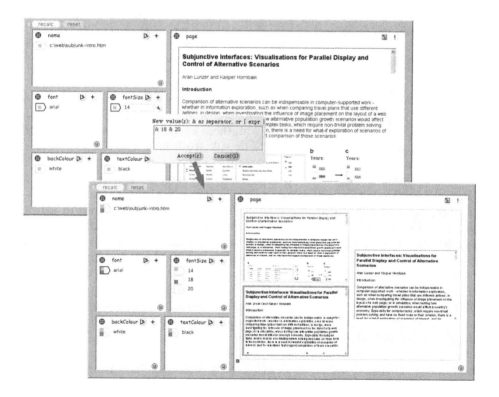

Fig. 1. Creating alternative scenarios on a RecipeSheet. The *page* cell shows a Web page formatted according to the style settings in the cells *font, fontSize, backColour* and *textColour*. The user edits the value in *fontSize*, specifying additional values by using the reserved & symbol. This results in creation of two extra scenarios, displayed alongside the first.

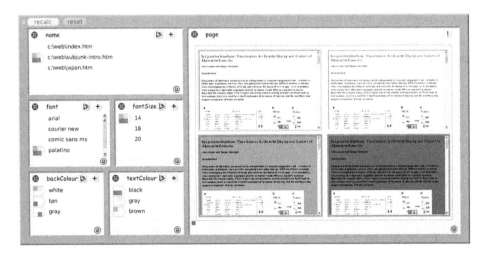

Fig. 2. User-chosen combinations of cell values. Having added alternative values to each of the style-settings cells, the user has manipulated the markers in the *backColour* and *textColour* cells to set up four scenarios with alternative colour combinations. All scenarios currently have the same value for file name, font and font size; to switch all scenarios to, say, the 20-point base font size, the user can simply click on that value.

tation and user interaction for some defined region, which typically constitutes a single widget. If that region would appear differently in the scenarios that have been set up, the multiplexer shows all those appearances. Each multiplexer shows its scenarios' various values side by side, to help a user compare values between scenarios.

Different kinds of widget call for different styles of multiplexer. In Figs. 1 and 2 most of the cells are for specifying text-string values; these display their scenario-specific values as a list, with markers to show which list item is used in which scenario. Just the *page* cell holds a richer type of content, that cannot be shown in a list; it shows its alternative values using zooming and spatial arrangement. However, all types of multiplexer use a common set of colours and arrangements to represent the various scenarios – so, for example, in Fig. 2 the colour of the square in the bottom-left of the marker next to 'tan' matches the border colour of the result at bottom left in the *page* cell. The intention of this is to help a user understand which values go to make up each scenario. The usability of widget multiplexers has been evaluated in a series of experiments [11].

Figure 2 shows a later stage in the use of the same recipe, when the user has introduced alternative values in all of the cells. This was done using a different mechanism from the scenario-copying approach described above, to avoid generating the huge number of scenarios that would result from a cross-product of all values. Instead, the markers beside the value lists support fine-grained manipulation to let the user choose how many scenarios exist and what values they contain. In this figure the user has created four scenarios, that differ just in their values for background and text colour.

A cell containing a list of values behaves somewhat like a menu, letting the user click on values or drag markers to change which value is assigned to which scenario. In the cells *name*, *font* and *fontSize* the user could click on a currently unmarked entry to switch all the existing scenarios to that value. This provides a rapid way to look at a number of alternative cases – for example, to see how each of the files would look with the specified set of colour combinations.

Figure 3 illustrates two further RecipeSheet features: first is the ability to set up, side by side, alternative ways to derive a cell's value; second is the potential for the system to assist in setting up alternative scenarios, such as by offering a simple 'pivot' facility that generates scenarios based on just the values set up in one cell (with all other values being held equal).

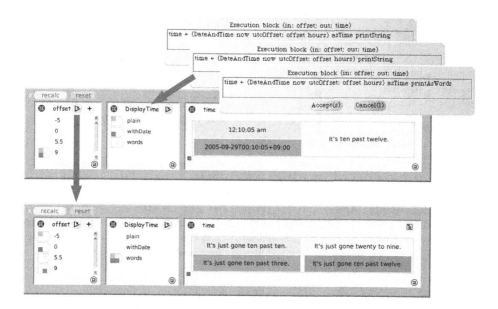

Fig. 3. Specifying variant procedures. This sheet includes a Smalltalk-based recipe to derive a string representing the current time at some given offset (in hours) from Greenwich Mean Time. The user has created a cell to visualise and edit the procedure for that recipe, creating three scenarios based on three alternative procedures. The *offset* cell also contains a range of values. Pressing the cell's 'pivot' button causes the sheet to switch to scenarios that differ purely according to the values within that cell.

This section has shown how the RecipeSheet supports the basic features of a subjunctive interface: multiple scenarios can exist at the same time, can be shown side by side, and can be adjusted in parallel. We have also shown how scenarios can differ in terms of the processing between cells, not just in terms of the cells' contents. In the next section we describe the programming abstraction that underlies these features.

3   Recipes

The programming abstraction that we have developed to support variation in data and in processing is called the recipe. In this section we provide an implementation-level definition.

3.1   The Basic Recipe

Figure 4 shows in schematic form a recipe's basic make-up and instantiation. A recipe is defined in terms of named ingredients (inputs) and results (outputs), and a single procedure that derives result values based on ingredient values (of course, the procedures of interest to us may also draw on external resources, such as the World Wide Web). The stored form of a recipe may include a default value for each ingredient, and for the procedure.

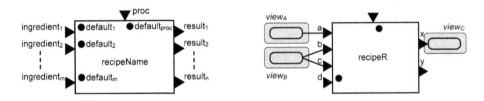

Fig. 4. Recipe form and instantiation. **Left:** Schematic for the canonical form of a recipe, with connections for a list of named ingredients, a list of named results, and a procedure. Optional default values for the procedure and for each ingredient are shown as black dots. **Right:** An instantiated recipe. The user has attached nodes to supply three of the ingredients (with a single node supplying both b and c), and a node to hold one of the results, and has set up views to act as the interfaces to those nodes. The recipe will be evaluated using default values for ingredient d and for the procedure.

For a recipe to be executed it must first be instantiated. This involves associating value holders, that we call nodes, with some or all of the recipe's ingredients and results. In later examples we will show how nodes may be shared between recipes, as the means for passing values from one recipe to another or for using the same value in multiple scenarios. At this stage we just note that in each scenario an ingredient or result may be associated with at most one node, and furthermore that a node may be associated with many ingredients but at most one result.

A node does not necessarily have a user interface; it's up to the user to specify which nodes should be represented by views, allowing the nodes' contents to be viewed or edited. The views on a RecipeSheet are referred to as cells.

3.2   Recipe Composition

Figure 5 illustrates recipe composition. The node that is associated with a result of one recipe can simultaneously be associated with one or more ingredients of

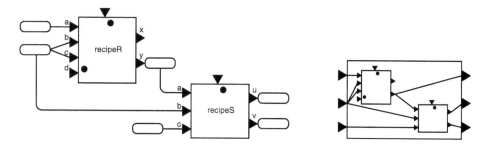

Fig. 5. Connecting recipes. **Left:** By declaring that recipeS's ingredient a will be supplied by the node for result y of recipeR, the user has connected the two recipes. **Right:** This composition represented as a single recipe, for use as-is or in further compositions. Note that result x of recipeR, which the user had not associated with a node, is therefore not a result of the composite.

other recipes. Each new value produced for this result will then be propagated automatically to those ingredients. It is currently the user's responsibility to ensure that an ingredient is only connected to a result whose values will be of suitable type, and that the overall graph of recipe connections is acyclic.

A graph of recipes instantiated and connected in this way can be treated (and stored) as a single composite recipe. The results, ingredients, and procedure for this composite recipe are defined as follows: every node within the graph that is associated with some result is also considered a result of the composite; all other nodes – i.e., nodes only associated with ingredients – are considered ingredients of the composite; the recipe's procedure is, in effect, a nested invocation of the execution mechanism described below.

3.3 Recipe Execution

The execution model for recipes mimics the dataflow-style behaviour of spreadsheets. When a recipe is first instantiated, it is executed with the ingredient values and procedure available at that time. Thereafter, in principle, a recipe should be re-executed whenever its procedure, or the value of one or more of its ingredients, is changed. In practice it makes sense to apply various optimisations – one being that, since a recipe graph is acyclic, re-execution of the graph in response to any ingredient-value changes can be scheduled such that each component recipe is executed just once. It can also be useful to let the user switch to a mode in which re-execution is triggered manually.

In theory the recipe model can support procedures written in any procedural language. Our current implementation supports just the use of Smalltalk, XQuery, Web services (through SOAP), and Web-application derivation captured using our C3W approach [3].

3.4 Recipe Variation

The recipe abstraction, by clarifying which aspects of result derivation are fixed and which are free to be varied, supports the setup and use of alternative pro-

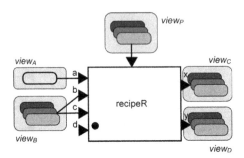

Fig. 6. Recipe variation. Three scenarios have been defined, each with its own instance of the procedure and of the node supplying ingredients b and c. Correspondingly, results x and y are also associated with three nodes each. Ingredient a is not affected by this variation, so a single node can serve all the scenarios.

cessing scenarios. Various degrees of freedom are possible; in our current work we define that the names and types of a recipe's ingredients and results are fixed, but that their values and the procedure used to derive the results are variable.

Figure 6 represents an example of recipe variation, showing three scenarios that involve the same recipe. All scenarios use the same source for one ingredient, but have independent sources for the other ingredients and for the recipe's procedure, allowing different values to be supplied for those elements.

Two types of procedure are supported: single-scenario and cross-scenario. A single-scenario procedure is written to accept a single value for each ingredient, and to produce a single value for each result. A cross-scenario procedure is written to accept a list of values for each ingredient, corresponding to that ingredient's values in all currently existing scenarios. For each named result it may either deliver a single aggregate value, or an independent value in each scenario.

When a single-scenario procedure is executed, the execution framework automatically handles the supply of ingredients and delivery of results for just one scenario; the procedure need not refer to scenarios at all. A cross-scenario procedure, on the other hand, must be written to expect ingredients as lists, and must deliver results that are clearly either aggregate values or scenario-dependent lists. The convention used to indicate this will typically depend on the programming language being used: for Smalltalk we have created a special collection class to hold cross-scenario result lists; for XQuery, a special XML tag. Given that recipes can have different procedures in different scenarios, we need the following rule for the use of cross-scenario procedures: when a recipe has variant procedures, any variant that is a cross-scenario procedure must deliver only aggregate result values.

4   Application to Web Resources

Having outlined what a RecipeSheet can do, we finish with some examples of how our existing prototype can handle Web-based resources.

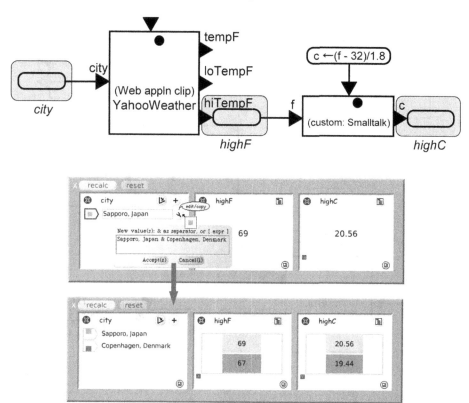

Fig. 7. Schematic and two displays of a simple composite recipe. The YahooWeather recipe offers three temperature values (today's high and low, and the current value) for a supplied city. The user has connected the high-temperature result, which is in Fahrenheit, to a custom recipe that converts this to Centigrade. Below, this composite is being used to look up Sapporo's temperature; when the user edits the *city* value and adds a second value, an extra scenario is created and the two are shown side by side.

Figure 7 illustrates the use of a simple recipe that was captured from the Yahoo! weather site. Because it was captured using C3W, the extracted results are pieces of HTML corresponding to a region within a Web page. For a result that is a piece of HTML, the RecipeSheet offers the following presentations: normal formatting as if in a browser (using an Internet Explorer view); the HTML markup as a string; just the content of text elements within the HTML; the text contents converted to a number. When setting up a cell to hold some result, the user is therefore given a choice among the available presentations; in this example the user chose numeric content. A similar choice is available when a result is connected as an ingredient for another recipe; again, here the numeric value is used as input to a custom Smalltalk recipe, which converts Fahrenheit values to Centigrade. Though not revealed explicitly in the current interface, the processing used to transform one type of result into another (e.g., HTML into a number) can also be implemented as a recipe.

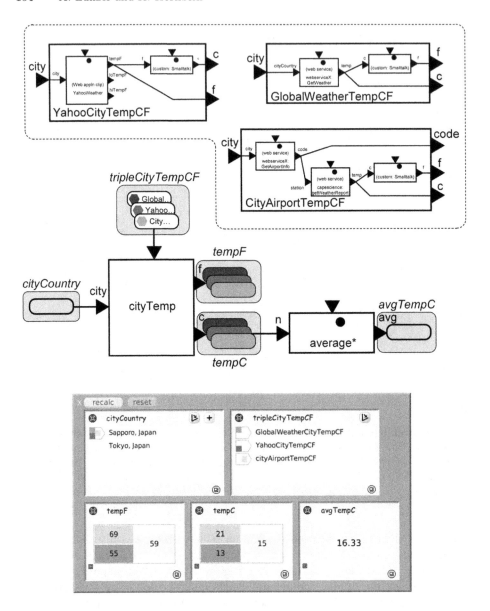

Fig. 8. Schematic and display of a recipe that includes variant procedures. Cells *tempF* and *tempC* gather the result nodes from three scenarios, each served by one of the composite recipes shown at the top. The composites' details have been simplified for presentation; one feature of interest is that one obtains a Fahrenheit value from the Web and converts it to Centigrade, while the others convert in the opposite direction. The asterisk on the recipe name 'average*' indicates that it is a cross-scenario recipe, providing the average of the values provided for its *n* ingredient.

In Fig. 8 the same combination of the Yahoo! application and temperature conversion (though this time on the result for the current temperature, rather than the day's high) is used as one of three alternative Web resources providing this information. The other two are based on Web services: one uses a service that delivers detailed information given a city name, and the other uses a combination of airport-code lookup followed by retrieval of information for the airport's weather station. In the execution shown here, the temperature reported by one recipe is dramatically different from the others (caused by a mismatch in when the weather conditions were sampled), revealing one benefit of seeing values side by side: although the average doesn't reveal the discrepancy, it is clear when looking at the contents of *tempC* and *tempF*.

We are currently evaluating the RecipeSheet with the help of a group at Hokkaido University who work with Web-based bioinformatics tools. A wide range of bioinformatics databases and services are now available over the Web, but the ad-hoc development of these tools has led to poor integration between them. A researcher or student who wants to use several tools in concert therefore faces challenges in selecting the aspects of the tools' behaviour that are of interest, in connecting the tools while accommodating any necessary data transformations and user interaction, and in generating and comparing the results for several scenarios. We are investigating how the RecipeSheet approach – in particular, its multi-scenario support – might help address these challenges.

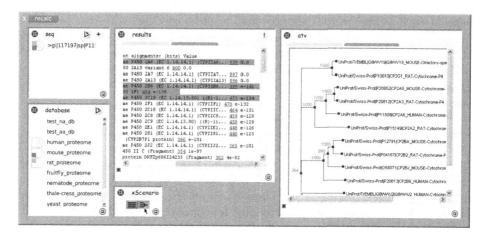

Fig. 9. A recipe that connects three bioinformatics tools: the homology-search tool BLAST, the phylogenetic-tree generator ClustalW, and the tree viewer ATV. This setup supports the user in running BLAST with alternative search sequences in cell *seq* and/or against alternative databases, then comparing the phylogenetic trees created by alternative selections among the BLAST results. In this figure the user has created three scenarios that search against three databases, has selected a few results from each search, and is running the tree-generation step in cross-scenario mode to aggregate those selections into a single phylogenetic tree.

Figure 9 shows a recipe built to a specification provided by our bioinformatics colleagues, embodying a typical sequence of processing steps. This recipe lets them see, side by side, scenarios involving different databases, then to aggregate selected results into a single view if wanted. Because our prototype RecipeSheet does not yet include support for commonly used glue languages such as Perl, our colleagues are not yet able to build such compositions for themselves. However, by collaborating on examples such as this we are building up our understanding of what is needed, and confirming the potential benefits of the recipe approach.

5   Conclusion and Future Work

A RecipeSheet is a spreadsheet-like environment, based on the principles of subjunctive interfaces, that supports users in creating, comparing and manipulating alternative scenarios. Its key concepts are a processing abstraction, called a recipe, that has explicit support for variation; a theoretically language-neutral framework for composing and executing recipes, potentially with variants that establish multiple scenarios; and an interface supporting recipe composition and the specification of variants. We have demonstrated our RecipeSheet prototype, developed in Squeak Smalltalk, that we are now evaluating in collaboration with our bioinformatics colleagues.

Much work lies ahead, on each of the key concepts. First is the recipe abstraction, for which we have yet to solidify the theoretical groundwork. Many aspects, such as how recipes are executed, must be specified with care to ensure properties such as determinacy and the avoidance of deadlocks. As a longer-term issue we would like to investigate allowing the variants of a recipe to differ at the level of ingredients becoming results, and vice versa. This would greatly enrich the model, but is also likely to lead to severe problems of interface complexity.

Second is the framework for composing and executing recipes across multiple scenarios. For the prototype we have postponed the resolution of various issues, instead using simplifications such as naive per-session caching of results, and by requiring manual triggering of recalculation when online resources are being used. We believe that we can find practical solutions to many such issues within existing research, especially in the domain of scientific workflow systems. We are also considering the addition of more glue languages (such as REXX and Perl), to broaden the user base in support of our evaluation work.

Third is the interface. The whole RecipeSheet project is part of our larger investigation of subjunctive interfaces, and their potential to change people's behaviour in evaluating and exploring results obtained in computer applications. Many questions remain unanswered regarding the willingness with which people will set up alternative scenarios, and how they would react to a system that automatically proposes alternatives alongside what they are doing. The RecipeSheet, as the richest manifestation of subjunctive interfaces to date, will become our vehicle for exploring these questions.

Acknowledgements

We gratefully acknowledge the efforts of the developers of the tools on which the current RecipeSheet implementation depends: Squeak, and its recently added bridge to .NET; the eXist implementation of XQuery; and the many bioinformatics tools, and other Web applications and Web services, that we have used as examples.

This work has been greatly facilitated by the supportive environment of the Meme Media Laboratory, including Jun Fujima's unstinting .NET programming support and late-night design discussions.

The development of the RecipeSheet is partly supported by JSPS grant-in-aid number 175000533602.

References

1. BookBurro. http://bookburro.org/.
2. Chi, E. H., Barry, P., Riedl, J., Konstan, J.: A Spreadsheet Approach to Information Visualization. *Proceedings of the IEEE Symposium on Information Visualization (InfoViz '97)*, pages 17–24.
3. Fujima, J., Lunzer, A., Hornbæk, K., Tanaka, Y.: Clip, Connect, Clone: Combining Application Elements to Build Custom Interfaces for Information Access. *Proc. ACM UIST,* pages 175–184. ACM Press, 2004.
4. Google Maps. http://maps.google.com.
5. Jankun-Kelly, T. J., Ma, K.-L.: Visualization Exploration and Encapsulation via a Spreadsheet-Like Interface. *IEEE Transactions on Visualization and Computer Graphics,* 7(3):275–287. IEEE Press, 2001.
6. Kuhlins, S., Tredwell, R.: Toolkits for Generating Wrappers – A Survey of Software Toolkits for Automated Data Extraction from Web Sites. *Lecture Notes in Computer Science (LNCS) 2591*, pages 184–198. Springer, 2003.
7. Laender, A. H. F., Ribeiro-Neto, B. A., da Silva, A. S., Teixeira, J. S.: A Brief Survey of Web Data Extraction Tools. *SIGMOD Record* 31(2):84–93. ACM Press, 2002.
8. Levoy, M.: Spreadsheets for Images. *Proceedings of ACM SIGGRAPH '94*, pages 139–146. ACM Press, 1994.
9. Lunzer, A.: Choice and comparison where the user wants them: Subjunctive interfaces for computer-supported exploration. In *Proc. IFIP TC. 13 International Conference on Human-Computer Interaction (INTERACT '99)*, pages 474–482. IOS Press, 1999.
10. Lunzer, A.: Benefits of Subjunctive Interface Support for Exploratory Access to Online Resources. In: G. Grieser, Y. Tanaka (eds.) *Intuitive Human Interfaces for Organizing and Accessing Intellectual Assets. LNAI 3359,* pages 14–32. Springer, 2004.
11. Lunzer, A., Hornbæk, K.: Usability studies on a visualisation for parallel display and control of alternative scenarios. In *Proceedings of AVI 2004*, pages 125–132. ACM Press, 2004.
12. MacManus, R., Porter, J.: Web 2.0 for Designers. *Digital Web Magazine*, May 2005. http://www.digital-web.com/articles/web_2_for_designers/.

13. Oinn, T., Addis, M., Ferris, J., Marvin, D., Greenwood, M., Carver, T., Pocock, M. R., Wipat, A., Li, P.: Taverna: A Tool for the Composition and Enactment of Bioinformatics Workflows. *Bioinformatics* 20(17):3045–3054. Oxford University Press, 2004.
14. Smedley, T. J., Cox, P. T., Byrne, S. L.: Expanding the Utility of Spreadsheets through the Integration of Visual Programming and User Interface Objects. *Proceedings of the workshop on Advanced visual interfaces (AVI '96)*, pages 148–155. ACM Press, 1996.
15. Terry, M., Mynatt, E.: Recognizing Creative Needs in User Interface Design. In *Proceedings of the fourth conference on Creativity and Cognition (C&C 2002)*, pages 38–44. ACM Press, 2002.
16. Truvé, S.: Dynamic What-If Analysis: Exploring Computational Dependencies with Slidercells and Micrographs. *Conference Companion of ACM Human Factors in Computing Systems (CHI '95)*, pages 280–281. ACM Press, 1995.
17. Wilson, S.:   Building a Visual Programming Language.   *MacTech* 13(4). http://www.mactech.com/articles/mactech/Vol.13/13.04/Spreadsheet2000/.
18. Yu, J., Buyya, R.: A Taxonomy of Scientific Workflow Systems for Grid Computing. *SIGMOD Record*, 34(3):44–49. ACM Press, 2005.

Knowledge Federation over the Web Based on Meme Media Technologies

Yuzuru Tanaka

Meme Media Laboratory, Hokkaido University,
Sapporo, 060-8628 Japan
tanaka@meme.hokudai.ac.jp

Abstract. This paper proposes a formal model for the aggregate ad hoc federation of geographically distributed intelligent resources accessible through the Web. We already proposed frameworks for one-by-one ad hoc federation of intelligent resources over the Web. They can define interoperation among intelligent resources over the Web as a set of interoperations between two intelligent resources. They allow us to define an overall federation by repetitively combining resources. This paper deals with a case in which we have large sets of intelligent resources accessible through the Web. Each set is assumed to consist of resources of the same type, and to be accessible through the Web in the same way. This paper focuses on how to define and to execute a large set of federations, each of which defines interoperation among resources taken from different sets of resources. Such federation is called aggregate federation. Our new framework for ad hoc aggregate federation will be formalized based on meta relations and their relational expressions, and enables users to flexibly select some resources satisfying a specified condition from each set of resources of the same kind, to define a relation of resources satisfying a specified condition as a subset of the Cartesian product of these different resource sets, and to define and to execute interoperation among resources in each tuple in the defined relation.

1 Introduction

The Web works not only as an open publishing repository of documents, but also as an open repository of distributed intelligent resources, i.e., computing resources. It treats each intelligent resource as a service, and publishes it either as a Web application or as a Web service. Such intelligent resources include not only services provided by Web servers, but also embedded and/or mobile intelligent resources connected to the Internet through wireless communication. Pervasive computing denotes an open system of intelligent resources in which users can dynamically select and interoperate some of these intelligent resources to perform their jobs satisfying their dynamically changing demands. Pervasive computing assumes the wide distribution of such intelligent resources, not only over the Web, but also in our physical environments.

In pervasive computing, the ad hoc definition and/or execution of interoperation among intelligent resources is called federation. While the integration

K.P. Jantke et al. (Eds.): Federation over the Web, LNAI 3847, pp. 159–182, 2006.

denotes interoperation among intelligent resources with standard interoperation interfaces designed in advance, federation denotes interoperation among intelligent resources without such advance design of interoperation interfaces. Ad hoc federation denotes such federation that can be defined on site at any time and any place by a non-programmer user. We define knowledge federation as federation of intelligent resources published in the form of documents.

Federation of intelligent resources over the Web is relevant to the interdisciplinary and international reuse and interoperation of heterogeneous intelligent resources, especially in scientific simulations [1], digital libraries [2], and research activities [3]. Federation of intelligent resources over pervasive computing environments is of interest for on-site instantaneous analysis, strategic planning, and immediate action that maximizes use of accessible resources, especially in risk management such as disaster relief and zoonosis control, finance, user-customizable security and management systems for office and home, strategic business analysis and management, customizable control of sensor and/or actuator networks, user-customizable monitoring and control of home electronic appliances, and so on. Federation of intelligent resources over pervasive computing environments requires ad hoc definability and an interactive easy way of finding appropriate resources and obtaining the proxies needed to utilize them.

Federation of intelligent resources may be classified into two types: autonomic federation defined by programs, and ad hoc federation by users. Most studies on federation have focused on the former type. Their approach is based on both the proposal of a standard communication protocol with a language to use it and a repository with a matching mechanism between service-providing programs and service-consuming programs [4]. The origin of such an idea can be found in the original tuple space model Linda [5, 6], which was then extended to Lime [7] to cope with mobile objects with dedicated tuple spaces. Federation of this type over the Web uses Web service technologies. In this paper, we focus on the latter type, i.e., federation defined by users. Such federation is defined by users in an ad hoc manner.

For ad hoc federation of intelligent resources accessible through the Web, we have already proposed the use of meme media technologies [8, 9] and the C3W framework [10] to clip out any portion of Web applications as visual components and to combine them through direct manipulation to create a new composite service. Such federation is defined one by one, and is called one-by-one federation. In this paper, we propose aggregate federation among sets of intelligent resources. Each set is assumed to consist of geographically distributed intelligent resources of the same type. Examples of such a set are a set of temperature sensors, a set of air conditioners, and a set of function calculation services including the one that converts a current room temperature value to the optimum air conditioner control parameter value to keep the most comfortable room temperature.

We assume that such a set of intelligent resources of the same type is designed to make their properties and IO (input and output) parameters accessible through the Web using one of the following representations:

1. as a textual list of items embedded in a Web document,
2. as a relation among an input form value of a Web application and a textual list of items embedded in its corresponding output Web page, or
3. as a relation between inputs and outputs of a Web service.

This paper proposes aggregate federation technologies based on our meme media architecture and frameworks to extract a 'Web view relation' of intelligent resources from the above three representations, and to functionally combine these Web view relations using relational expressions for defining a federation among sets of intelligent resources in an ad hoc way. A Web view relation works similarly to a view relation. The latter is defined by a query over a relational database and is treated as a database relation, while the former is defined by HTML path expressions over Web documents and/or Web applications, and is, likewise, treated as a database relation.

2   Basic Idea of Our Approach

The approach to one-by-one ad hoc federation developed by us requires a technique for extracting the IO relation of each intelligent resource as a meme media object, and defining a federation among intelligent resources by combining their corresponding meme media objects [9, 10]. Aggregate ad hoc federation, on the other hand, requires a technique for extracting sets of IO relations as a 'Web view relation', and defining a set of federations among sets of intelligent resources by combining their corresponding view relations using relational expression such as those used for relational databases.

Each Web view relation defines rules to obtain a relation from the Web. It is a non materialized relation, and becomes a materialized relation when evaluated. Web view relations can be treated as relations in databases. A relational expression of view relations defines another Web view relation, which also becomes a relation when evaluated.

For a set of intelligent resources whose information is published as a textual list in a Web document, we can apply some Web wrapper technology to extract a Web view relation over a specified set of attributes about these intelligent resources. Each record, or each tuple, in such a Web view relation represents a single intelligent resource, and provides the value of each of its attributes. For a Web document on a set of sensors of different categories at different locations, we may extract a Web view relation with the sensor identifier, the sensor type, the sensor location, and the current sensor value as its attributes. In this example, the sensor identifier attribute works as a primary key of this relation. The evaluation of a Web view relation first accesses the Web page and extracts a materialized relation. The evaluation of the same Web view relation may result in different relations at different times if this Web page is periodically updated by its server.

For a set of intelligent resources whose information is published as a Web application, we can apply the same method we have proposed [11] for one-by-one federation to the Web application to extract an IO relation as a meme media object, which works as a proxy object of this Web application. Such a meme media object representing an IO relation, when provided with a set of possible input values for each extracted input field, defines a materialized relation. Therefore, it also defines a Web view relation whose input domains should be specified in advance.

For a set of intelligent resources whose information is published as a Web service, we propose a new method for automatically analyzing the WSDL description of its interface, asking a user to specify IO items to extract an IO relation from the Web service, and automatically creating a meme media object with IO ports for the extracted IO relation. This meme media object works as a proxy object of the Web service, enabling only a subset of the original IO ports. Such an IO relation, when provided with a set of possible input values for each extracted input item, defines a materialized relation. Therefore, it also defines a Web view relation whose input domains should be specified in advance.

Using a relational expression over such Web view relations, we will be able to define an aggregate federation among sets of intelligent resources, where each set consists of intelligent resources of the same type.

3   Web View Relations for Web Applications and Web Services

3.1   Meme Media as an Enabling Technology

IntelligentPad is an instance of the meme-media architecture, based on a two-dimensional representation. For our current purposes, its architecture can be roughly summarized as follows: Instead of directly dealing with component objects, IntelligentPad wraps each object with a standard pad wrapper, i.e., a software module with a standard visual representation and a standard functional linkage interface, and treats it as a media object called a pad. Each pad has both a standard user interface and a standard connection interface. The user interface of every pad has a card-like view on the screen and a standard set of operations like 'move', 'resize', 'copy', 'paste', and 'peel'. As a connection interface, every pad provides a list of slots that work as IO ports, and a standard set of messages 'set', 'gimme', and 'update'. Each pad designates one of its slots as its primary slot. Most pads allow users to change the primary-slot designation.

You may paste a pad on another pad to define a parent-child relationship between these two pads. The former becomes a child of the latter. When you paste a pad on another, you can select one of the slots provided by the parent pad, and connect the child pad to this selected slot. The selected slot is called the connection slot. Using a 'set' message, each child pad can set the value of its primary slot to the connection slot of its parent pad. Using a 'gimme' message, each child pad can read the connection slot value of its parent pad, and update its primary slot with this value. Whenever a pad has a state change, it sends an 'update' message to each of its child pads to notify that there has been a state change. Whenever a pad receives an 'update' message, it sends a 'gimme' message to its parent pad to read the recent value of the slot to which it is connected. For each slot connection, you can independently enable or disable each of the three standard messages, 'set', 'gimme', and 'update'. By pasting pads on another pad and specifying slot connections, you may easily define both a compound-document's layout design and functional linkages among these pads. Further details on its architecture, its applications, and its extension to a meme-media instance with three-dimensional representation can be found in [8].

3.2   Web View Relations for Web Applications

Our C3W framework, proposed in 2004 [11], allows a user to clip arbitrary HTML elements from Web pages visited through a sequence of navigation operations, and to paste these clips, represented as pads, onto a single special pad called a C3WsheetPad. The pasted pads capture not just the appearance of the clipped elements, but also the functional relationships between them in the original navigation. Figure 1 shows an application of this framework to the CNN Money stock-quote information service Web page. The Web browser used here is also a pad, that wraps Internet Explorer. This browser pad supports clipping by providing a highlight that follows the mouse pointer, indicating the region of the nearest surrounding HTML element; if the user starts a mouse drag, the highlighted document portion is clipped as a pad.

In Fig. 1, we first clipped the company-name input field as a pad and pasted it on a C3WsheetPad. Then we entered a company name in the input field on the original Web page, and submitted it to the Web application. The Web application updated the page to show the current stock quote of this company. Then we clipped the stock-quote value from this page, and pasted it as another pad on the same C3WsheetPad. The first clip holds the url of the original Web page and the HTML path expression that specifies the selected element within this page.

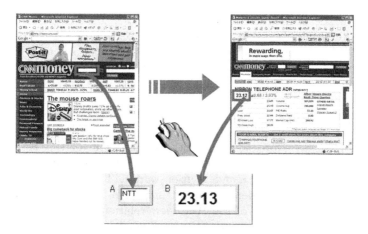

Fig. 1. Clips extracted from more than one page in a single navigation and their recombination on a C3WsheetPad

The second clip holds all the user operation events between the first and second clipping, and the HTML path expression specifying the second selected portion on the current Web page. When these clips are pasted on the C3WsheetPad, it uses their HTML path expressions, and the sequence of user actions between the clipping operations, to relate the clips as inputs and outputs of the Web application. It also assigns each clip a unique cell name such as A, B, C, ..., Z, A1, B1, ... , and generates a corresponding slot, i.e., a slot #A for the cell A. The value of each slot is typically the HTML description of the HTML element shown by the clip connected to this slot. However, for convenience, the slot values for simple clips are defined differently: clips of non-numerical input fields and non-numerical text strings have slot values that correspond to their textual contents; numerical input fields and numerical text strings have numerical slot values.

The C3WsheetPad used in the example shown in Fig. 1 works as a pad, with two slots #A and #B, even after we peel off the two clips. It accepts a company name through slot #A and returns the current stock quote of the company through slot #B. Therefore, it works as a virtual database relation over the two attributes <company name> and <stock quote>, where someone must specify externally the domain of the attribute <company name>. We may consider this pad as a Web view relation V(<company name>*, <stock quote>), where the asterisk in <company name>* indicates that the domain of this attribute needs to be specified externally.

Suppose that there is a large set of geographically distributed sensors, and that the current output values of these sensors can be accessed through a dedicated Web application. We further assume the following about this Web application: It has an input field for specifying a sensor identifier, and a submit button to issue a query to the server. After evaluating each query, the server updates the Web page to return the current status of the specified sensor. For simplicity, we assume that it returns a single output value.

Our C3W framework, when applied to this Web application, allows us to first clip out the sensor identifier input form, then to click the submit button on the original Web page, and to clip out the sensor value from the updated Web page. The pasting of these two clips on the same C3WsheetPad creates two slots, slot #A for the sensor identifier input and slot #B for the sensor value output. After we peel off these clips, this C3WsheetPad works as a Web view relation V1(<sensor identifier>*, <sensor value>), in which the domain of the attribute <sensor identifier> needs to be specified externally. Let S(<sensor identifier>) be a unary relation that specifies a set of sensor identifiers. Then an expression defining a natural join of the Web view relation V1 and the relation S defines a new Web view relation over two attributes, <sensor identifier> and <sensor value>. The evaluation of this expression takes one sensor identifier at a time from S and inputs this to the <sensor identifier> attribute of the Web view relation V1 to obtain the corresponding <sensor value> attribute value, and returns a relation over these two attributes.

3.3 Web View Relations for Web Services

If a Web service is provided with a WSDL description of its interface, we can simply syntactically analyze this description to obtain the complete list of its input and output ports. This analysis and the listing can be easily automated. In order to automate the wrapping of an arbitrary Web service to obtain its proxy pad with slots for arbitrarily selected IO ports, we need to automate the code generation for defining slots for selected IO ports. This can be automated by analyzing each IO port type in the WSDL description and by applying standard code generation for each port type. Based on these operations we have developed a pad wrapper for Web services. When applied to a Web service, this pad wrapper pops up a complete list of its IO ports, and asks its user to select some of them to work as slots. When the user specifies a selection, it automatically generates a pad that works as a proxy object of this Web service.

Suppose that there is a large set of geographically distributed sensors, and that the properties and the current values of these sensors can be accessed through a Web service. We further assume the following about this Web service: Its interface includes the sensor identifier input, the sensor-category output, the sensor-location output, and the current sensor-value output. The pad obtained as a proxy of this Web service by using the above-mentioned service wrapper technology will have <sensor identifier>, <sensor category>, <sensor location> and <sensor value> as its slots. This pad can work as a Web view relation V2(<sensor identifier>*, <sensor category>, <sensor location>, <sensor value>) in which the domain of the attribute <sensor identifier> needs to be specified externally. An expression defining a natural join of this Web view relation and the unary relation S(<sensor identifier>) used in the previous section defines a Web view relation over the attributes <sensor identifier>, <sensor category>, <sensor location> and <sensor value>. The evaluation of this expression accesses the Web service as many times as the cardinality of the relation S to obtain the same number of tuples.

4 Web View Relations for Lists in Web Documents

Tools for the extraction of a Web view relation from a Web document, a Web application, or a Web service are generically called Web wrappers. There are quite a few research studies on Web wrappers for Web documents, as will be discussed in Sect. 7. Here we propose a new type of Web wrapper based on the relational model of databases. Such a Web wrapper is represented as a meta relation, which is a relation with meta values as its attribute values. Meta values include texts, numerical values, HTML path expressions, and urls.

Figure 2 shows a Web document with a table showing the career averages of an NBA basketball player. The first attribute <year> of the first record in this table has '97-98' as its textual value, and is identified by an HTML expression /html[1]/body[1]/table[1]/tr[2]/td[1]/, while the second attribute <team> of the same tuple has SAC as its value, and is identified by an HTML path expression /html[1]/body[1]/table[1]/tr[2]/td[2]/. It should be noticed here that the

YEAR	TEAM	G	GS	MPG	FG%	3P%	FT%	OF
97-98	SAC	59	16	16.3	.403	.211	.672	
98-99	SAC	49	49	24.6	.435	.286	.691	
99-00	ORL	46	46	26.2	.433	.095	.762	
99-00	DEN	15	10	24.9	.389	.500	.738	
99-00	--	61	56	25.9	.424	.130	.756	
00-01	DEN	29	12	14.5	.387	.400	.583	
01-02	DEN	20	12	20.9	.379	.500	.750	
01-02	DAL	4	0	6.0	.000	.000	.000	
01-02	--	24	12	18.4	.374	.500	.727	
02-03	DAL	14	0	14.6	.466	.000	.500	
Career		236	145	20.4	.417	.237	.703	

Fig. 2. A Web document with a table showing the career averages of an NBA basketball player

first row in the career average table showing attribute names corresponds to the HTML path expression /html[1]/body[1]/table[1]/tr[1]/, and the tuples are listed from the second row at /html[1]/body[1]/table[1]/tr[2]/. Similarly to the first tuple, the two attribute values of the second tuple are identified respectively by the following HTML path expressions, /html[1]/body[1]/table[1]/tr[3]/td[1]/ and /html[1]/body[1]/table[1]/tr[3]/td[2]/. Instead of copying these four values for filling in a newly defined relation R(<year>, <team>) as shown in Fig. 3(a), let us fill in this new relation with their HTML path expressions as shown in Fig. 3(b). We call this latter relation a meta relation. This meta relation defines two rules to extract the first and second tuples from the Web page. Our basic idea is to generalize these two rules to a single rule to extract not only the first two tuples, but all the tuples from the Web page.

The generalization of the two HTML path expressions of the first attribute, /html[1]/body[1]/table[1]/tr[2]/td[1]/ and /html[1]/body[1]/table[1]/tr[3]/td[1]/ is what is called their antiunification, and results in /html[1]/body[1]/table[1] /tr[x]/td[1]/, whereas the generalization of the two HTML path expressions of the second attribute results in /html[1]/body[1]/table[1]/tr[y]/td[2]/. Here we used different variables for these two generalizations since they are independently performed. However, they are not independent with each other since the first candidate of the first generalization corresponds to the first candidate of the second generalization, and likewise for subsequent candidates. We must use the same variable for these two generalizations.

This constraint among attribute values in the same generalized tuple is called the aggregation constraint. We need to generalize meta values in each attribute to satisfy the aggregate constraint. We can deal with the aggregate constraint in the generalization for each attribute by keeping a record of which values are generalized to each variable. We use a special notation $x(u, v)$ to represent a

R	\<year\>	\<team\>
97-98	SAC
98-99	SAC

(a) A relation consisting of the first two tuples with the first two attributes of the table in Figure 2.

R	\<year\>	\<team\>
/html[1]/body[1]/table[1]/tr[2]/td[1]/	/html[1]/body[1]/table[1]/tr[2]/td[2]/
/html[1]/body[1]/table[1]/tr[3]/td[1]/	/html[1]/body[1]/table[1]/tr[3]/td[2]/

(b) A meta relation with two rules to extract the two tuples in (a) from the table in Figure 2.

R	\<year\>	\<team\>
/html[1]/body[1]/table[1]/tr[$x(2,3)$]/td[1]/	/html[1]/body[1]/table[1]/tr[$x(2,3)$]/td[2]/

(c) A meta relation obtained by the generalization of the two tuples in (b)

Fig. 3. A relation and a meta relation that are manually extracted from a table in a Web document

variable that generalizes two values, u in the first candidate and v in the second candidate. For example, in the generalization for the first attribute in the above example, the variable x is a generalization of the two indices '2' in the first candidate and '3' in the second candidate. In order to keep this record, we use a notation $x(2,3)$ for this variable instead of x. For the variables in the same tuple, i.e., for the variables subject to the aggregate constraint, we use the same symbol x in this variable notation $x(u,v)$. Now, the generalizations for the first and second attributes become /html[1]/body[1]/table[1]/tr[$x(2,3)$]/td[1]/ and /html[1]/body[1]/table[1]/tr[$x(2,3)$]/td[2]/ as shown in Fig. 3(c). Because there are two occurrences of the same variable $x(2,3)$, they are always instantiated with the same value. The notation $x(2,3)$ also denotes that the variable's instantiation sequence starts at '2' and changes in increments of 1. When $x(2,3)$ in /html[1]/body[1]/table[1]/tr[$x(2,3)$]/td[1]/ is instantiated with '2', '3', ... in this order, its occurrence in /html[1]/body[1]/table[1]/tr[$x(2,3)$]/td[2]/ is also simultaneously instantiated with '2', '3', ... to extract the first two columns of the career average table in the Web page and to create a relation R(\<year\>, \<team\>).

The generalization of the two tuples mentioned above can be explained in terms of meta relations and meta values as follows. First, you create an empty new meta relation R(\<year\>, \<team\>) with a relation name R and attribute names \<year\> and \<team\>. This meta relation specifies a relation you will create from values extracted from a Web page. You may specify the first column of the first tuple in the career average table on the Web page, and associate it with the first attribute of the first record in R. Then you may specify the second column of the first tuple in the career average table on the Web page, and associate it with the second attribute of the first record in R. These operations create the first tuple with meta values in R as shown in Fig. 3(b). Then you may repeat similar operations to associate the first two column values of the second tuple

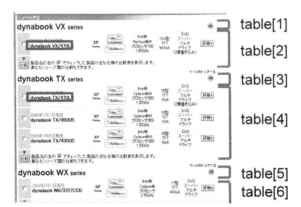

Fig. 4. A list of notebook PC products of Toshiba, where the header and the list of different models in each PC series are each represented as HTML table fragments parenthesized with table tags

in the career average table on the Web page with the second tuple in R. These operations create the second meta value tuple in R as shown in Fig. 3(b). Now you can apply a generalization operation to the first two meta value tuples in R, which merges two tuples in R to a single tuple as shown in Fig. 3(c). The meta relation thus obtained in Fig. 3(c) defines the rule for a Web wrapper.

Figure 4 shows a list of notebook PC products of Toshiba, where the header and the list of different models in each PC series are both represented as HTML table fragments parenthesized with table tags. In order to extract all model names of notebook PCs from this Web page, we need to specify as extraction candidates the first model name in the first series, the first model name in the second series, and the second model name in the second series. Their path expressions /html[1] /body[1] /table[2] /tr[1]/td[2]/, /html[1]/body[1] /table[4] /tr[1] /td[2]/, /html[1]/body[1]/table[4]/tr[2]/td[2]/ are used as meta values of a meta relation PC(<model name>). The generalization of the second and third tuples in this relation is /html[1]/body[1]/table[4]/tr[$x(1,2)$]/td[2]/. The further generalization of this and the first tuple is /html[1]/body[1]/table[$x(2,4)$]/tr[$x(1,2)$]/td[2]/, where the generalization of '1' and '$x(1,2)$' becomes '$x(1,2)$' since the latter includes the former (Fig. 5). The meta relation PC(<model name>) with a single tuple /html[1]/body[1] /table[$x(2,4)$]/tr[$x(1,2)$]/td[2]/ thus obtained works as a Web wrapper to extract all the model names from this page. The two variables $x(2,4)$ and $x(1,2)$ are independently instantiated respectively with 2, 4, 6, ... , and with 1, 2, 3, ...

In the above examples, we extracted only such items that are arranged in a tabular form in the source Web pages. However, their generalization uses only the regularity among the HTML path expressions of the items extracted for the same attribute, and the regularity of relative locations of the HTML nodes extracted for the different attributes of the same tuple. Therefore, the items to be extracted need not be arranged in a tabular form in the source Web page. The

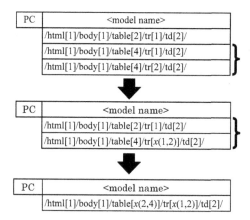

Fig. 5. A generalization of two tuples in the same series, and a generalization of two different series

extraction of book information items such as the title, the authors, the publisher, the year, and the price from an amazon.com or Barnes&Noble.com book search result is such a case. Furthermore, such a list from which to extract a relation may continue across more than one page.

In order to extend our method for extracting a relation from a list on multiple pages, we extend a meta relation to include an additional dummy attribute <url>. This attribute may take a navigation path expression as its value. A navigation path expression is recursively defined as follows: A url is a navigation path expression. Suppose that a is a navigation path expression; if b is an HTML path expression identifying an anchor node in the Web page identified by a, then ab/click/ is a navigation path identifying the target Web page. If b is an HTML path expression identifying an input field in the Web page identified by a, then ab/submit(v)/ is a navigation path identifying the target Web page that is obtained by the submission of v through this input field.

Figure 6 shows a Barnes&Noble book search result for two keywords, 'meme' and 'media'. This result consists of more than one page. We want to extract the title, the front cover image, and the price of each book from the whole search result. We will construct a meta relation with a <url> attribute as follows. Using the first search result page, we will extract all the attribute values for the first and second candidate tuples, and obtain their HTML path expressions to define a meta relation as shown in Fig. 7(a). We will then generalize these two tuples, and replace them with a single generalized tuple as shown in Fig. 7(b). Now we will set the url of this first result page to the <url> attribute of the first tuple in the meta relation with the <url> attribute. Then we will extract the anchor to the next page and put its navigation path, ending with /click/, in the <url> attribute of the second tuple in the meta relation. We may specify the other attributes of the second tuple to have the same meta values as the first tuple. This is shown in Fig. 7(c). Now we will gener-

Fig. 6. A Barnes&Noble book search result for two keywords, 'meme' and 'media'

alize these two tuples to obtain a single tuple whose <url> attribute value is url1$x(\varepsilon$, /html[1]/.../click/), where url1 is equal to http://search .barnesand-noble.com/booksearch/results.asp?SAT=11&WRD=meme+media (Fig. 7(d)). This variable $x(\varepsilon$, /html[1] /.../click/) denotes that its value is first instantiated with an empty string ε, then secondly with /html[1]/.../click/, thirdly with /html[1]/.../click/html[1]/.../click/, and so on in this order. Thus the first page, second page, third page, ..., are sequentially processed to extract all the records in this order. The processing will terminate automatically if the last page has no corresponding anchor.

The generalization of multiple HTML path expressions can be computed using an antiunification algorithm. Antiunification for general cases has been studied by Reynolds [12], and also by Plotkin under the name 'generalization' [13]. In our system implementation, we used LCS (Longest Common Sequence) algorithm for antiunification.

When applied to a Web page with a list of properties and current statuses of distributed intelligent resources, meta relations thus defined to extract some of these entities work as Web view relations. They represent data extraction rules, and can be evaluated to become relations. Web view relations thus obtained have no attributes whose domains need to be externally specified.

Suppose that there exists a Web page with a list of properties and current statuses of distributed sensors. This list shows the identifier, category, location, and current value of each sensor, and periodically updates itself. Following the procedures described above, we can easily extract these values of all these sensors in the form of a meta relation Sensor(<identifier>, <category>, <location>, <current value>). This meta relation works as a Web view relation, and can be joined with other Web view relations.

Book	<title>	<front cover image>	<price>
	/html[1]/body[1]/table[6] /tbody[1]/tr[2]/td[3] /table[2]/tbody[1] /tr[3]/td[1]/table[1] /tbody[1]/tr[3]/td[2]/a[1]/	/html[1]/body[1]/table[6] /tbody[1]/tr[2]/td[3] /table[2]/tbody[1] /tr[3]/td[1]/table[1] /tbody[1]/tr[5]/td[2] /a[1]/img[1]/	/html[1]/body[1]/table[6] /tbody[1]/tr[2]/td[3] /table[2]/tbody[1] /tr[3]/td[3]/table[1] /tbody[1]/tr[4]/td[3]/
	/html[1]/body[1]/table[6] /tbody[1]/tr[2]/td[3] /table[3]/tbody[1] /tr[3]/td[1]/table[1] /tbody[1]/tr[3]/td[2]/a[1]/	/html[1]/body[1]/table[6] /tbody[1]/tr[2]/td[3] /table[3]/tbody[1] /tr[3]/td[1]/table[1] /tbody[1]/tr[5]/td[2] /a[1]/img[1]/	/html[1]/body[1]/table[6] /tbody[1]/tr[2]/td[3] /table[3]/tbody[1] /tr[3]/td[3]/table[1] /tbody[1]/tr[4]/td[3]/

(a) A meta relation with the first and second candidate tuples.

Book	<title>	<front cover image>	<price>
	/html[1]/body[1]/table[6] /tbody[1]/tr[2]/td[3] /table[$x(2,3)$]/tbody[1] /tr[3]/td[1]/table[1] /tbody[1]/tr[3]/td[2]/a[1]/	/html[1]/body[1]/table[6] /tbody[1]/tr[2]/td[3] /table[$x(2,3)$]/tbody[1] /tr[3]/td[1]/table[1] /tbody[1]/tr[5]/td[2] /a[1]/img[1]/	/html[1]/body[1]/table[6] /tbody[1]/tr[2]/td[3] /table[$x(2,3)$]/tbody[1] /tr[3]/td[3]/table[1] /tbody[1]/tr[4]/td[3]/

(b) Generalization of the two tuples in (a).

Book	<url>	<title>	<front cover image>	<price>
	http://search .barnesandnoble.com /booksearch/results .asp?SAT=11& WRD=meme+media	/html[1]/body[1]/... /table[$x(2,3)$]/... /tr[3]/td[2]/a[1]/	/html[1]/body[1]/... /table[$x(2,3)$]/... /tr[5]/td[2] /a[1]/img[1]/	/html[1]/body[1]/... /table[$x(2,3)$]/... /tr[4]/td[3]/
	http://search .barnesandnoble.com /booksearch/results .asp?SAT=11& WRD=meme+media /html[1]/body[1] /table[6]/tbody[1] /tr[2]/td[3]/table[12] /tbody[1]/tr[6]/td[1] /a[2] /click/	/html[1]/body[1]/... /table[$x(2,3)$]/... /tr[3]/td[2]/a[1]/	/html[1]/body[1]/... /table[$x(2,3)$]/... /tr[5]/td[2] /a[1]/img[1]/	/html[1]/body[1]/... /table[$x(2,3)$]/... /tr[4]/td[3]/

(c) Use of the <url> attribute to deal with a list across more than one page.

Book	<url>	<title>	<front cover image>	<price>
	http://search.... ?SAT=11& WRD=meme+media $x(\varepsilon$, /html[1]/body[1] /table[6]/tbody[1] /tr[2]/td[3]/table[12] /tbody[1]/tr[6]/td[1] /a[2] /click/)	/html[1]/body[1]/ ... /table[$x(2,3)$]/... /tr[3]/td[2]/a[1]/	/html[1]/body[1]/ ... /table[$x(2,3)$]/... /tr[5]/td[2] /a[1]/img[1]/	/html[1]/body[1]/ ... /table[$x(2,3)$]/... /tr[4]/td[3]/

(d) Generalization of the tuples in (c).

Fig. 7. A meta relation to extract a Web view relation from a list across more than one page

5 Web View Relations for Web Applications That Return Lists

The Barnes&Noble.com example in Fig. 6 used a meta relation with a <url> attribute to extract a Web view relation from a list embedded in more than one Web page. However, this example is actually a Web application, and accepts different search keywords to output different lists. In this section, we will explain how we can use a meta relation to extract a Web view relation with the new attribute <keyword> in addition to the three attributes <title>, <front cover image> and <price>.

When you input a keyword, the Barnes&Noble site returns a new page whose url includes a query at the end of a url address. Here, we will define a meta relation BookSearch with two attributes <keyword> and <url> as shown in Fig. 8(a). The <keyword> attribute and the <url> attribute of the first tuple take the first-candidate input keyword 'meme' and the url of the corresponding search result page. These two attributes of the second tuple take the second-candidate input keyword 'Web' and the url of the corresponding search result page. Figure 8(a) shows these two tuples. The generalization of these two tuples results in a meta

BookSearch	<keyword>*	<url>
	meme	http://search.barnesandnoble.com/booksearch/results.asp?WRD=meme
	Web	http://search.barnesandnoble.com/booksearch/results.asp?WRD=web

(a) Two search results of Barnes&Noble.com for two different keywords 'meme' and 'Web' have two different urls.

BookSearch	<keyword>*	<url>
	x(meme, Web)	http://search.barnesandnoble.com/booksearch/results.asp?WRD= x(meme, Web)

(b) The two meta tuples in (a) can be generalized to a single tuple.

<keyword>*	<url>	<title>	<front cover image>	<price>
x(meme, Web)	http://search .barnesandnoble.com /booksearch/results.asp ?WRD=x(meme, Web) x(ε , /html[1]/.../a[2] /click/)	/html[1]/body[1] /... /table[x(2,3)]/... /tr[3]/td[2]/a[1]/	/html[1]/body[1] /... /table[x(2,3)]/... /tr[5]/td[2] /a[1]/img[1]/	/html[1]/body[1] /... /table[x(2,3)]/... /tr[4]/td[3]/

(c) The generalization join of the meta relation in (b) and the meta relation in Figure 7 (d) gives this meta relation.

Fig. 8. Extraction of a relation between each keyword and the result-page url as a meta relation, and its generalization join with the meta relation that works as a wrapper to extract a relation from each search result

relation with a single tuple as shown in Fig. 8(b). This meta relation works as a Web view relation BookSearch(<keyword>*, <url>) whose <keyword> attribute domain needs to be externally specified.

In order to combine this meta relation with the meta relation Book to define a meta relation over <keyword>*, <url>, <title>, <front cover image> and <price>, we need a special operation BookSearch**Book, which is similar to a natural join. The operation R**S is called a generalization join, and defined as follows:

$$R**S = \{t1**t2 \mid t1 \in R, t2 \in S\},$$

where t1**t2 is dfined to take the least generalized value of t1 and t2 for the join attributes, the same value as t1 for other attributes of t1, and the same value as t2 for other attributes of t2. The generalization join BookSearch**Book becomes a meta relation as shown in Fig. 8(c). This generalization join works as a Web view relation over <keyword>*, <url>, <title>, <front cover image> and <price>. The domain of its <keyword> attribute needs to be externally specified.

Suppose that distributed sensors are made accessible through a Web application of this type, in which we specify, for example, a category to obtain a list of sensors across more than one page. The specification of a category corresponds to a specification of a keyword in the Barnes&Noble.com example. The above-mentioned method enables us to interactively extract a Web view relation, such as Sensor(<category>*, <id>, <location>, <value>), from this Web application.

6 Aggregate Federations as Relational Expressions of Web View Relations

Like view relations, Web view relations can be treated in the same way as relations. When evaluated, Web view relations become relations. Their evaluation accesses the source Web pages to extract actual attribute values of all the tuples. Relational expressions of Web view relations may use the same set of relational operations defined for relations. These operations include projection, selection, restriction, join, union, and intersection operations. This paper uses Codd's notation for relational operations, i.e., R[A, B] for the projection of a relation R to a set of attributes A and B, R[A='v'] for a selection of a relation R with respect to the condition that the value of the attribute A must be 'v', R[A=B] for a restriction of a relation R with respect to the condition that the values of the two attributes A and B must be the same, and R[A=C]S for a join of two relations R and S with respect to the condition that a tuple t1 in R is joined with a tuple t2 in S iff the A attribute value of t1 is equal to the C attribute value of t2.

Relational expressions of Web view relations are not evaluated unless the evaluation is explicitly applied. The evaluation of a relational expression E of Web view relations is denoted by $eval(E)$.

Suppose we have a set of distributed room sensors including temperature sensors and a set of distributed actuators including air conditioners. We assume that each room has only one sensor of a specific category and only one actuator of a specific category. We assume that a list of sensors and a list of air conditioners are both documented in the two Web pages D1 and D2. The information in these lists includes the identifier, category, location of each sensor and each air conditioner. Locations are specified by room numbers. Suppose also that there is a Web application A1 that returns the current value of a specified sensor. Suppose also that there is a Web service S1 that controls a specified actuator with a specified control value. We also assume that there is a library of functions including a special function with 'optimal-air-conditioning' as its name, which calculates the optimal air-conditioner control-value for the current room temperature. We assume that this library is provided by a Web service S2, and that each function name uniquely determines a function in this library.

Applying our meta relation method to the Web documents D1 and D2, we can interactively extract Web view relations R1(<sensorID>, <sensorCategory>, <room>) and R2(<actuatorID>, <actuatorCategory>, <room>) respectively from D1 and D2. The attributes <sensorID> and <actuatorID> work as key attributes of R1 and R2 respectively.

For the Web application A1, we can apply our C3W framework to clip out its sensor-identifier input field and the current sensor value from the result page. When pasted with these clips, a C3WsheetPad creates two corresponding slots, and works as a Web view relation R3(<sensorID>*, <currentValue>) whose first attribute domain needs to be externally specified. The <sensorID> attribute works as the key of this Web view relation.

For the Web service S1, our Web service wrapper analyses its WSDL description and asks the user to select some of its IO ports. We may select the two input ports for inputting the actuator identifier and the actuator control-value. Then the wrapper automatically creates a pad with these two ports as its slots. This pad works as a Web view relation R4(<actuatorID>*, <controlValue>*) whose two attribute domains need to be specified externally. The attribute <actuatorID> works as the key attribute of this Web view relation.

Similarly, the function library can be extracted from the Web service S2 as a Web view relation R5(<functionName>*, <input>*, <output>) whose first two attributes' domains need to be specified externally. The attribute <functionName> works as the key attribute of this Web view relation.

In order to define a new Web view relation WV1(<sensorID>, <room>) about all the temperature sensors in R1, we may apply a relational selection operator to R1 as follows:

WV1 ← R1[<sensorCategory>='temperature'][<sensorID>, <room>].

Using this Web view relation WV1 to specify the domain of the Web view relation R3, we can define a new Web view relation WV2(<sensorID>, <room>, <currentValue>) as follows:

WV2 ← (WV1[<sensorID>=<sensorID>*]R3)[<sensorID>, <room>,
      <currentValue>],

where the two Web view relations WV1 and R3 are joined with respect to their
<sensorID> attributes.

Similarly, we can define a new Web view relation WV3(<actuatorID>, <room>,
<controlValue>*) about all the air conditioners in R2 as follows:

WV3 ← ((R2[<actuatorCategory>='air conditioner'][<actuatorID>, <room>])
      [<actuatorID>=<actuatorID>*]R4)[<actuatorID>, <room>,
      <controlValue>*].

Now each temperature sensor in the Web view relation WV1 is associated
with an air conditioner installed in the same room by defining a new Web view
relation WV4(<sensorID>, <currentValue>, <actuatorID>, <controlValue>*) as
follows:

WV4 ← (WV2[<room>=<room>]WV3) [<sensorID>, <currentValue>,
      <actuatorID>, <controlValue>*].

The Web view relation WV4 defines which temperature sensor is associated
with which air conditioner in the aggregate federation we want to establish,
without specifying the functional interoperation among them. The current value
of each sensor is not used yet to specify the control value of the associated air
conditioner. Each sensor output is used to calculate the optimal control value
for the associated air conditioner. This calculation is performed by one of the
functions in the function library provided by the Web service S2. This function
is obtained as the single tuple in the following Web view relation WV5(<input>*,
<output>):

WV5 ← R5[<functionName>*='optimal-air-conditioning'][<input>*, <output>].

Now, we can relate the current value of each sensor to the control value
of the associated air conditioner by converting the former to the latter using
the function in WV5. The Web view relation WV6(<sensorID>, <currentValue>,
<actuatorID>, <controlValue>) defined as follows establishes the aggregate fed-
eration we want:

WV6 ← (WV4[<currentValue>=<input>* and <controlValue>*=<output>]WV5)
      [<sensorID>, <currentValue>, <actuatorID>, < controlValue>].

When evaluated periodically, this Web view relation thus defined using intermediate Web view relations WV1, WV2, WV3, WV4 and WV5 makes each
room-temperature sensor interoperate with the air conditioner in the same room
by periodically sending the current value output of the former to the control
value input of the latter through the conversion function named 'optimal-air-

conditioning'. We use the notation $eval^*(E, t)$ to denote such periodic evaluation of a relational expression E of Web view relations at a time interval t. The time interval t must be larger than the minimum time required to evaluate E by accessing the Web.

For any aggregate federation over the Web that includes neither recursion nor loops in its interoperations, we can always use a relational expression of Web view relations to specify this aggregate federation in an ad hoc manner. Our methods to extract Web view relations about intelligent resources from the Web and the use of relational expressions involving them enable us to define and execute aggregate federations among intelligent resources over the Web in an ad hoc way.

7 Related Work

A typical example system to which our aggregate federation technologies can be applied may be such a wireless sensor network accessible through the Web as described in [14]. The current sensor networks are assumed to be designed for specific applications, having data communication protocols strongly coupled to applications. Sensor networks of the future, however, are envisioned as comprising heterogeneous devices that offer assistance for a wide range of applications. To achieve this goal, a new architecture approach is needed, having application-specific features separated from the data communication protocol, while influencing its behavior. Some people propose a Web Services approach for the design of sensor networks, in which sensor nodes are service providers and applications are clients of such services [15]. Their main goal is to enable a flexible architecture in which sensor networks data can be accessed by users spread all over the world.

In this paper we have aimed at a similar flexible architecture in which we can dynamically select sensors and actuators from existing sensor networks and actuator networks, and make them interoperate with each other together with other intelligent resources over the Web. Such a technology for the ad hoc aggregate federation of various intelligent resources that are accessible through the Web has not been well studied yet.

Once sensor networks' data are accessible through Web services, their interoperation might be defined as the coordination of Web services that has been studied in [16, 17, 18]. Such coordination is also called orchestration [19, 20] or choreography [21] of Web services.

We consider that there are three modes for creating and coordinating functional combinations of available Web applications and/or Web services: static federation, dynamic federation, and ad hoc federation. Each mode involves selecting intelligent resources within some defined scope, making them interoperate with each other, and coordinating them to satisfy given demands. For a static demand and a static scope of resources, the selection, interoperation, and coordination of intelligent resources can also be statically defined. However, if either the demand or the scope of resources may change dynamically, then the selection, interoperation, and coordination of intelligent resources requires dynamic or ad hoc definition. Dynamic definition can be used if the demand is static, or its dynamic change can be predicted and specified in advance; ad hoc definition is required if the demand cannot be predicted.

A static federation uses a static description to relate each component of a new composition with the component of some available resource that may be explicitly specified or semantically quantified. Semantic Web [22] technologies such as RDF [23] were introduced for this purpose. Composition with existing Web documents using RDF defines a portal site, but cannot make more than one Web application interoperate with each other through parameter bindings. Semantic Web technologies can define parameter bindings only among Web services through an agent program. This technology is called Semantic Web Service.

The Semantic Web Service technology [24, 25, 26] aims to enable a wide variety of agent technologies for automated Web service discovery, execution, composition, and interoperation. It is based on both Semantic Web technologies and agent technologies over the Web such as the Web agent technology [27] and the softbot [28]. The Semantic Web service framework enables us to program an agent for a dynamic federation of more than one Web service.

Dynamic federation based on the Semantic Web service framework uses an agent program for the discovery, execution, composition, interoperation, and coordination of Web services. Therefore, both the quantification conditions for discovery, and the way of interoperation must be predictable for us to program them in the agent. Dynamic federation is different from ad hoc federation. The latter deals with the case in which the quantification conditions for discovery, and the way of interoperation are not predictable, and cannot be programmed.

Dynamic federation technology, however, cannot enable us to combine two Web applications that we come across and wish to combine for assistance with our current task. Even if the same two functions are also provided as Web services, we need to develop an agent for their interoperation before we can utilize the composite function. This is not only time consuming as well as cost-inefficient, but also troublesome since it breaks the continuity of our thought in our current task. We need a new technology for instantaneous federation that can be defined immediately on site at any place and any time in an ad hoc way.

Ad hoc federation of intelligent resources requires ad hoc definability of interoperation and coordination, and an interactive easy way of finding appropriate resources and obtaining the proxies needed to utilize their functions. We are not aware of technologies for ad hoc federation other than those proposed by our group [11, 29].

These frameworks we proposed in [11, 29] for ad hoc federation are, however, applicable only to one-by-one federation. They can define interoperation among intelligent resources over the Web as a set of interoperations between two intelligent resources. They allow us to define an overall federation by repetitively combining resources. This paper deals with a case in which we have large sets of intelligent resources accessible through the Web. Each set is assumed to consist of resources of the same type, and to be accessible through the Web in the same way. This paper deals with how to define and to execute a large set of federations simultaneously, each of which defines interoperation among resources taken from different sets of resources. Such federation is called aggregate federation. Our ad hoc aggregate federation framework enables users to flexibly select some resources satisfying a specified condition from each set, to define a relation of resources satisfying a specified condition as a subset of the Cartesian product of these resource sets, and to define and to execute interoperation among resources in each tuple in the defined relation.

Our meta relation works as a Web wrapper. There are lots of preceding research studies on Web wrappers. Some of them are based on programming by demonstration (PBD) technologies on Web pages. Internet Scrapbook [30] allows users to re-edit Web documents by demonstrating how to change the layout of a Web page into a customized one. Internet Scrapbook applies the same editing rule whenever the Web page is later accessed for refreshing. Such a tool enables the manipulation of layouts, but not the extraction and functional connection of components. Bauer and Dengler [31, 32] have also introduced a PBD method by which even naive users can configure their own Web based information services satisfying their individual information needs. They have implemented the method in terms of InfoBeans. By accessing an InfoBox with an ordinary Web browser, users can wrap Web applications. By connecting channels among InfoBeans on the InfoBox, users can also integrate them functionally. However, it seems difficult for a user to reuse a part of a composite Web application defined by some other user.

WebVCR [33] and WebView [34] provide a familiar VCR-style interface to record and replay users' actions. Users can create and update 'smart bookmarks', which are shortcuts to Web contents that require a series of Web-browsing actions, by pressing a record button on their Web browser. Smart bookmarks can therefore be used to record hard-to-reach Web pages that have no fixed URLs. However, WebVCR does not support the definition of I/O ports for Web applications. For example, end-users cannot modify the parameters supplied to an input form. WebView allows definition of customized views of Web contents. When a user records a smart bookmark, he or she can indicate if some field in a form is to be requested at playback time, rather than stored with the bookmark. However it seems difficult for end-users to create a new view that integrates different Web applications.

Sometimes Web applications revise the format of front-end HTML pages. There are lots of preceding research studies on the induction of Web wrappers based on examples of extraction from Web pages. However, there is little research on allowing end-users to wrap Web applications and to define functional linkage in the same environment.

W4F [35], which is a semi-automatic wrapper generator, provides a GUI support tool to define an extraction. The system creates a wrapper class written in Java from a user's demonstration. To use this wrapper class, users need to write program code. DEbyE [36] provides more powerful GUI support tool for the wrapping of Web applications, and stores the extracted text portions in an XML repository. Users have to use another XML tool to combine extracted data from Web applications. LExIKON [37] learns an underlying relation among objects within a Web page from a user-specified ordered set of text strings in the page. There is no GUI support tool for the join of two extracted relations.

8   Concluding Remarks

This paper has proposed a formal model for the aggregate ad hoc federation of geographically distributed intelligent resources accessible through the Web. We already proposed frameworks for ad hoc federation in [11, 29]. They are, however, applicable only to one-by-one federation. They can define interoperation among intelligent resources over the Web as a set of interoperations between two intelligent resources. They allow us to define an overall federation by repetitively combining resources. This paper has dealt with a case in which we have large sets of intelligent resources accessible through the Web. Each set is assumed to consist of resources of the same type, and to be accessible through the Web in the same way. This paper has focused on how to define and to execute a large set of federations, each of which defines interoperation among resources taken from different sets of resources. Such federation is called aggregate federation. Our new framework for ad hoc aggregate federation is formalized based on meta relations and their relational expressions, and enables users to flexibly select some resources satisfying a specified condition from each set of resources of the same kind, to define a relation of resources satisfying a specified condition as a subset of the Cartesian product of these different resource sets, and to define and to execute interoperation among resources in each tuple in the defined relation.

A typical example system to which our ad hoc aggregate federation technologies can be applied may be wireless sensor and actuator networks accessible through the Web. Today's sensor and actuator networks are assumed to be designed for specific applications, having data communication protocols strongly coupled to those applications. The sensor and actuator networks of the future, however, are envisioned as comprising heterogeneous devices that offer assistance for a wide range of applications. Sensors and actuators in such networks need to interoperate not only with each other, but also with other resources over the Web. Some applications using these networks may require instantaneous analysis, strategic planning, and immediate action that maximizes the use of accessible resources. Example applications may include risk management such as disaster relief and zoonosis control, user-customizable security and management for office and home, customizable control of sensor and/or actuator networks, user-customizable monitoring and control of home electronic appliances, and so on.

Our framework for ad hoc aggregate federation provides a new formal basis for instantaneous interactive definition and execution of interoperations among more than one set of widely distributed intelligent resources for unpredictable missions.

References

1. Miller, J.A., Seila, A.F., Tao, J.: Finding a substrate for federated components on the web. In: WSC '00: Proceedings of the 32nd conference on Winter simulation, San Diego, CA, USA, Society for Computer Simulation International (2000) 1849–1854
2. Feng, L., Jeusfeld, M.A., Hoppenbrouwers, J.: Towards knowledge-based digital libraries. SIGMOD Rec. **30** (2001) 41–46
3. Bass, M.J., Branschofsky, M.: Dspace at mit: meeting the challenges. In: JCDL '01: Proceedings of the 1st ACM/IEEE-CS joint conference on Digital libraries, New York, NY, USA, ACM Press (2001) 468
4. Eugster, P.T., Felber, P.A., Guerraoui, R., Kermarrec, A.M.: The many faces of publish/subscribe. ACM Comput. Surv. **35** (2003) 114–131
5. Gelernter, D.: Mirror Worlds. Oxford University Press (1992)
6. Gelernter, D.: Generative communication in linda. ACM Trans. Program. Lang. Syst. **7** (1985) 80–112
7. Picco, G.P., Murphy, A.L., Roman, G.C.: Lime: Linda meets mobility. In: ICSE '99: Proceedings of the 21st international conference on Software engineering, Los Alamitos, CA, USA, IEEE Computer Society Press (1999) 368–377
8. Tanaka, Y.: Meme Media and Meme Market Architectures: Knowledge Media for Editing, Distributing, and Managing Intellectual Resources. John Wiley & Sons, Inc., New York, NY, USA (2003)
9. Tanaka, Y., Ito, K.: Meme media architecture for the reediting and redistribution of web resources. In: FQAS. (2004) 1–12
10. Tanaka, Y., Fujima, J., Ohigashi, M.: Meme media for the knowledge federation over the web and pervasive computing environments. In: Advances in Computer Science - ASIAN 2004, Lecture Notes in Computer Science, 3321. (2004) 33–47
11. Fujima, J., Lunzer, A., Hornbæk, K., Tanaka, Y.: Clip, connect, clone: combining application elements to build custom interfaces for information access. In: UIST '04: Proceedings of the 17th annual ACM symposium on User interface software and technology, New York, NY, USA, ACM Press (2004) 175–184
12. Reynolds, J.C.: Transformational systems and the algebraic structure of atomic formulas. In Meltzer, B., Mitchie, D., eds.: Machine Intelligence. (1970) 135–151
13. Plotkin, G.D.: A note on inductive generalization. In Meltzer, B., Mitchie, D., eds.: Machine Intelligence. (1970) 153–165
14. Delicato, F.C., Pires, P.F., Pirmez, L., da Costa Carmo, L.F.R.: A flexible web service based architecture for wireless sensor networks. In: ICDCSW '03: Proceedings of the 23rd International Conference on Distributed Computing Systems, Washington, DC, USA, IEEE Computer Society (2003) 730
15. Hill, J., Horton, M., Kling, R., Krishnamurthy, L.: The platforms enabling wireless sensor networks. Commun. ACM **47** (2004) 41–46
16. Terai, K., Izumi, N., Yamaguchi, T.: Coordinating web services based on business models. In: ICEC '03: Proceedings of the 5th international conference on Electronic commerce, New York, NY, USA, ACM Press (2003) 473–478
17. Tai, S., Khalaf, R., Mikalsen, T.: Composition of coordinated web services. In: Proceedings of the 5th ACM/IFIP/USENIX international conference on Middleware, New York, NY, USA, Springer-Verlag New York, Inc. (2004) 294–310
18. Gudgin, M.: Secure, reliable, transacted: innovation in web services architecture. In: SIGMOD '04: Proceedings of the 2004 ACM SIGMOD international conference on Management of data, New York, NY, USA, ACM Press (2004) 879–880

19. Tsalgatidou, A., Pilioura, T.: An overview of standards and related technology in web services. Distrib. Parallel Databases 12 (2002) 135–162
20. Zirpins, C., Lamersdorf, W., Baier, T.: Flexible coordination of service interaction patterns. In: ICSOC '04: Proceedings of the 2nd international conference on Service oriented computing, New York, NY, USA, ACM Press (2004) 49–56
21. Foster, H., Uchitel, S., Magee, J., Kramer, J.: Compatibility verification for web service choreography. In: ICWS '04: Proceedings of the IEEE International Conference on Web Services (ICWS'04), Washington, DC, USA, IEEE Computer Society (2004) 738
22. Burners-Lee, T., Hendler, J., Lassila, O.: The semantic web. Scientific American 284 (2001)
23. Brickley, D., Guha (Eds), R.V.: "resource description framework (RDF) schema specification 1.0". W3C Recommendation (2000) http://www.w3.org/TR/2000/CR-rdf-schema-20000327/.
24. McIlraith, S., Son, T., Zeng, H.: Semantic web services (2001)
25. Howard, R., Kerschberg, L.: Brokering semantic web services via intelligent middleware agents within a knowledge-based framework. In: IAT '04: Proceedings of the Intelligent Agent Technology, IEEE/WIC/ACM International Conference on (IAT'04), Washington, DC, USA, IEEE Computer Society (2004) 513–516
26. Benbernou, S., Hacid, M.S.: Resolution and constraint propagation for semantic web services discovery. Distrib. Parallel Databases 18 (2005) 65–81
27. Waldinger, R.: Deductive composition of web software agents. In: Proc. NASA Goddard Workshop Formal Approaches to Agent-Based Systems, Lecture Notes in Computer Science, 1871. (2001)
28. Etzioni, O., Weld, D.: A softbot-based interface to the internet. Commun. ACM 37 (1994) 72–76
29. Ito, K., Tanaka, Y.: A visual environment for dynamic web application composition. In: HYPERTEXT '03: Proceedings of the fourteenth ACM conference on Hypertext and hypermedia, New York, NY, USA, ACM Press (2003) 184–193
30. Sugiura, A., Koseki, Y.: Internet scrapbook: automating web browsing tasks by demonstration. In: UIST '98: Proceedings of the 11th annual ACM symposium on User interface software and technology, New York, NY, USA, ACM Press (1998) 9–18
31. Bauer, M., Dengler, D.: InfoBeans-configuration of personalized information. In: Proceedings of the International Conference on Intelligent User Interfaces. (1999) 153–156
32. Bauer, M., Dengler, D., Paul, G.: Instructible information agents for web mining. In: IUI '00: Proceedings of the 5th international conference on Intelligent user interfaces, New York, NY, USA, ACM Press (2000) 21–28
33. Anupam, V., Freire, J., Kumar, B., Lieuwen, D.: Automating web navigation with the webvcr. In: Proceedings of the 9th international World Wide Web conference on Computer networks : the international journal of computer and telecommunications netowrking, Amsterdam, The Netherlands, The Netherlands, North-Holland Publishing Co. (2000) 503–517
34. Freire, J., Kumar, B., Lieuwen, D.: Webviews: accessing personalized web content and services. In: WWW '01: Proceedings of the 10th international conference on World Wide Web, New York, NY, USA, ACM Press (2001) 576–586
35. Sahuguet, A., Azavant, F.: Building intelligent web applications using lightweight wrappers. Data Knowl. Eng. 36 (2001) 283–316

36. Golgher, P.B., Laender, A.H.F., da Silva, A.S., Ribeiro-Neto, B.A.: An example-based environment for wrapper generation. In: ER '00: Proceedings of the Workshops on Conceptual Modeling Approaches for E-Business and The World Wide Web and Conceptual Modeling, London, UK, Springer-Verlag (2000) 152–164

37. Grieser, G., Jantke, K.P., Lange, S., Thomas, B.: A unifying approach to html wrapper representation and learning. In: DS '00: Proceedings of the Third International Conference on Discovery Science, London, UK, Springer-Verlag (2000) 50–64

Towards Understanding Meme Media Knowledge Evolution

Roland Kaschek[1], Klaus P. Jantke[2,3], and István-Tibor Nébel[4]

[1] Massey University, Department of Information Systems ,
Private Bag 11 222, Palmerston North, New Zealand
R.H.Kaschek@massey.ac.nz
[2] FIT Leipzig, Forschungsinstitut für InformationsTechnologien,
Postfach 30 11 66, 04251 Leipzig, Germany
jantke@fit-leipzig.de
[3] Hokkaido University Sapporo, Meme Media Laboratory,
Kita 13, Nishi 8, Kita-ku, Sapporo, 060-8628 Japan
jantke@meme.hokudai.ac.jp
[4] Universität Leipzig, AG Medizinische Lern- und Informationssysteme,
Ph.-Rosenthal-Straße 27, 04103 Leipzig, Germany
nebt@medizin.uni-leipzig.de

Abstract. Successful communication involves the individual utterances being interpreted within a suitable context. Systems that fail to acquire and share the context required for some topic are likely to fail to communicate successfully about that topic. Software systems populating an open medium such as the Web are unlikely to have been designed or otherwise prepared to communicate with each other, so if they are to communicate they face this challenge of acquiring and sharing the necessary context. We consider this situation for software systems implemented as meme media objects that contain representations of human knowledge. The mentioned acquisition can be understood as an enhancement of the knowledge representation they contain. Thus we consider establishing successful communication among meme media objects on the Web as an instance of knowledge evolution. The paper provides a conceptual framework for studying knowledge evolution. That framework is based on a particular interpretation of the concept of model. We give an example of use of the framework in an e-learning case study within a medical context.

1 Introduction

In the sequel we are going to talk about systems without elaborating on the definition of that term, or the properties of systems. An elementary introduction into the system concept is in [3–ch. 4]. Capabilities of a system may include the particular capability to respond to a given stimulus in different ways. An explanation model for that is the existence of an inner system parameter that is involved in the generation of the response to that stimulus. In particular if it is assumed that that parameter is changing in its value or structure or both it is an

K.P. Jantke et al. (Eds.): Federation over the Web, LNAI 3847, pp. 183–201, 2006.

obvious consequence that the system's stimulus-response behavior may be a rich one. It may even never respond twice in the same way to a given stimulus that appears repeatedly. For us **knowledge** is that inner system parameter as well as the capability to use it adequately. Representations of knowledge may be considered for knowledge processing and its analysis. Represented knowledge may be structured and that structure may result from the particular way of encoding chosen for representation purposes. There is, however, more to it. Knowledge can be distinguished as being focal or subsidiarily, i.e., as being that what corresponds to the concern currently at hand or to its context respectively. It is well understood that the subsidiary knowledge can be focused at and thus become, focal, see, e.g. [39–p. 14]. However, in that case there will be a context to it. That context gives it a connotation different from the one it had when it was used as subsidiary knowledge. The consequence of that conception is, as Polyani has put it (see [39–p. 6] "we can know more than we can tell".

Presupposing information systems theory (IST), as outlined in [9], we can define communication as the process in which communicators exchange signals in a medium. According to Shannon (cited after [9–p. 43]) "the fundamental problem of communication is that of reproducing at one point either exactly or approximately a message selected at another point." As noise occurs in the medium and disturbs the signal the mentioned reproduction is not a trivial task. The information used for reproducing the message is considered part of the communication context. The communication is considered as successful if at least one of the communicators achieves its communication goals. Clearly, if these goals involve that a sender of a signal wants the receiver of it to do something particular then the context required for understanding that particular thing and actually doing it may be substantial for the communication to be successful. We are going to focus on only one communicator and propose a theoretical framework for encoding and understanding its focal knowledge. We are going to take the position of an observer who has access to the communicator's knowledge.

Memetics is seen as outlined in the books by Richard Dawkins [10], Susan Blackmore [5] and Yuzuru Tanaka [37]. Richard Dawkins has directed the world's attention to the phenomena involved in cultural inheritance and has introduced his seminal concept named "meme". Susan Blackmore has taken the initiative to discuss the relevance of Dawkins' perspective from a psychological and from a somehow philosophical point of view telling us all that we are affected by Dawkins' work. It is, naturally, up to you whether or not you feel personally affected by memetics. The second author's paper [18] may be seen as a further contribution to this discussion. Yuzuru Tanaka, fortunately, has seized Dawkins' suggestion and developed it towards concepts, implementations and applications in computer science. He has coined the key term **meme media**. The present approach relies on Tanaka's trend-setting work taking Dawkins' and Blackmore's contributions seriously. We contribute to federations over the Web, i.e., a Web-mediated communication and cooperation of software agents that are neither designed nor prepared for that task. We also contribute to the adaptation of a software assistant to a human user. For both of these we suggest a particular way of understanding knowledge and its evolution.

As predicted by Mark Stefik [36], there is a tendency towards externalization of knowledge into interactive electronic media, a trend which is considerably boosted by the spread of the Internet. Stefik expounds that the most commonly understood goal of AI is to build intelligent, autonomous thinking machines. Obviously it is a reasonable alternative to focus more on collectives of intelligent systems that interact with each other in a knowledge medium. The latter enables what we call meme media pools (for pools of medical therapy planning knowledge, see [11], [26] and [21], e.g.). Meme media pools are mushrooming.

Meme media objects or meme media, for short, are the inhabitants of these pools. In [18], we asked: How are they? Are they doing well? Today, we are able to have a closer look and to ask a little more precisely: How do they evolve? Taking Dawkins' and Blackmore's contributions [10] and [5] seriously means to ask for the evolution of knowledge. In the spirit of Tanaka [37], every pool of meme media brings with it the potential of knowledge evolution. A meme media pool is set up properly, only if the represented knowledge evolves. Since without adapting to the changing conditions the value or usability of knowledge will diminish and we have set up just another heap of data. That problem is familiar to all large enterprizes. They all have huge data bases, but suffer from a lack of knowledge.

When Tanaka's book [37] appeared, it seemed that the time has come for our data –or, at least, for some of them– to wake up and begin to evolve. But does this really happen today? Where are the pools of evolving knowledge media? We do need a framework to talk about the knowledge that is externalized, to discuss potentials and problems in much more detail, to identify core mechanisms of knowledge evolution (see [20], [19]), and to validate evolution. The state of the art is such that knowledge resides mainly in humans, who also serve as the sources of new knowledge. Meme media technologies provide the tools for representing externalized human knowledge, making the meme media representations accessible to wide human communities, so that humans can share, edit and re-distribute meme media objects, thus, fostering knowledge evolution.

Our approach goes beyond the limits of that state of affairs. We focus on knowledge of systems such as software agents. Since we use human knowledge processing as archetypical for knowledge processing of systems in general we use models in two roles. Firstly, models serve as representations of focal knowledge. Secondly, models serve as the unit of change or evolution, i.e., as meme objects. Below we are going to presuppose a particular conception of model that appears as useful for understanding knowledge evolution. In that conception, however, models are composite objects, i.e., sets of so-called judgments. For illustration, we refer to medical therapy knowledge and planning as in [11], [21] and [26].

Paper Outline. In the next section we focus on certain aspects of information systems development. In section 3 we propose a framework of modeling. In sections 4 and 5 we discuss knowledge evolution and a case of knowledge evolution in an e-learning application respectively. We conclude the paper with a summary and suggestions in section 6.

2   Aspects of Information Systems Development

Historically, following a very wide definition (that according to [14], p.11, is due to Langefors) the term information system (IS) was defined as "...a technically implemented medium for the purpose of recording, storing, and disseminating linguistic expressions as well as for the support of inference making." With a wide understanding of language in mind and interpreting the term 'linguistic expressions' as valid sentences in given languages this definition is still wide enough to cover kinds of computer application that nowadays are considered as different from each other, such as database systems, workflow management systems, knowledge management systems, entertainment systems, learning systems, and the like.

Certain problems in the context of this paper would be considered as non-trivial, meaning that they can be decomposed into subproblems until a level of nesting is achieved at which the problem solver still oversees how to combine the solutions of subproblems for achieving a solution to the initial problem, and such that all the simple problems, i.e., those that are not decomposed into other problems, can be solved. It is clear that the class of problems that are trivial for humans is not empty; everyday problems belong to it such as "print a particular file", "reply to your partner's email from last Monday". It is also clear that the class of problems that are non-trivial for humans is not empty. It contains ,for example, the so-called wicked problems. Wicked problems are those problems whose definition or concept of solution are very likely to change as soon as actual problem solving starts. A typical example of a wicked problem is the creation of a computer application that is supposed to aid humans in doing a task that previously was not done with computer aid. Since there is no experience in that area regarding what aid a computer application could provide, it is likely that the 'whole thing' will be considered differently by the potential users once they have had access to a prototype application and can gather experience regarding what helps and what doesn't.

Planning in complex dynamic environments, such as planning to resolve disturbances in large technical installations is typically a wicked problem [1]. You necessarily start with incomplete information about the problem you are facing, and during planning you repeatedly learn that your understanding of the task to be resolved needs revision. There are recent attempts to attack planning problems for medical therapy [11], [21] and [26], another complex, dynamic domain, using meme media technologies. Wicked problems are related to knowledge evolution issues. We feel that a computer application suited to aiding the solution of trivial problems could best be referred to as a 'tool', comparable to a hammer, scissors, etc. On the other hand we feel that a computer application best suited for aiding the solution of non-trivial problems should be referred to as 'assistant'. In short tools are controlled by humans, whereas assistants provide cooperative aid for human thinking.

The problems for which tools and assistants are used differ from each other. This has considerable impact on what these application kinds are, and how they are used. By their nature, assistants need to be more interactive than tools. They also need to be more capable of adapting themselves to users, as well as developing the capability to figure out an appropriate substitute for the intended message from the disturbed signal that is actually perceived during the communication. The single characteristic that best shows the difference between tools and assistants is how one may judge their successful use. A tool was used successfully if it achieved what the human asked it to do. An assistant was used successfully if it actively helped the human to achieve his or her goal. As most humans do not have the capability of saying clearly what they want in a complex situation the limitations of tool usage are obvious and a demand for assistants is growing. Adaptivity and intelligence in our view are properties required for modern computer applications because of the inherent limitations of tool usage given the ever growing complexity of tasks to be solved with computer aid.

3   A Framework for Modeling

We relate modeling to knowledge evolution, as we consider the knowledge to evolve in a context of interacting systems that aim at exchanging knowledge and therefore represent parts of it as models. For that to take place it must be assured that the rules for encoding and decoding models are shared among the communicators. A well-known mechanism for achieving that is the use of consensually defined and agreed-on semantic models, i.e., conceptual frameworks for conceptualizing domains. As the context of utterances cannot be made fully explicit the represented knowledge in question must not be misunderstood as comprising objective, general laws. Rather it needs to be understood as culture-dependent conventions and consequences thereof. Knowledge about an object is then represented in a model of that object in so far as the model correctly reflects those conventions and their consequences.

Modeling in this paper is understood as creating, using, analyzing, maintaining, and retiring models. We model object O by a model M if we want to know something about O but for one or another reason cannot, must not, dare not (or similar) investigate O itself, or if it would be possible but not economical to investigate O itself. Modeling is thus about creating and using substitute objects M for original objects O. To be more specific, the substitute objects M in this paper are conceptual, i.e., they are often perceived as cognitive entities. The original O can be a real world object or a cognitive object. We do not go into more detail regarding when one should follow a realistic approach (according to which real world objects exist independent of whether humans or other cognitive beings observe them) or a constructivist approach (according to which objects are creations of individual minds). We do limit ourselves to the models being individual mental constructions.

Following Stachowiak [33, 34, 35], we consider the following properties as characteristic for models:

1. **Mapping property**, saying that every model is a model of something, its original.

2. **Truncation property**, saying that models usually lack of certain characteristics that their originals have and that this makes them useful for modelers.
3. **Pragmatic property**, saying that the justification of using a model is subject to a certain purpose, usage conditions, a period of time, a particular user and the like.

Stachowiak [34] has put forward the so-called principle of methodological order according to which the original always temporally precedes the model. We do not share his view, because it excludes a standard terminology in which one talks about design models. These do in fact temporally precede their original, i.e., the actual implementation. Wieringa [41] distinguished descriptive models from prescriptive ones. We concur with his distinction, but express it slightly different. In our view, being descriptive, prescriptive, and the like is not a property of the model. Rather, these terms are **reference modes** for how the model is related to its original, expressing that modelers use the model to describe the original, or to prescribe it, and so on. We identify further reference modes such as idealizing, forecasting, and constituting. We distinguish our position on models from that of Stachowiak in one further respect: He focused on the truncation property, seeing in it an important ingredient of models. While we accept this importance, we also believe that models in general have certain properties that their originals don't have and that this is often crucial for their usability. For example, in [22] it was argued that the usability of a map significantly depends on the material from which it is made. We refer to that property of models as the **plenty property**.

The analysis and synthesis method of the ancient Greek philosophers (see, e.g. Polya, [31–pp. 141] can be made effective for modeling information system. Thus the modeling procedure that is known as the method of Langefors consists then in modeling the system components by their input-output behavior and the components' interaction as a flow- or message exchange[5]. If the components and their interaction are modeled properly, they allow the reconstruction of the input-output behavior of the system as a whole. It is often considered an essential feature of systems that the interaction of their components gives rise to properties that cannot be attributed to a single one of the system components. Such properties are called emergent.

So far we have taken a relational approach to explaining the term model, i.e., we have related models to originals and provided a brief discussion of the properties of that relationship. We take now an ontological approach to the concept 'model' and define it in terms of a more elementary concept. We make use of a naive understanding of the concept 'concept' (a more profound treatment of it is available in the work of Pfänder [30] and Kamlah and Lorenzen [23]). We reuse the theory of judgment in the form published by Alexander Pfänder in 1921, [30]. A **judgment** according to Pfänder's theory is a tuple $U = (S, P, C, I)$. Its meaning is that actor I relates the predicate notion P to the instances of the subject notion S in a way specified by the copula C. The copula C specifies whether the predicate notion is accredited to or denied from

---

[5] It would be more correct to use the term signal exchange. See, for example [32], for a more in-depth discussion of this point.

the instance set of the subject notion, i.e., the extent of S. The copula also specifies whether the predicate notion is related to all instances of the subject notion or only to particular ones. Pfänder defines the modality of a judgment as the degree of confidence of the I in the judgment. The judgments (employing the obvious notation) (*Gretchen, graut es vor Heinrich, +, Gretchen*) and (*Katze, grau in der Nacht, A+, Peter*) mean that Gretchen and Peter judge respectively "Heinrich, I am terrified by you!"[6] and "All cats are gray in the dark." Provided a judgment is uttered then according to Austin's speech-act-theory it would be considered as **verdictive utterance**, see [2–p. 169]. Note finally that in our view the subject notions that give rise to a proper judgment are culture-depending, as is the case with the predicate notions and the copulae.

A **signature** is a 4-tuple $\Sigma = (\Omega, \mathcal{F}, \mathcal{R}, A)$ such that $\Omega = \{\Omega_1, \ldots, \Omega_m\}$, $\mathcal{F} = \{\mathcal{F}_1, \ldots, \mathcal{F}_n\}$, $\mathcal{R} = \{\mathcal{R}_1, \ldots, \mathcal{R}_o\}$ are respectively sets of sort symbols, function symbols, and relation symbols, and A is a mapping. The maping associates with each function symbol f and each relation symbol r non-negative integers $a(f)$ and $a(r)$ and so-called **arities** $A(f) = (i_1, \ldots, i_{a(f)}, i)$, and $A(r) = (j_1, \ldots, j_{a(r)})$ where $i_1, \ldots, i_{a(f)}, i \in \{1, \ldots, m\}$, and $j_1, \ldots, j_{a(r)} \in \{1, \ldots, m\}$. A **structure** $\mathcal{S}$ over a signature $\Sigma = (\Omega, \mathcal{F}, \mathcal{R}, A)$ is a triple $\mathcal{S} = (S, \mathcal{F}_S, \mathcal{R}_S)$ such that $S = \{S_1, \ldots, S_m\}$, $\mathcal{F}_S = \cup\{f_S^1, \ldots, f_S^{b(f)} \mid f \in F, \ b(f) \ a \ positive \ integer\}$, $\mathcal{R}_S = \cup\{r_S^1, \ldots, r_S^{b(r)} \mid r \in R, \ b(r) \ a \ positive \ integer\}$ is a set of sets, functions, and relations, such that $f_S : S_{i_1} \times \ldots \times S_{i_{a(f)}} \to S_i, \ \forall f_S \in \mathcal{F}_S$, with $A(f) = (i_1, \ldots, i_{a(f)}, i)$, and $r_S \subseteq S_{j_1} \times \ldots S_{j_{a(r)}}, \ \forall r_S \in \mathcal{R}_S$, with $A(r) = (j_1, \ldots, j_{a(r)})$. Given such a structure $\mathcal{S} = (S, \mathcal{F}_S, \mathcal{R}_S)$ the set $\cup S$ is called its **support** and, if no confusion is likely, $\mathcal{S}$ is referred to as S. For each function $f \in \mathcal{F}_S$ and for each relation $r \in \mathcal{R}_S$, the tuples $A(f)$ and $A(r)$ are called the **signature** of f and r respectively. For each $s \in S$ the elements of s are said to be of **sort** s. Note that we allow for multiple instantiation of function symbols and relation symbols by functions and relations respectively for simpler encoding of semantic models as structure over a signature.

For an illustration of practical relevance, consider the perhaps best known semantic model: the ER-model. We introduce the signature $(\Omega, \mathcal{F}, \mathcal{R}, A)$ with $\Omega = \{entity \ type, value \ type, relationship \ type\}$, $\mathcal{F} = \emptyset$, and $\mathcal{R} = \{role, c_E, c_R\}^7$. The arities are $a(role) = a(c_E) = a(c_R) = 2$, and $A(role) = (relationship \ type, entity \ type)$, $A(c_E) = (entity \ type, \ value \ type)$, $A(c_R) = (relationship \ type, value \ type)$. An entity-relationship diagram is then a structure over that signature. Consider for an illustration the example in figure 1.

The schema in figure 1 is a structure $\mathcal{S} = (S, \mathcal{F}_S, \mathcal{R}_S)$ over the signature given above, i.e., $S = \{entity \ type, relationship \ type, value \ type\}$ with $entity \ type = \{project, high \ risk \ project, classified \ project, employee, department, group\}$, $relationship \ type = \{is \ involved \ in, \ A_1, \ A_2, \ G_1, \ G_2\}$, and $value \ type = \emptyset$.

---

[6] Johann Wolfgang von Goethe, Faust, Part I, see [31], line 4610: "Heinrich! Mir graut's vor Dir."

[7] As the role concept is frequently used and fairly understood we only briefly explain c_E and c_R. These are characteristics that associate value types with entity types or relationship types respectively.

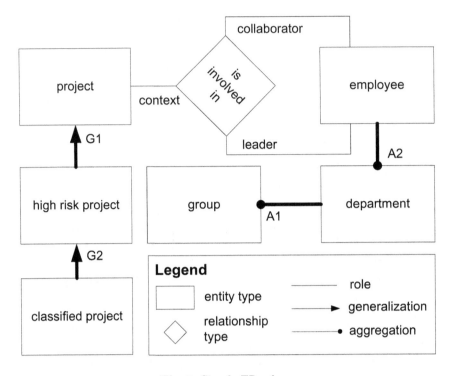

Fig. 1. Simple ER-schema

We have furthermore $\mathcal{F}_S = \emptyset$, and $\mathcal{R}_S = \{roles, c_{ES}, c_{RS}\}$ with $roles = \{context, leader, collaborator, super, sub, whole, part\}$. We make here use of the convention that the roles occurring in aggregation and generalization are not explicitly represented in an ER-schema. We deviate from common practice, however, by explicitly showing names for aggregations and generalizations in schemas. In the example we have $c_{ES} = \emptyset = c_{RS}$ as well as $context = \{(is\ involved\ in\ ,\ project\ )\},\ collaborator = \{(is\ involved\ in\ ,\ employee\ )\},\ leader = \{(is\ involved\ in\ ,\ employee\ )\},\ super = \{(G_1\ ,\ project),\ (G_2, highrisk\ project\ )\},\ sub = \{(G_1, high\ risk\ project\ ),\ (G_2, classified\ project\ )\},\ whole = \{(A_1, group),\ (A_2, department)\},$ and $part = \{(A_1, department), (A_2, employee)\}$.

A database over an entity relationship schema is an interpretation of the schema in the category of sets with relations as morphisms.[8] Such an interpretation means that all graphical items in the schema apart from its roles and characteristics are interpreted as sets and the roles and characteristics are interpreted as relations between these sets.

Let I be a modeler, $\Sigma = (\Omega, \mathcal{F}, \mathcal{R}, A)$ a signature, and $\mathcal{S} = (S, \mathcal{F}_S, \mathcal{R}_S)$ a structure over Σ. Then I can encode the structure $\mathcal{S}$ uniquely as a set of judgments. The following sets of judgments together yield what is required:

---

[8] One might wish to refer to [8] as an introduction to category theory.

- $\{(s, \exists, +, I) \mid s \in S\} \cup \{(f_S, \exists, +, I) \mid f_S \in \mathcal{F}_S\} \cup \{(r_S, \exists, +, I) \mid r_S \in \mathcal{R}_S\}$;
- $\{(f_S, A_{f_S}, +, I) \mid f_S \in \mathcal{F}_S\}$, where A_{f_S} is the predicate 'the function f_S has the signature $f_S : S_{i_1} \times \ldots \times S_{i_{a(f)}} \to S_i$ if the function symbol f that it instantiates has the arity $A(f) = (i_1, \ldots, i_{a(f)}, i)$';
- $\{(r_S, A_{r_S}, +, I) \mid r_S \in \mathcal{R}_S\}$, where A_{r_S} is the predicate 'the relation r_S has the signature $r_S \subseteq S_{i_1} \times \ldots \times S_{i_{a(r)}}$ if the relation symbol r that it instantiates has the arity $A(r) = (S_{i_1}, \ldots, S_{i_{a(r)}})$';

where it is assumed that the predicate notion '$\exists$' means that I with respect to a universe of discourse, UoD, has obtained a definition of the subject notion that allows him or her to classify the phenomena in UoD as either belonging to the extent of the subject notion or not. For other semantic models such as class diagrams, Petri Nets, and State Charts constructions work that are similar to the one used here for the ER model. Below we can thus focus on structures over a signature as generic conceptual framework for describing the majority of models that occur for example in systems development.

4   Modeling Knowledge Evolution

A modeler will in general need several attempts to arrive at a satisfactory solution. If the problem were simple one then he would not start modeling in the first place. He will make his later solution attempts depend on what he has learned from earlier ones. That way he can invest the acquired knowledge to make new and better models. To better understand such modeling processes we take a linguistic view and consider models (and in particular structures over a signature) as language artifacts. We then may discuss models in terms of their syntax, semantics, and pragmatics.[9] Since we have to consider sequences of models we are going to analyze modeling processes in these terms. Modeling thus can be understood as a trajectory in a three-dimensional space with dimensions:

- **syntax**, i.e., modeling activities target the model's compliance to the current signature or to a newly chosen one;
- **semantics**, modeling activities target the model's meaning; and
- **pragmatics**, i.e., modeling activities target the appropriate use the modeler can make of the model.

In this paper we focus on the semantics dimension and only briefly touch the other dimensions. For explaining the syntax dimension we consider software development as an example of a modeling process. In a software process one will, in one way or another, and whether documented as a physical artifact or not, create a requirements model (describing the customer requirements), a conceptual model (prescribing the application or business content of the system that is to be implemented), a design model (prescribing a computer

---

[9] Refer for example to [27] for an explanation of these basic linguistic concepts.

based system for implementing the conceptual model), and an implementation. The software process provides means for model mapping, i.e., for creating a model M' that in that software process follows immediately model M. To explain the pragmatics dimension we consider first the planning processes. Obviously plans are supposed to be proceeding models used in a prescriptive reference mode. Constructing a single model, i.e., a plan may be a complex process. The construction of a model may last quite some time, as complex reasoning is necessary. In some cases the time needed to create the model cannot be ignored for example, because the plan must be executed in a changing universe of discourse. A plan may be worthless if creating it takes too much time.

Our second point regarding the pragmatics concerns the role of models as substitute objects. That role suggests that in modeling one needs to have a mapping that allows the reformulation of a problem specified in terms of the original into a problem as specified in terms of the model. The model would be considered as satisfactory if for that problem a solution can be found and propagated back into the original, thus delivering a solution for the original problem. Following terminology used by Stachowiak [35], here we give the name icomorphism to the pair of mappings that enables this propagation and back propagation. It is clear that, in the case where a model is not satisfactory all the parameters mentioned here may be modified.

With respect to the semantics dimension design primitives (see for example [38,6,4]) are suggested in order to realize a controlled and stepwise mode of model manipulation. That view also is present in [19]. What we want to call knowledge evolution is the trajectory of modeling processes as projected onto the semantics dimension. In considering knowledge evolution, we therefore presuppose a signature $\Sigma = (\Omega, \mathcal{F}, \mathcal{R}, A)$ and consider a sequence $\{M_i\}_{i \in I}$ of structures over that signature.

In modeling, one can try to benefit from methods like simulated annealing by following a trial-and-error approach in which for exploration purposes all design primitives are applied in a round-robin-style, the quality of the solutions that become possible is assessed, and then, as a direction for improving the model, whichever design primitive implies the largest gradient of solution improvement is actually imposed on the model. Obviously that approach can be tailored by associating weighting factors to the design primitives that impact the solution assessment. That way the application of some of the design primitives may be favored or disadvantaged. If one were to include deterioration of knowledge, using some appropriate infrastructure, and combine that with a refreshment strategy –like the one just described– then it should become possible to simulate knowledge evolution.

If knowledge evolution is considered as a co-evolution of human understanding of a problem and machine awareness of what the human partner wants then it is clear that a formal conception of machine awareness in the sense of semantics of artifacts does not work, as in general one cannot check whether a model that is formally represented in a computer is equivalent to the model that a human actually is using.[10] Also it cannot be guaranteed that humans use consistent models.

In approaches to wrapper induction as used for illustration in [19], elementary steps of enhancement mean to replace some plug-in meme media object that represents a certain formal language by another one. In terms of logic programming, a definition of a formal language defining predicate is substituted by another one. In algebraic terms, this is easy to circumscribe. The signature of the cited wrapper induction problem has a finite number of sorts for certain delimiter languages. Definitions of a constant of one sort are modified to transform some model M into a successor version M'. Termination of the resulting sequence of successor models is only guaranteed under certain strong assumptions [13].

Instead of a summary of the rather wide discussion above, let us contrast the approach developed to more conventional 'Algorithmic' or 'Computational Learning Theory' [18]. When systems learn, one might assume that this is seen as acquiring some knowledge. In fact, the underlying main scenario is well-structured:

1. There is assumed some target object to be learned.
2. The learning system is fed in information.
3. In response, it constructs hypotheses.
4. A hypothesis is true, if it correctly describes or sufficiently approximates the target object.

In such a scenario, the knowledge is sitting in the system's hypothesis and its quality is determined by a semantic mapping from hypotheses to originals. There are, for sure, problems to which such an approach is appropriate. However, the authors address more difficult –even wicked– problems where we would like to be able to say 'he has got it'. Whether or not some partner –a human or an 'intelligent' computer assistant– understands me, my needs and my desires is rarely describable by pointing to a particular point in a semantic space. Instead, it shows when we are talking to each other, when we are working together, or when we arrive together at some problem solution.

The following section sketches a case study in e-learning (in a medical context) where the evolution of knowledge can hardly be understood as arriving at a point where a certain data structure determines a particular target object. The system can be deemed to have 'got it', if it successfully guides a human, who is both a learner and a patient, through a particular virtual problem solving scenario.

---

[10] Problems of this type are inherent to computer science, because application domains which are usually not formal at all are reflected by completely formal models that are mathematical in spirit, as long as they remain on a conceptual level, and that are discrete, finite and even digitalized, when they are reaching the level of implementation. A typical representative is known as Church's Thesis claiming the unprovable equivalence of 'the computable' and what is computable, at least on a conceptual level, by means of any of the classical computational apparatus such as Church's λ-Calculus, Post's Algorithms, Partial-Recursive Functions, Turing Machines and the like.

5   A Case of e-Learning in a Medical Context

One of the problems in certain medical domains is to educate and train patients
to behave appropriately when particular symptoms of a specific disease they are
suffering from suddenly occur. For German patients who are suffering from dia-
betes mellitus, a hypoglycemia education program [28, 29] has been developed,
implemented, brought into regular applications and evaluated. For more detail,
interested readers are directed to the references. Using this program, learners
are supposed to deepen their knowledge and understanding of how to behave
in a case of a severe hypoglycemia. So, at a first glance, we are dealing with a
rather simple e-learning task in a fairly restricted domain. However, the majority
of patients are elderly people with low or literally no computer literacy. They
need particularly careful treatment. It is desirable not just to present them with
a learning tool, but to provide a computer system that assists them by being
intelligent in the sense of adapting to each patient's peculiarities.

The key idea is to exploit the fact that all learners are at the same time
patients within a rather limited medical context. As soon as a learner gets in
contact with the e-learning system, she or he is seen as a patient. Medical domain knowledge is used to infer knowledge about the patient. Figure 2 shows
an additional development tool that is available for knowledge evolution studies.
A certain learner / patient overlay model is assumed. Window A of figure 2 is

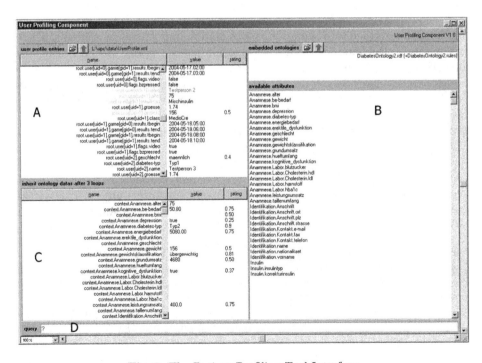

Fig. 2. The Patient Profiling Tool Interface

showing the original model. Domain knowledge is called upon to complete the recent variant of the user model. Window B gives an impression of the underlying ontology's terms. The system's inference module may be called upon for user model completion. The history of this approach [28, 29] may be described in terms of logic and inference as inductive completion of a model over one signature by employing knowledge about another related signature.

Though this knowledge is always hypothetical to some extent, it is used to tailor the system's behavior. When the system learns or guesses successfully, the human-computer interaction proceeds more smoothly. This is reflected in the human learner/patient having less of a need to ask back (see figure 3). The human-computer interaction becomes more pleasant and satisfactory. Satisfaction and fun, not torture, is seen as a key to engaging a learner's mind [25]. The crux is the way in which a current (learner / patient) model may be changed. The mechanisms of model manipulation are seen as the key to knowledge evolution [19].

In our present case study, there is an initial model M_0 of the learner containing only those data from her / his patient database record that is taken for granted. The signature is fixed and is mostly determined by the list of parameters taken into account. In traditional terms, those parameters may be called attributes. If M_i is a patient model and a is an attribute, then its current value is denoted as $M_i.a$. Attributes may be null. The provided values, however, are pairs of some ground value of the respective sort and some confidence c. For convenience, instead of null attributes one might assume any default value with confidence 0. In practice, initial models M_0 are usually highly incomplete. In the medical domain, the underlying domain knowledge frequently originates from large clinical trials. This knowledge rarely provides 'truth' in an objective sense. Rather, it consists of models that are felt to be supported by evidence obtained from the trials. Based on data in a model M_i and on domain knowledge, one may employ rules that suggest $M_{i+1}.a = (v_{i+1}, c_{i+1})$. If then $M_i.a = (v_i, c_i)$ and $c_{i+1} > c_i$ then the assignment $M_{i+1}.a := (v_{i+1}, c_{i+1})$ is executed.

Figure 3 is taken from [28], and shows results from a careful evaluation. The system that uses learner model induction was run in parallel with a static system without this type of adaptivity. In the conventional system, the system's knowledge underlying the human-computer interaction does not change. In contrast, the original learner model of the adaptive system usually changes during human-machine interaction. The system's knowledge evolves.

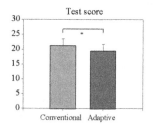 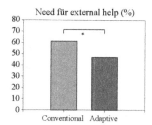 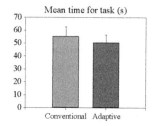

Fig. 3. Evaluation by Comparison to a System Version without Learning

6   Summary and Suggestions

In this paper modeling is understood as creating, using, analyzing, maintaining, and retiring models. The crux is that we are making the step from modeling being performed by humans to computerized modeling. When humans gain knowledge through modeling, there should be cases in which computers come up with new knowledge through modeling as sketched above.

From a memetic point of view, we are releasing meme media objects for a life in the wild of computer networks [18]. We may expect knowledge evolution to take place. If this truly happens, we have left behind the state of the art where mostly humans played the role of knowledge sources [36]. The main aim of the present paper is to introduce a suitable terminology seeing modeling from a sufficiently general perspective. According to the authors' terminology, modeling –and knowledge evolution– may proceed in three different dimensions named syntax, semantics, and pragmatics.

The approach is still having teething troubles. Though there is already an application sketched in section 5, the treatment in the preceding sections is still preliminary. The authors confined themselves to an investigation of only semantics. Even for that dimension, supplements and completions are necessary. The transition steps from a model M to its successor M' deserve some more in-depth investigation. For instance, the case study of section 5 enjoys a termination property within the dimension semantics. Over a given medical context, only finitely many model enhancements are possible. This is due to four important facts. First, every enhancement changes one (or only a finite number of) attribute value(s). Second, attribute values are only changed in cases where the new value has a higher confidence than the value before. Third, confidence values have a step width with a fixed finest granularity, due to characteristics of clinical trials. Fourth, there is a maximal confidence value assumed. It seems that the case study under consideration has a peculiarity which, in terms of rewriting [16], may be seen as termination or even as confluence.

One might go even further and expect that the rewriting systems perspective is setting the stage for investigation of fundamental problems in knowledge evolution. Let us give an example. In rewriting systems one carefully distinguishes confluence from local confluence [16]. In cases where systems are locally confluent, but not confluent, early rewriting steps may be decisive for what can be reached in the future. This may be critical when knowledge evolution is seen as rewriting and confluence is not guaranteed.

Future research work should focus on a more holistic approach investigating the proposed three dimensions in their mutual interdependence, thus, seeing knowledge evolution along pathways through this three-dimensional space.

Among the many interesting phenomena to be studied, the authors are very much interested in templates of pathways, whether or not those exist and what they might possibly reveal about the way in which knowledge evolves. However, to speculate, we need a language to express our dreams, our guesses and our doubts. For meme media knowledge evolution, we propose a terminology like the one sketched here.

6.1   Continuing Discussion

The evolution metaphor can be extended somewhat to address more fully how the process of knowledge change works. In Biology one uses the two levels of phenotype and genotype and locates the driving forces and possibilities of explanation of observed modifications on the genotype. It seems that by analogy one can relate phenotype and focal knowledge, and genotype and subsidiary knowledge. Therefore an observer of a system that embodies evolving knowledge, if he or she does not have privileged access to the subsidiary knowledge of the observed system, might be prevented from understanding the system behavior, and in particular its communication.

Model evolution must not be confused with knowledge evolution, as knowledge does not reside in the models. Knowledge may result from a usage of the evolving models. There is no knowledge without the models' usage. This is similar to the need to play a record (nowadays, one would say a CD or DVD) in order to "get the music out", as discussed at length by Hofstadter [15].

As discussed in more detail above, the judgments made to build a model usually do not reflect anything so ambitious as the 'truth'. They represent opinions on which a learning system's activities are to be based. The quality of the model is not its relation to some particular semantic target, but the quality of the system's behavior relying on those judgments. When an assistant system succeeds in modeling to some extent such that our cooperation –between me and the system– also succeeds, this does not necessarily mean that the system got any 'truth' about me. It just means that the judgments that were made work well for the particular purpose. They can be evaluated only with respect to this purpose. There are good reasons to regard the system's knowledge as evolving if it collects judgments such that after a certain time it assists its user better than before.

6.2   Towards Insights and Messages

What does the discussion above buy us? There is a need to answer this question, if not today, then at least in the near future, at least. Here is the authors' first attempt. If you compose meme media objects, for instance, if you plug IntelligentPad objects together, you may arrive at something new you have never had before. It may turn out to be useful. You may keep it, others may (re-)use it, there may be dissemination and re-editing of what you built, and it may last for a long time. But it seems misleading to say that the knowledge is externalized and located in your composite meme media object. There is no way to squeeze any drop of knowledge out of the construct. We need to see knowledge evolution from the higher perspective of the media objects' application. This is one important insight and a guideline for research. Implications are as follows. Data mining, statistics, probability theory or whatever you use in modeling is never a discipline of 'knowledge discovery', 'knowledge construction', 'knowledge evolution' or anything like that. No doubt, all these disciplines are important. But in the best case, they provide only the technicalities needed for model construction along dimensions like semantics or syntax. We arrive at the knowledge evolution issue, when we deal with the technicalities for the purpose of problem solving in a particular domain. Therefore, it does not make sense to evaluate particular model construction techniques for their potential to support knowledge evolution. Evaluation with respect to knowledge evolution needs to be domain specific. The evaluation problem deserves further research and experimentation.

To go even further, it seems possible to talk about 'understanding each other' with the particular meaning that models that are created, and judgments that are built provide a basis of pleasant cooperation between a human user and an IT system that was designed to be the user's assistant. The question of understanding each other bridges between the research reported here and the topic of 'federation over the Web'. The focus of research and development under the banner of federation is on scenarios where systems meet that have not been designed and prepared to meet each other. One might see 'understanding each other' as the key problem to be resolved for federation over the Web .

6.3   A Case of Learner Classification

The fact that the present approach does indeed matter can be illustrated by means of a case of learner classification. In [12], the authors carefully discuss the state of the art in learner modeling for adaptive e-learning. The citations about the different perspectives and their discussion of the need of learner modeling may be seen as being very informative.

Esposito et al. [12] develop an approach to learner classification that adopts a data mining perspective [7, 24]. They rely on the assumption that every learner is of a certain learner type and that this type has to be discovered. This sounds a bit like the idea of finding out some ultimate truth about a human learner with the aim of taking this truth as a basis for a system's subsequent adaptation. There is a certain profiling framework in which every learner or, more precisely, her / his profile may be represented as a vector over a given list of attributes. This is coming close to conventional overlay models.

Esposito et al. aim at measuring the accuracy of the profile extractor, i.e. evaluating how close their profile extractor's learner model approaches the truth. According to [12–p. 44], evaluation was performed by a domain expert who classified the students. His classification was compared to the computer system's learner model. The system was been found to model quite well. However, according to the present authors' approach outlined above, there is no truth to be discovered. Consequently, there is nothing against which the models generated may be directly compared. Instead, a learner model seen and represented as a finite set of judgments is evaluated by investigating the effect it has on the quality of human-computer interaction. From the perspective of the present approach to modeling, the system's knowledge evolution may advance from one set of judgments to another one without any convergence to an ultimately true target.

References

1. Oksana Arnold. Die Therapiesteuerungskomponente einer wissensbasierten Systemarchitektur für Aufgaben der Prozeßführung, volume 130 of DISKI. infix, 1996.
2. John Longshaw Austin. Zur Theorie der Sprechakte. Philip Reclam jun., Stuttgart,1979.
3. Niv Ahituv, Seev Neumann. Principles of Information Systems for Management. Wm. C. Brown Publishers, Dubuque, IA, third edition, 1990.
4. Carlo Batini, Stefano Ceri, and Shamkant Navathe. Conceptual Database De-sign. The Benjamin / Cummings Publishing Company; Inc., Redwood City, California, 1992.
5. Susan Blackmore. The Meme Machine. Oxford University Press, 1999.
6. Michael Blaha and William Premerlani. Object-Oriented Modeling and Design for Database Applications. Prentice-Hall, Inc., Upper Saddle River, New Jersey, 1998.
7. Max A. Bramer, editor. Knowledge Discovery and Data Mining. IEE Professional Applications of Computing Series 1. The Institution of Electrical Engineers, 1999.
8. Michael Barr, Charles Wells. Category Theory for Computing Science. Prentice Hall, New York, 1990.
9. John F. Cragan, Donald C. Shields. Understanding Communication Theory: The Communicative Forces for Human Action. Allyn and Bacon, Boston et al., 1998.
10. Richard Dawkins. The Selfish Gene. Oxford University Press, 1976.
11. Volker Dötsch, Kimihito Ito, and Klaus P. Jantke. Human-agent cooperation in accessing and communicating knowledge media? A case in medical therapy planning. In Gunter Grieser and Yuzuru Tanaka, editors, International Workshop on Intuitive Human Interface for Organizing and Accessing Intellectual Assets, International Workshop, Dagstuhl Castle, Germany, March 1-5, 2004, Proceedings, volume 3359 of Lecture Notes in Artifical Intelligence, pages 68 - 87, Berlin, Heidelberg, New York, 2005. Springer-Verlag.
12. Floriana Esposito, Oriana Licchelli, and Giovanni Semeraro. Discovering Student Models in e-learning Systems. Journal of Universal Computer Science, 10 (1): 47 - 57, January 2004.
13. Gunter Grieser, Klaus P. Jantke and Steffen Lange. Consistency Queries in Information Extraction. In Nicolò Cesa-Bianchi, Masayuki Numao and Rüdiger Reischuk, editors, Proc. 13th International Conference on Algorithmic Learning Theory, volume 2533 of Lecture Notes in Artificial Intelligence, pages 173 - 187, Berlin, Heidelberg, NewYork, 2002. Springer-Verlag.
14. Rudy Hirschheim, Heinz K. Klein, and Kalle Lyytinen. Information Systems Development and Data Modeling, Conceptual and Philosophical Foundations. Cambridge University Press, Cambridge, 1995.
15. Douglas R. Hofstädter. Gödel, Escher, Bach: an Eternal Golden Braid. Basic Books, 1979.
16. Gerard Huet and Derek C. Oppen. Equations and Rewrite Rules: A Survey. In Ronald V. Book, editor, Formal Language Theory: Perspectives and Open Problems, pages 349 - 405. Academic, 1980.
17. Sanjay Jain, Daniel Osherson, James S. Royer, and Arun Sharma. Systems That Learn. The MIT Press, 1999.
18. Klaus P. Jantke. The biotope issue in meme media implementations. In Gunter Grieser and Yuzuru Tanaka, editors, International Workshop on Intuitive Human Interface for Organizing and Accessing Intellectual Assets, International Workshop, Dagstuhl Castle, Germany, March 1-5, 2004, Proceedings, volume 3359 of Lecture Notes in Artificial Intelligence, pages 99 - 107, Berlin, Heidelberg, NewYork, 2005. Springer-Verlag.

19. Klaus P. Jantke. Inductive modeling: a roadmap. Technical Report, Forschungsinstitut für Informations Technologien Leipzig e.V., Forschungsbericht 2005-02, January 2005.
20. Klaus P. Jantke. Principles, potentials and problems of inductive reasoning in meme media technology applications (invited keynote). In Yuzuru Tanaka, editor, Proc. 2nd International Symposium on Ubiquitous Knowledge Network Environment, March 16 - 18, 2005, Sapporo Convention Center, Sapporo, Japan, pages 29 - 43. Hokkaido University Sapporo, Japan, Meme Media Lab., 2005.
21. Klaus P. Jantke and Nataliya Lamonova. Assistance and induction ? the therapy planning case. In S. Hartmann, R. Kaschek, Kinshuk, K.-D. Schewe, J.M. Turull Torres, and R. Whiddett, editors, First International Workshop on Perspectives of Intelligent Systems? Assistance, PISA 2005, Palmerston North, New Zealand, March 3 - 5, 2005, pages 72 - 85. Massey University, Dept. of Information Systems, 2005.
22. Roland Kaschek. Modeling ontology use for information systems. In Klaus-Dieter Althoff, Andreas Dengel, Ralph Bergmann, Markus Nick , Thomas Roth-Berghofer Th., editors, Professional Knowledge Management. LNCS 3782 Springer Verlag, 2005.
23. Wilhelm Kamlah and Paul Lorenzen. Logische Propädeutik: Vorschule des vernünftigen Redens. Verlag J. B. Metzler, Stuttgart, Weimar, 1996.
24. Willi Klösgen and Jan M. Zytkow, editors. Handbook of Data Mining and Knowledge Discovery. Oxford University Press, 2002.
25. Raph Koster. A Theory of Fun for Game Design. Paraglyph Press, Inc.,2005.
26. Nataliya Lamonova, Kimihito Ito, and Yuzuru Tanaka. From planning tools to intelligent assistants: Meme Media and logic programming technologies. In S. Hartmann, R. Kaschek, Kinshuk, K.-D. Schewe, J. M. Turull Torres, and R. Whiddett, editors, First International Workshop on Perspectives of Intelligent Systems? Assistance, PISA 2005, Palmerston North, New Zealand, March 3 - 5, 2005, pages 143 - 152. Massey University, Dept. of Information Systems, 2005.
27. Angelika Linke, Markus Nussbaumer, and Paul R. Portmann; Transscript Linguistics, (In German). Max Niemeyer Verlag, Tübingen, 4th. unchanged edition 2001.
28. Istvan-Tibor Nebel. Patient and learner adaptation in technology enhanced learning by induction based on medical context. Technical report, Forschungsinstitut für Informations Technologien Leipzig e.V., Forschungsbericht 2004 - 02, December 2004.
29. Istvan-Tibor Nebel. From planning tools to intelligen tassistants: Meme Media and logic programming technologies. In S. Hartmann, R. Kaschek, Kinshuk, K.-D. Schewe, J. M. Turull Torres, and R. Whiddett, editors, First International Workshop on Perspectives of Intelligent Systems' Assistance, PISA 2005, Palmerston North, New Zealand, March 3 - 5, 2005, pages 176 - 186. Massey University, Dept. of Information Systems, 2005.
30. Alexander Pfänder. Logik. Verlag von Max Niemeyer, Halle a.d. Saale, 1921.
31. George Polya. How to Solve It. Princeton University Press, Princeton, New Jersey, 1988.
32. Michael J. Reddy. The conduit metaphor: A case of frame conflict in our language about language. In Andrew Ortony, editor, Metaphor and Thought, 4th. printing of second edition of 1992. Cambridge University Press, 1998.
33. Herbert Stachowiak. Allgemeine Modelltheorie. Springer, 1973.
34. Herbert Stachowiak. Erkenntnisstufen zum Systematischen Neopragmatismus und zur Allgemeinen Modelltheorie. In Herbert Stachowiak, editor, Modelle: Konstruktionen der Wirklichkeit, pages 87 - 146. Wilhelm Fink Verlag, München, 1983.

35. Herbert Stachowiak. Modell. In Helmut Seiffert and Gerard Radnitzky, editors, Handlexikon zur Wissenschaftstheorie, pages 219 - 222. Deutscher Taschenbuch Verlag GmbH&Co. KG, München, 1992.
36. Mark Stefik. The next knowledge medium. AI Magazine, 7(1):34 - 46, 1986.
37. Yuzuru Tanaka. Meme Media and Meme Market Architectures. IEEE Press and Wiley-Interscience, 2003.
38. Bernhard Thalheim. Entity-Relationship Modeling. Springer-Verlag, Berlin, Heidelberg, 2000.
39. Haridimos Tsoukas. Do we really understand tacit knowledge? Retrieved from http://www.is.lse.ac.uk/events/esrcseminars/tsoukas.pdf on 31 August 2005.
40. Erich Trunz, editor. Goethe. Faust. C. H.Beck, 1996.
41. Roelf Wieringa. Algebraic foundations for dynamic conceptual models. PhD thesis, Free University of Amsterdam, Amsterdam, The Netherlands, Mai 1990.

Mechanisms of Knowledge Evolution for Web Information Extraction

Carsten Müller

SAP AG
Neurottstr. 16, 69190 Walldorf, Germany
carsten.mueller@sap.com

Abstract. The knowledge that is needed in Web information extraction can, under certain assumptions, be characterized as the knowledge held by wrappers that are used to extract the semantics of documents. The evolution of this knowledge can be divided into the phase of initial learning of the wrappers and the later phase of wrapper maintenance. In this paper we will focus only on the initial learning phase. Based on the LExIKON System, the principal structure of learning algorithms for island wrappers is explained.

1 Motivation

In times of a continual growing flood of information knowledge, management systems gain more and more importance. Of course, standard text-retrieval systems are specially designed to provide easy access to all this information. However, they have no access to the semantics of the documents and, therefore, lose quality when they have to manage billions of documents. With the help of information extraction programs, known as wrappers, the search results can be improved in terms of quality, as wrappers can assist search engines by providing that necessary access [17].

In order to determine the semantics of documents, wrappers need some knowledge about those documents. The kind of knowledge they need strongly depends on the type of documents that is focused on. In the case of free-text documents, typical approaches are based on linguistic information. With regard to semi-structured documents, wrappers usually take advantage of XPATH expressions or – as in our case – pattern languages. Of course, wrappers can acquire this knowledge directly from the user; this is the case if wrappers are programmed manually. Alternatively, the process of knowledge acquisition can be carried out by assistance systems.

The LExIKON system, presented in [7, 22], is such an assistance system. One of the main goals that the developers of the LExIKON system pursued was the development of a system that can be handled even by users who do not have any knowledge about Information Extraction. The only task that the users have to perform is to indicate their opinion on documents that are presented in their Web browser, and to teach the system until it has completely learned their opinion. The whole process of wrapper learning is hidden from the user.

K.P. Jantke et al. (Eds.): Federation over the Web, LNAI 3847, pp. 202–214, 2006.
© Springer-Verlag Berlin Heidelberg 2006

The acceptance of a learning system for wrappers strongly depends on the quality of the generated wrappers. This means that the system has to be able to learn wrappers for as many Web pages as possible. As Web pages have become more and more complex, the hidden learning processes have to be quite sophisticated.

The following sections deal with the mechanisms of knowledge evolution by wrappers. First of all some background knowledge about the LExIKON system will be provided in Section 2. Based on this knowledge a simple learning algorithm will be presented in Section 3. This learning algorithm will be studied more precisely in Section 4. After a short overview in Section 5 that shows how to deal with negative examples, some test results will be presented in Section 6.

2   The LExIKON Framework

The LExIKON system [7, 22] is an assistance system for generating wrappers that perform extraction with the help of pattern languages. The previously mentioned goal of developing a system that can also be handled by users with no knowledge about Information Extraction was achieved by the use of a simple query scenario [6].

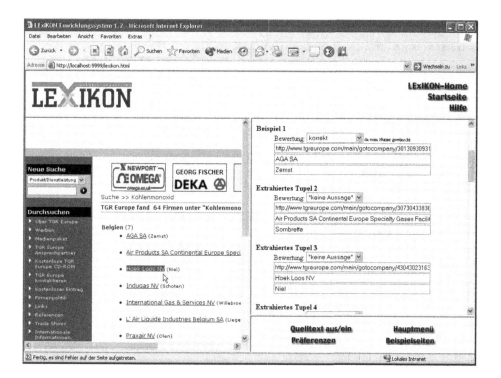

Fig. 1. The LExIKON system at work

At the beginning of such a scenario the user has to mark the so-called positive examples in his/her web browser (see Fig. 1). These positive examples constitute part of the information in which the user is interested. Based on these examples the LExIKON system generates some hypotheses that reflect its overall view on the document. By means of these hypotheses the system creates a wrapper that is then applied to the document, and the results of this extraction process are presented to the user. If the user is satisfied with these results, the process of wrapper learning is completed. Otherwise the user can request a further learning step by supplying LExIKON with more examples. Along with additional positive examples, the user can specify so-called negative examples by rejecting results that the system has offered. With each learning step the wrapper's knowledge about the user's interests increases. The evolution of this knowledge does not end until the user is satisfied with the results of the extraction process.

The wrappers that are generated by the LExIKON system belong to the class of island wrappers [28]. The name island wrapper comes from the assumption that the relevant information is always embedded between particular strings, the so-called left and right delimiters. These strings can be summarized as delimiter languages that in the simplest cases are just sets of strings, and in more complex cases may be patterns. For our purposes, advanced elementary formal systems (AEFS) turned out to be the best programming language for Island Wrappers [8, 21]. The reason is that delimiter languages and structural constraints can both be expressed in a very compact form (see Fig. 2).

$$\mathrm{extract}(X_1,X_2,X_3,Y_0L_1X_1R_1Y_1L_2X_2R_2Y_2L_3X_3R_3Y_3) \leftarrow l_1(L_1),\ \mathrm{nc\text{-}}r_1(X_1),\ r_1(R_1),$$
$$\mathrm{nc\text{-}}l_2(Y_1),$$
$$l_2(L_2),\ \mathrm{nc\text{-}}r_2(X_2),\ r_2(R_2),$$
$$\mathrm{nc\text{-}}l_3(Y_2),$$
$$l_3(L_3),\ \mathrm{nc\text{-}}r_3(X_3),\ r_3(R_3).$$

$\mathrm{nc\text{-}}r_1(X) \leftarrow \mathrm{not}\ \mathrm{c\text{-}}r_1(X).$		
$\mathrm{c\text{-}}r_1(X) \leftarrow r_1(X).$	$\mathrm{c\text{-}}r_1(XY) \leftarrow \mathrm{c\text{-}}r_1(X).$	$\mathrm{c\text{-}}r_1(XY) \leftarrow \mathrm{c\text{-}}r_1(Y).$
$\mathrm{nc\text{-}}l_2(X) \leftarrow \mathrm{not}\ \mathrm{c\text{-}}l_2(X).$		
$\mathrm{c\text{-}}l_2(X) \leftarrow l_2(X).$	$\mathrm{c\text{-}}l_2(XY) \leftarrow \mathrm{c\text{-}}l_2(X).$	$\mathrm{c\text{-}}l_2(XY) \leftarrow \mathrm{c\text{-}}l_2(Y).$
$\mathrm{nc\text{-}}r_2(X) \leftarrow \mathrm{not}\ \mathrm{c\text{-}}r_2(X).$		
$\mathrm{c\text{-}}r_2(X) \leftarrow r_2(X).$	$\mathrm{c\text{-}}r_2(XY) \leftarrow \mathrm{c\text{-}}r_2(X).$	$\mathrm{c\text{-}}r_2(XY) \leftarrow \mathrm{c\text{-}}r_2(Y).$
$\mathrm{nc\text{-}}l_3(X) \leftarrow \mathrm{not}\ \mathrm{c\text{-}}l_3(X).$		
$\mathrm{c\text{-}}l_3(X) \leftarrow l_3(X).$	$\mathrm{c\text{-}}l_3(XY) \leftarrow \mathrm{c\text{-}}l_3(X).$	$\mathrm{c\text{-}}l_3(XY) \leftarrow \mathrm{c\text{-}}l_3(Y).$
$\mathrm{nc\text{-}}r_3(X) \leftarrow \mathrm{not}\ \mathrm{c\text{-}}r_3(X).$		
$\mathrm{c\text{-}}r_3(X) \leftarrow r_3(X).$	$\mathrm{c\text{-}}r_3(XY) \leftarrow \mathrm{c\text{-}}r_3(X).$	$\mathrm{c\text{-}}r_3(XY) \leftarrow \mathrm{c\text{-}}r_3(Y).$

$l_1(\mathbf{href} ='').$
$l_1(\mathbf{href} =').$
$r_1('').$
$r_1(').$
$l_2(>).$
$r_2(< /\mathbf{a} >).$
$l_3((().$
$r_3(). < /\mathbf{li} >).$

Fig. 2. AEFS

An AEFS wrapper, as it is presented here, consists of three parts. The first part of the wrapper contains a pattern $(Y_0 L_1 X_1 R_1 Y_1 L_2 X_2 R_2 Y_2)$ that defines the order in which the components, the delimiter languages and the remaining strings take their place within the document. The variables X_i, $i \in \{1 \dots n\}$ represent the components of a positive example. The variables L_i and R_i stand for left and right delimiter languages. The remaining text fragments of the document are represented by the variables Y_j, $j \in \{0 \dots n\}$.

The second part of an AEFS wrapper is a set of constraints. These constraints describe how the extraction process is to be performed. Words of the right delimiter languages R_i, for instance, must not be subwords of the component X_i of any positive example. As far as the left delimiter languages L_i, $i \in \{2 \dots n\}$ are concerned, there is, moreover, a rule defining that words of these delimiter languages must not be contained in the remaining strings Y_{i-1}.

The last part of an AEFS wrapper is formed by the words of the delimiter languages. Figure 2 shows that the delimiter languages can be written as a list of words. Alternatively, they can also be written in the form of a regular pattern.

Most of the targeted Web pages are based on pre-defined html templates and only differ in their semantic content. As a result, wrappers for many of these pages contain the same pattern and the same constraints; only the delimiter languages are different. Consequently, the knowledge that is necessary in order to extract the semantics of those documents is mostly provided by the delimiter languages. In the context of Web information extraction this means that the process of knowledge evolution can be reduced to the process of delimiter learning. This task will be explained in the following sections.

3   The Process of Knowledge Aquisition

In order to understand the process of delimiter learning, the interface between the LExIKON system and the learning algorithms has to be described first. The LExIKON framework strictly defines the input and output parameters of the learning algorithms. Available input parameters are the example document and the lists of positive and negative examples. Each example is a tuple $(x_1, \dots, x_n)$ which is complemented by the position of its components $(p_1, \dots, p_n)$ (see Fig. 3). Moreover, each example contains a flag m that indicates whether it has a positive or a negative rating. The output parameter of each learning algorithm is an Island Wrapper written in AEFS.

$$[(x_1, p_1, x_2, p_2, \dots x_n, p_n, m), (x_1, p_1, x_2, p_2, \dots x_n, p_n, m), \dots]$$

Fig. 3. List of examples

However, the learning algorithms need the information in a particular format. Therefore, a data preparation step has to be carried out before the learning can begin. Hence, all existing learning algorithms can be divided into a data preparation step and a delimiter learning step (see Fig. 4).

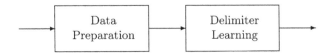

Fig. 4. Common structure of learning algorithms

Normally, the data preparation starts with the division of the list of examples into lists of positive and negative ones. In the easiest case the learning of the wrapper is only based on the list of positive examples, while the role of the negative examples is restricted to the validation of the learned wrapper. In the next step the list of positive examples is used to generate a list of text fragments for each delimiter language. These text fragments are prefixes or suffixes of the strings that surround the components. This means that any text fragment between two consecutive components x_i and x_{i+1} is divided into two parts. The left part is added to the list of the right delimiter r_i, while the right part is added to the list of the left delimiter l_{i+1}.

During the learning step these lists of text fragments are used to find suitable delimiters. In the case where some left delimiter language L_i is to be learned, suffixes from the words of the list for L_i are selected. During the selection processs the constraints that are specified in AEFS have to be considered. Thus selection of suffixes is restricted to those that, if regarded as subwords, appear just once within the words of the list. Similarly, when looking for right delimiters the constraints of AEFS must be fulfilled by prefixes of the words in the lists; only prefixes that do not occur inside components are selected. Among all the selected prefixes and suffixes only the most suitable ones are used as delimiters. The delimiters can now be embedded into an AEFS program, either directly or after having been generalized into the form of a pattern language.

However, a learning algorithm at this stage of development will fail with regard to many documents. On the one hand, this situation can be improved by modifying the data preparation step; on the other hand, better results can be achieved by profiting from synergy effects between delimiter languages. The optimization of learning algorithms is the subject of our next section.

4   Wrapper Induction Schemes

One of the crucial points within the learning algorithm described in Sect. 3 is located within the data preparation step: it is the generation of the list of candidates for the words of the delimiter languages. In this context, the rules according to which the division of the text fragments between two consecutive components takes place are of highest importance. Test results showed that rules following heuristics such as "division into parts of equal length" result in wrappers of poor quality.

Better results can be achieved if more attention is paid to the constraints of AEFS. According to these constraints the left delimiter language L_i must not be contained in the string Y_{i-1}, $i = [2..n]$. Moreover, X_i must not be contained in R_i, $i = [1..n]$. As the information for learning L_{i+1} and R_i is derived from the same strings, there are synergy effects between these two delimiters. However, in the case where a learning algorithm is structured in a way that the information for all delimiters is prepared before any delimiter is learned, these synergy effects are lost. Consequently, it might be possible that the AEFS constraints cannot be fulfilled even though it would normally be possible to learn an Island Wrapper for the document. In order to avoid this situation either the left or the right delimiters must be learned first. The strings between X_i and X_{i+1}, reduced by the delimiters that have been learned already, can then be used for learning the remaining delimiters. This leads us to a new scheme for learning algorithms.

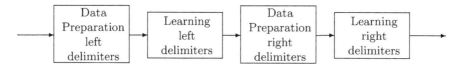

Fig. 5. Left delimiters before right delimiters

In the scheme represented in Fig. 5 all left delimiter languages are learned before any right delimiter is taken into consideration. A problem that arises with this scheme is that the remaining string between X_i and L_{i+1} might be too short to learn the right delimiter language R_i due to the constraints of AEFS. This problem is avoided if the right delimiters are learned before the left ones (see Fig. 6).

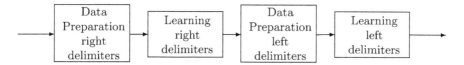

Fig. 6. Right delimiters before left delimiters

A starting-point for optimization is the selection of candidates for delimiter languages. When the candidates that do not follow the constraints of AEFS are eliminated, very often more than one candidate remains as a possible delimiter. Consequently, criteria for selection are necessary. The two most suitable selection heuristics seem to be either to prefer candidates with 'minimal length' or those with 'maximal length'. A delimiter has 'minimal length' if it is just long enough to fulfill the constraints of AEFS. Regarding left delimiters l_i (suffixes), this means that they must not be part of any intermediate string Y_{i-1}. For right delimiters r_i (prefixes) it means that they must not be part of any component X_i. A left delimiter (suffix) with 'maximal length' contains, of course, the left delimiter with 'minimal length'. Moreover, it contains the longest common subsequence [11] that is a prefix of the 'left delimiter with minimal length'. The right delimiter (prefix) with 'maximal length' is similarly defined.

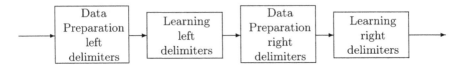

Fig. 7. Left/right delimiters of minimal length

Preferring only delimiters of minimal length has the advantage that where there is the possibility to learn an Island Wrapper this will surely be achieved. However, the query scenario will involve many steps and the learning algorithm has to handle many negative examples.

Preferring only delimiters of maximal length has the advantage that the query scenario converges very rapidly. This means that the user does not need to provide many positive and negative examples in order to obtain a satisfactory wrapper. However, when right delimiters are learned before left ones, it may happen that the intermediate strings Y_{i-1} are too short for learning the left delimiters L_i according to the constraints of AEFS. In this case the algorithm might need to be run for a second time with an adapted data preparation strategy (see Fig. 8).

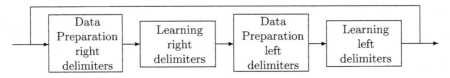

Fig. 8. Right delimiters before left delimiters with loop-back

With the help of a combination of the two strategies (delimiters with maximal length and delimiters with minimal length), the disadvantages described above can be avoided. One possibility is, for instance, to generate the delimiter languages with minimal length first. After that, these delimiter languages can be extended to those with maximal length (see Fig. 9).

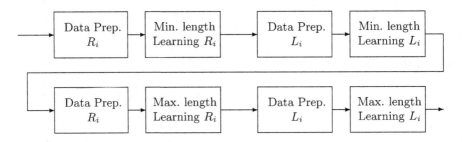

Fig. 9. First minimal length, then maximal length

However, the question arises as to whether such a complex scheme is really necessary for a sucessful learning process. Can the same results not also be achieved by another scheme? So far only the results for learning all delimiters with minimal length or with maximal length were discussed. One possibility that combines these approaches could be to learn left delimiters with minimal length before learning right delimiters with maximal length. The disadvantage of this approach becomes obvious when considering that left delimiters are usually much longer than right ones. The reason for this is that the intermediate strings are much longer than the components. Consequently, the probability that a delimiter cannot fulfill the AEFS constraints is much higher where left delimiter languages are concerned.

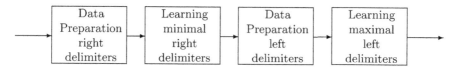

Fig. 10. Minimal right delimiters before maximal left delimiters

To avoid this problem there remains the alternative of learning right delimiters with minimal length followed by left delimiters with maximal length (see Fig. 10). Test results have shown that this is sufficient to achieve a level of quality that is as high as the level of the scheme in Fig. 9. The test results in Sect. 6 were achieved using an algorithm based on this scheme.

5 Dealing with Negative Examples

So far, the learning of the wrapper was performed without paying attention to negative examples. But before an approach for using negative examples within the learning algorithm can be presented, some basic thoughts have to be discussed. Basically, negative examples are extracted tuples that were rejected by the user. In terms of structure they are built in the same way as positive examples. However, they differ in their negative rating.

As the negative rating refers to each tuple as a whole, a question arises as to which component is responsible for the user's rejection. When thinking about island wrappers the situation is even worse. Even if the component is known, two delimiter languages remain of which either (or both) may be the reason for rejection.

So how can negative examples be embedded in the learning algorithm? One possibility is that the wrapper is only learned with the help of positive examples. If the new wrapper does not extract the negative examples any more, the learning task ends. If there are still negative examples that are extracted by the new wrapper, the wrapper has to be adapted. This learning algorithm is built according to the scheme in Fig. 11.

The goal of the adaptation process is, of course, that the negative examples will not be extracted any more. To achieve this task it is sufficient if any single

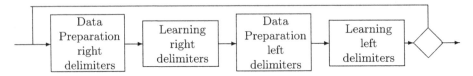

Fig. 11. Learning algorithm with consistency check

component of the negative example is no longer extracted. This can be accomplished by extending one of the delimiter languages. The crucial point is to find out which delimiter language has to be changed in order to meet the user's needs.

As there is no AEFS constraint that must be fulfilled for L_1, one possibility could be to always modify L_1. Tests showed that this heuristic is quite satisfactory. If the rejection is based on a delimiter language other than L_1, the user can moreover influence the system's behaviour by providing a positive example.

Alternatively, the component that is responsible for the rejection has to be determined. This can be done by statistical calculations. One possibility could be to find out which negative component has the smallest similarity to its corresponding positive components. Kushmerick [19] defined some similarity measures that can be used for this task.

However, the question remains as to whether the right or left delimiter language is responsible for the rejection. With the help of statistical features, this problem can also be solved. If the similarity between the negative component and its corresponding positive ones is very small, the left delimiter language has to be changed.

However, negative examples are not only of use for testing a wrapper that was learned using just positive examples. Negative examples can also be used during the learning process. One possibility is to compare the components of the negative examples with those of the positive ones. If a component of a negative example is also part of a positive example, it cannot be the reason for the rejection. Consequently, the corresponding left and right delimiter languages are working correctly. This means that if the negative example is still extracted, the delimiter languages of another component must be changed.

If it is known which component is responsible for the rejection, the selection process of the delimiter candidates can be adapted. This means that the candidates for delimiters not only have to fulfill the AEFS constraints but also must not be prefixes or suffixes of the negative components.

6   Test Results

We tested our learning algorithm by generating wrappers for the Web pages of Google, Yahoo!, Yahoo! Finance, Amazon, EBay, AltaVista and Lycos. It became obvious that the learning algorithm can generate wrappers for all of these pages. Moreover, the algorithm converges very rapidly. This means that only a few learning steps are necessary in order to create a satisfactory wrapper.

As far as the result pages of Google and Yahoo! were concerned, we tried to extract the document title, the content snippet and the link for each search result. Where all these components were available, the extraction was performed well. In cases where one of the components was missing, either the corresponding search result did not get extracted as a whole or a tuple was extracted containing a mixture of two search results. The reason for this is that an AEFS wrapper can only extract tuples if no delimiter languages are missing.

Regarding the Web page of Yahoo! Finance, the learning task was to create a wrapper for the table in which the current market prices of companies are displayed. As there was no delimiter language missing, the generated wrappers achieved a high quality.

With respect to the Web portal of Amazon we created a wrapper for extracting book title, author and price. This worked very well. Only a few learning steps were necessary to create the wrapper. Again, there was the problem with the missing delimiter languages. The same results were achieved for EBay, AltaVista and Lycos.

To summarize these results one can say that a wrapper could be learned for each Web page. Moreover, only a few learning steps were necessary in order to create this wrapper. The quality of the wrapper was good if all delimiter languages were available.

7   Summary and Future Work

The LExIKON system, as described in this paper, may be seen as a powerful assistant to the user. With the help of LExIKON the task of wrapper generation, which could formerly only be performed by specialists in the area of Information Extraction, can now be carried out by any user who has some basic knowledge about computers.

This goal could only be achieved with the help of intelligent algorithms for knowledge evolution. The problems that have to be solved in the area of knowledge evolution for information extraction were illustrated by taking a basic algorithm as an example. Based on this algorithm the concept of wrapper induction schemes was developed. With the help of these schemes new structures for learning algorithms could be invented. These learning algorithms optimized the learning of AEFS wrappers to a high degree.

On the one hand, the tests showed that the wrappers are already powerful enough to extract the semantics of many documents. On the other hand, there are still some problems to be solved. Those problems, including the problem of missing delimiter languages and the problem of changes within the order of the components, cannot only be solved by learning delimiter languages; the whole structure of the AEFS wrapper has to be changed. This will be the topic of our further research in the area of wrapper learning.

So far only the task of the initial wrapper learning was discussed. But when we think about knowledge evolution there is still one more aspect that has to be mentioned. Evolution means a continual process of further development. This phenomenon can also be observed with regard to the Internet. As Web pages change over time, the wrappers deployed to extract their semantics have to be adapted to the pages' new structure. The process of relearning, called wrapper maintenance, will also be a topic of further research.

Acknowledgements

The author acknowledges the very fruitful cooperation with Professor Jantke from FIT-Leipzig, with his former LExIKON research and development team and with partners from research groups at the Darmstadt University of Technology, at the University of Koblenz-Landau, at the University of Leipzig and at the DFKI in Saarbrücken.

Bernd Thomas did pioneering work on Island Wrappers. Klaus Jantke, Gunter Grieser and Steffen Lange invented the concept of AEFS which turned out to be essential. Kathrin Speich, Gunter Grieser and Jörg Herrmann contributed their own ideas to formal language learning for information extraction.

For the present work with SAP I have to thank Klaus Kreplin, Wolfgang Degenhardt and the whole TREX team who allowed me to experiment with the search engine SAP TREX. With their help we were able to turn LExIKON into an efficient assistant for Information Extraction, that is already used by SAP TREX and many other SAP solutions.

References

1. D. Angluin and C. H. Smith. A survey of inductive inference: Theory and methods. *Computing Surveys*, 15:237–269, 1983.
2. D. Angluin and C. H. Smith. Inductive inference. In Stuart C. Shapiro, editor, *Encyclopedia of Artificial Intelligence. Second Edition (Volume 1)*, pages 672–682. John Wiley & Sons, Inc., 1992.
3. B. Chidlovskii. Information extraction from tree documents by learning subtree delimiters. In Subbarao Kambhampati and Craig A. Knoblock, editors, *Proceedings of IJCAI-03 Workshop on Information Integration on the Web (IIWeb-03), August 9-10, 2003, Acapulco, Mexico*, pages 3–8, 2003.
4. E.M. Gold. Limiting recursion. *Journal of Symbolic Logic*, 30:28–48, 1965.
5. E.M. Gold. Language identification in the limit. *Information and Control*, 10:447–474, 1967.
6. G. Grieser, K.P. Jantke, and S. Lange. Consistency queries in information extraction. In N. Cesa-Bianchi, M. Numao, and R. Reischuk, editors, *ALT2002*, volume 2533 of *LNAI*, pages 173–187. Springer-Verlag, 2002.
7. G. Grieser, K.P. Jantke, S. Lange, and W. Niehoff. LExIKON – Systemarchitekturen zur Extraktion von Information aus dem Internet. In *Proc. 42nd IWK*, pages 913–918. Technische Universität Ilmenau, 2000.
8. G. Grieser, K.P. Jantke, S. Lange, and B. Thomas. A unifying approach to HTML wrapper representation and learning. In *Proc. 3rd Int. Conf. on Discovery Science*, LNAI 1967, pages 50–64. Springer-Verlag, 2000.
9. G. Grieser and S. Lange. Learning approaches to wrapper induction. In *Proc. 14th Int. Florida AI Research Society Conference*, pages 249–253. AAAI Press, 2001.

10. G. Grieser and S. Lange. Changing the perspective: Interaction scenarios that take the needs of the machine into account. In R. Kaschek, editor, *Intelligent Assistant Systems: Concepts, Techniques and Technologies*. Idea Group Inc., 2005.

11. D. Hirschberg. A linear space algorithm for computing maximal common subsequences. *Communications of the ACM*, 18:341–343, 1975.

12. S. Jain, D. Osherson, J. S. Royer, and A. Sharma. *Systems That Learn*. The MIT Press, 1999.

13. K. P. Jantke. Formalisms underlying intuitiveness in human-computer interaction. In Yuzuru Tanaka, editor, *Proc. 3rd International Workshop on Access Architectures for Organizing and Accessing Intellectual Assets, March 5–7, 2003, Sapporo, Japan*. Meme Media Laboratory, Hokkaido University, 2003.

14. K. P. Jantke. Informationsbeschaffung im Internet. Lerntechnologien für die Extraktion von Information aus semistrukturierten Dokumenten. *electrosuisse Bulletin SEV/VSE*, 94(1):15–22, 2003.

15. K. P. Jantke. Wissensmangement im Internet. auf dem Weg zum Digitalen Assistenten für das e-Learning. *Global Journal of Engineering Education*, 7(3):259–266, 2003.

16. K. P. Jantke, G. Grieser, and S. Lange. Adaptation to the learners' needs and desires by induction and negotiation of hypotheses. In Michael E. Auer and Ursula Auer, editors, *International Conference on Interactive Computer Aided Learning, ICL 2004, Sept. 29 – Oct. 1, 2004, Villach, Austria (CD-ROM)*, 2004.

17. K.P. Jantke and C. Müller. Wrapper induction programs as information extraction assistance. In S. Hartmann, R. Kaschek, Kinshuk, K.-D. Schewe, J.M. Turull-Torres, and R. Whiddett, editors, *First International Workshop on Perspectives of Intelligent Systems' Assistance, PISA 2005, Palmerston North, New Zealand, March 3-5, 2005*, pages 86–101, Massey University, Dept. Information Systems, 2005.

18. R. Klette and R. Wiehagen. Research in the theory of inductive inference by GDR mathematicians - A survey. *Information Sciences*, 22:149–169, 1980.

19. N. Kushmerick. Regression testing for wrapper maintenance. In *AAAI/IAAI*, pages 74–79, 1999.

20. N. Kushmerick. Wrapper induction: Efficiency and expressiveness. *Artificial Intelligence*, 118:15–68, 2000.

21. S. Lange, G. Grieser, and K.P. Jantke. Advanced elementary formal systems. *TCS*, 298:51–70, 2003.

22. S. Lange, K.P. Jantke, G. Grieser, and W. Niehoff. LExIKON – Lernszenarios für die Extraktion von Information aus dem Internet. In *Proc. 42nd IWK*, pages 901–906. Technische Universität Ilmenau, 2000.

23. K. Lerman, S.N. Minton, and C.A. Knoblock. Wrapper maintenance: A machine learning approach. *Journal of Artificial Intelligence Research*, 18:149–181, 2003.

24. A. Maedche and S. Staab. Ontology learning for the semantic web. *IEEE Intelligent Systems*, 16:72–79, 2001.

25. I. Muslea, S.N. Minton, and C.A. Knoblock. Hierarchical wrapper induction for semistructured information sources. *Autonomous Agents and Multi-Agent Systems*, 4:93–114, 2001.

26. S. Soderland. Learning information extraction rules for semi-structured and free text. In *Machine Learning*. 34(1–3):233-272, 1999.

27. A. Stephan and K. P. Jantke. Wissensextraktion aus dem Internet mit Hilfe gelernter Extraktionsmechanismen. In *online 2002, Düsseldorf, Proc., Vol. VI*, pages C612.01–C612.12. ONLINE GmbH, 2002.

28. B. Thomas. Anti unification based learning of T-wrappers for information extraction. In *Proc. of AAAI Workshop on Machine Learning for IE*, pages 190–198. AAAI, 1999.

29. B. Thomas. Token-templates and logic programs for intelligent web search. *Journal of Intelligent Information Systems*, 14:241–261, 2000.

Author Index

Lecture Notes in Artificial Intelligence (LNAI)

Vol. 3601: G. Moro, S. Bergamaschi, K. Aberer (Eds.), Agents and Peer-to-Peer Computing. XII, 245 pages. 2005.

Vol. 3596: F. Dau, M.-L. Mugnier, G. Stumme (Eds.), Conceptual Structures: Common Semantics for Sharing Knowledge. XI, 467 pages. 2005.

Vol. 3593: V. Mařík, R. W. Brennan, M. Pěchouček (Eds.), Holonic and Multi-Agent Systems for Manufacturing. XI, 269 pages. 2005.

Vol. 3587: P. Perner, A. Imiya (Eds.), Machine Learning and Data Mining in Pattern Recognition. XVII, 695 pages. 2005.

Vol. 3584: X. Li, S. Wang, Z.Y. Dong (Eds.), Advanced Data Mining and Applications. XIX, 835 pages. 2005.

Vol. 3581: S. Miksch, J. Hunter, E.T. Keravnou (Eds.), Artificial Intelligence in Medicine. XVII, 547 pages. 2005.

Vol. 3577: R. Falcone, S. Barber, J. Sabater-Mir, M.P. Singh (Eds.), Trusting Agents for Trusting Electronic Societies. VIII, 235 pages. 2005.

Vol. 3575: S. Wermter, G. Palm, M. Elshaw (Eds.), Biomimetic Neural Learning for Intelligent Robots. IX, 383 pages. 2005.

Vol. 3571: L. Godo (Ed.), Symbolic and Quantitative Approaches to Reasoning with Uncertainty. XVI, 1028 pages. 2005.

Vol. 3559: P. Auer, R. Meir (Eds.), Learning Theory. XI, 692 pages. 2005.

Vol. 3558: V. Torra, Y. Narukawa, S. Miyamoto (Eds.), Modeling Decisions for Artificial Intelligence. XII, 470 pages. 2005.

Vol. 3554: A.K. Dey, B. Kokinov, D.B. Leake, R. Turner (Eds.), Modeling and Using Context. XIV, 572 pages. 2005.

Vol. 3550: T. Eymann, F. Klügl, W. Lamersdorf, M. Klusch, M.N. Huhns (Eds.), Multiagent System Technologies. XI, 246 pages. 2005.

Vol. 3539: K. Morik, J.-F. Boulicaut, A. Siebes (Eds.), Local Pattern Detection. XI, 233 pages. 2005.

Vol. 3538: L. Ardissono, P. Brna, A. Mitrović (Eds.), User Modeling 2005. XVI, 533 pages. 2005.

Vol. 3533: M. Ali, F. Esposito (Eds.), Innovations in Applied Artificial Intelligence. XX, 858 pages. 2005.

Vol. 3528: P.S. Szczepaniak, J. Kacprzyk, A. Niewiadomski (Eds.), Advances in Web Intelligence. XVII, 513 pages. 2005.

Vol. 3518: T.-B. Ho, D. Cheung, H. Liu (Eds.), Advances in Knowledge Discovery and Data Mining. XXI, 864 pages. 2005.

Vol. 3508: P. Bresciani, P. Giorgini, B. Henderson-Sellers, G. Low, M. Winikoff (Eds.), Agent-Oriented Information Systems II. X, 227 pages. 2005.

Vol. 3505: V. Gorodetsky, J. Liu, V.A. Skormin (Eds.), Autonomous Intelligent Systems: Agents and Data Mining. XIII, 303 pages. 2005.

Vol. 3501: B. Kégl, G. Lapalme (Eds.), Advances in Artificial Intelligence. XV, 458 pages. 2005.

Vol. 3492: P. Blache, E.P. Stabler, J.V. Busquets, R. Moot (Eds.), Logical Aspects of Computational Linguistics. X, 363 pages. 2005.

Vol. 3490: L. Bolc, Z. Michalewicz, T. Nishida (Eds.), Intelligent Media Technology for Communicative Intelligence. X, 259 pages. 2005.

Vol. 3488: M.-S. Hacid, N.V. Murray, Z.W. Raś, S. Tsumoto (Eds.), Foundations of Intelligent Systems. XIII, 700 pages. 2005.

Vol. 3487: J.A. Leite, P. Torroni (Eds.), Computational Logic in Multi-Agent Systems. XII, 281 pages. 2005.

Vol. 3476: J.A. Leite, A. Omicini, P. Torroni, P. Yolum (Eds.), Declarative Agent Languages and Technologies II. XII, 289 pages. 2005.

Vol. 3464: S.A. Brueckner, G.D.M. Serugendo, A. Karageorgos, R. Nagpal (Eds.), Engineering Self-Organising Systems. XIII, 299 pages. 2005.

Vol. 3452: F. Baader, A. Voronkov (Eds.), Logic for Programming, Artificial Intelligence, and Reasoning. XI, 562 pages. 2005.

Vol. 3451: M.-P. Gleizes, A. Omicini, F. Zambonelli (Eds.), Engineering Societies in the Agents World V. XIII, 349 pages. 2005.

Vol. 3446: T. Ishida, L. Gasser, H. Nakashima (Eds.), Massively Multi-Agent Systems I. XI, 349 pages. 2005.

Vol. 3445: G. Chollet, A. Esposito, M. Faúndez-Zanuy, M. Marinaro (Eds.), Nonlinear Speech Modeling and Applications. XIII, 433 pages. 2005.

Vol. 3438: H. Christiansen, P.R. Skadhauge, J. Villadsen (Eds.), Constraint Solving and Language Processing. VIII, 205 pages. 2005.

Vol. 3430: S. Tsumoto, T. Yamaguchi, M. Numao, H. Motoda (Eds.), Active Mining. XII, 349 pages. 2005.

Vol. 3419: B.V. Faltings, A. Petcu, F. Fages, F. Rossi (Eds.), Recent Advances in Constraints. X, 217 pages. 2005.

Vol. 3416: M.H. Böhlen, J. Gamper, W. Polasek, M.A. Wimmer (Eds.), E-Government: Towards Electronic Democracy. XIII, 311 pages. 2005.

Vol. 3415: P. Davidsson, B. Logan, K. Takadama (Eds.), Multi-Agent and Multi-Agent-Based Simulation. X, 265 pages. 2005.

Vol. 3413: K. Fischer, M. Florian, T. Malsch (Eds.), Socionics. X, 315 pages. 2005.

Vol. 3403: B. Ganter, R. Godin (Eds.), Formal Concept Analysis. XI, 419 pages. 2005.

Vol. 3398: D.-K. Baik (Ed.), Systems Modeling and Simulation: Theory and Applications. XIV, 733 pages. 2005.

Vol. 3397: T.G. Kim (Ed.), Artificial Intelligence and Simulation. XV, 711 pages. 2005.

Vol. 3396: R.M. van Eijk, M.-P. Huget, F.P. M. Dignum (Eds.), Agent Communication. X, 261 pages. 2005.

Vol. 3394: D. Kudenko, D. Kazakov, E. Alonso (Eds.), Adaptive Agents and Multi-Agent Systems II. VIII, 313 pages. 2005.

Vol. 3392: D. Seipel, M. Hanus, U. Geske, O. Bartenstein (Eds.), Applications of Declarative Programming and Knowledge Management. X, 309 pages. 2005.

Vol. 3374: D. Weyns, H. V.D. Parunak, F. Michel (Eds.), Environments for Multi-Agent Systems. X, 279 pages. 2005.